A Literary Letter for Every Day of the Year

A Literary Letter FOR EVERY DAY OF THE YEAR

EDITED BY
LIZ ISON

BATSFORD

First published in the United Kingdom
in 2025 by
Batsford
43 Great Ormond Street
London
WC1N 3HZ

An imprint of B. T. Batsford Holdings Limited

ISBN 978 1 84994 944 6

A CIP catalogue record for this book is available from the British Library.

10 9 8 7 6 5 4 3 2 1

Reproduction by Mission Productions, Hong Kong
Printed and bound by Elma Basim, Turkey

This book can be ordered direct from the publisher at
www.batsfordbooks.com, or try your local bookshop

Distributed throughout the UK and Europe by
Abrams & Chronicle Books, 1 West Smithfield, London EC1A 9JU and
57 rue Gaston Tessier, 75166 Paris, France

www.abramsandchronicle.co.uk
info@abramsandchronicle.co.uk

Contents

Introduction

'Letters are the only solace of my life at present, except sardines and omelettes,' wrote Edward Lear, comic poet, of his love of receiving letters. The idea of letters as sustenance is also echoed by prolific letter writer Fanny Burney, author of the epistolary novel *Evelina*, who declared she would rather give up 'a month's allowance of meat, than my week's allowance of an epistle'.

The central place of letters in people's lives is - or was - no overstatement. In the days before the telephone, the fax machine, email, the smart phone and its plethora of messaging apps, writing and sending letters to friends and family was a way of life and a part of the daily routine. From the personal to the political, from expressing love and loss and everything in between, sending and receiving letters could stave off loneliness and isolation: when people were physically separated it was the means of human connection (as Samuel Richardson describes it, 'the pen [...] makes distance, presence').

This is an anthology of what I've termed 'literary letters': the letters of poets, playwrights, novelists and other writers. I have selected them for their literary qualities, whether that be a brilliant turn of phrase, a well-structured sentence or a dazzling description; and also for what the letters reveal about the personality, values or concerns of its writer. Sometimes I have chosen letters that hold a sort of revelation: be that the young writer's precocious expression of a sense of ambition or destiny, perhaps a foreshadowing of later success ('What am I thinking about?' asks a young John Milton, 'So help me God, of immortality'); or the writer knowingly or unconsciously communicating something essential about their philosophy of writing or its themes (famously, John Keats coining the phrase 'negative capability' in a letter to his brothers in which he defined it as 'when a man is capable of being in uncertainties, mysteries, doubts, without any irritable reaching after fact and reason'). Or the letter might be written in a literary style or form that we recognize as quintessentially theirs (Dylan Thomas, for example, doesn't disappoint with 'a mockturtle gabble of wrecked convivial hydrographers tangled with polyps and blind prawns'). Here are also letters reflecting on the process of letter writing itself: the joys and consolations of letters (reading Mary Shelley's letter 'is almost like folding you to my heart', writes her husband, poet Percy Shelley) as well as the excuses that are sometimes made for not replying to a letter (Wordsworth is relatable when admitting that 'procrastination became irresistible to me').

Frequently biographers and researchers turn to writers' correspondences to gain insights into the life story of their subjects, and there is often much rich material to be harvested about, for example, friendships and fallings-out, dealings with publishers or events of the day. Some of this type of content is to be found here. But I am often drawn to letters that transcend the writers' times, and which can be enjoyed without historical context or biographical knowledge. These are letters that give glimpses into the heart and soul of the writer, that strip away the aura of fame to reveal the human being and that cover all the many reasons that we write to each other: for news sharing, staying in touch, giving advice, educating, arguing, flirting, making love, breaking up, mending bridges, moralizing and entertaining.

I have been on the lookout for letters – or more accurately, parts of letters – that work like a poem does, or a short story, whether it is a letter that has flashes of brilliance, seduces or cajoles, skims the surface or ponders the complex. Edna St Vincent Millay recognized such qualities in her mother's letters, telling her 'they are so lovely that very often I read parts of them aloud to people, just as literature'. Many of the letters are literary in a broader sense: writers corresponding with each other or writers discussing or praising other great writers of the past or present. We can imagine the thrill of being the original intended recipient(s) but the letters can hit home for us, today, the unintended, unknown reader receiving it out of context, removed from its time and place and transposed from its original form. In other words, these are letters that deserve to be read and savoured not only for their merit and interest as correspondence but also as stand-alone literary gems.

A note on the editing: most of the letters I've included are extracts which I've lightly edited (a gentle polish to make the gems shine and gleam). I have created a title for each one, often using a quote from the text. On occasion, punctuation and line breaks have also been modified and formatting standardised though I often retain original spelling variations and idiosyncratic punctuation or spacing. I have included the date or month the letter was written where this is known and matches the entry for that day; at other times, when the letter is included to fit with a theme around previous or subsequent entires, to mark a particular occasion or for other reasons, only the year of composition is specified. I have also included short biographies of each letter writer at the end of the book.

There are also a number of letters from literature: who could resist one of Mr Micawber's letters from Dickens's *David Copperfield* or Captain Wentworth's written declaration of love in Jane Austen's *Persuasion*? Some poems have also been selected: poets sometimes inserted early drafts of recently completed poems in their correspondence to friends. In other cases, you'll find poems about letter writing or epistolary poems: a kind of hybrid poem-and-letter-in-one that used to be a popular poetic form.

I hope you enjoy exploring these literary letters.

Liz Ison

JANUARY

1 JANUARY

The art of letter-writing

Virginia Woolf to John Lehman

From *A Letter to a Young Poet* (1932)

Did you ever meet, or was he before your day, that old gentleman - who used to enliven conversation, especially at breakfast when the post came in, by saying that the art of letter-writing is dead? The penny post, the old gentleman used to say, has killed the art of letter-writing. We rush, he went on, spreading his toast with marmalade, to the telephone. We commit our half-formed thoughts to the postcard.

But when the post came in this morning and I opened your letter stuffed with little blue sheets written all over in a cramped but not illegible hand - I replied - Nonsense.

Naturally when a letter cost half a crown to send, it had to prove itself a document of some importance; it was read aloud; it was tied up with green silk; after a certain number of years it was published for the infinite delectation of posterity.

But your letter only cost three-halfpence to send. Therefore you could afford to be intimate, irreticent, indiscreet in the extreme. What you tell me about poor dear C. and his adventure on the Channel boat is deadly private; your ribald jests at the expense of M. would certainly ruin your friendship if they got about; I doubt, too, that posterity, unless it is much quicker in the wit than I expect, could follow the line of your thought from the roof which leaks ('splash, splash, splash into the soap dish'); to Siamese cats ('Wrap their noses in an old stocking my Aunt says if they howl'); so to Gerard Hopkins; so to gold-fish; and so with a sudden alarming swoop to 'Do write and tell me where poetry's going, or if it's dead?'

2 JANUARY

Your jar of marmalade: a token of friendship

Samuel Johnson to Mrs Boswell

1777

Madam

Though I am well enough pleased with the taste of sweetmeats, very little of the pleasure which I received at the arrival of your jar of marmalade arose from eating it. I received it as a token of friendship, as a proof of reconciliation, things much sweeter than sweetmeats, and upon this consideration I return you, dear Madam, my sincerest thanks. By having your kindness I think I have a double security for the continuance of Mr Boswell's, which it is not to be expected that any man can long keep, when the influence of a lady so highly and so justly valued operates against him. Mr Boswell will tell you that I was always faithful to your interest, and always endeavoured to exalt you in his estimation. You must now do the same for me. We must all help one another, and you must now consider me, as,

Dear Madam, your most obliged, and most humble servant,
Sam Johnson

3 JANUARY

Letters, sardines and omelettes

Edward Lear to Lady Wyatt

San Remo, Italy, 1870

My dear Lady Wyatt

My only remaining fig tree was accidentially smashed by a lad with a ladder, so that figuratively speaking I now cut a figless figure.

Letters are the only solace of my life at present, except sardines and omelettes.

Believe me,

My dear Lady Wyatt,

Your's sincerely
Edward Lear

4 JANUARY

I strongly disapprove of your recipe

E Nesbit to Mavis Carter; shortly before the author's death

1924

I strongly disapprove of your marmalade recipe.
Far better cut up each orange in eight - don't squeeze - and soak before cutting up.
But, dear me, marmalade is far behind me.

The only reason I ever write a letter is out of desperation

Edna St Vincent Millay to Professor Herbert C Lipscomb

Austerlitz, New York, January 1946

... there is practically nothing under the sun or moon which I would not rather do than write any letter to any person whatsoever on earth: I would rather wash dishes all day; I would rather do a big washing on an old-fashioned scrubbing board; I would rather lay a pipe-line; I would rather dig a grave. The reason I never write a letter to anybody, is not, as you might think, that as a child my nurse stabbed me with a pen, or that my typing is verminous - no; as for pens, I use them rather often in my own work, and my typing is usually pretty good. But enough of that ... much too much.

The only reason I ever write a letter to anybody is out of desperation, a fear that some person, whose friendship I esteem and cherish, not understanding my continued silence, may become lost to me.

My earnest friendly greetings to you,
Edna St. Vincent Millay

6 JANUARY

Cloud of fog and flow of soul

Thomas Hardy to Edmund Gosse
Piccadilly, London, 6 January 1889

My dear Gosse

Here am I at the Savile in a pillar of a cloud of fog - there is my wife in Manchester Street - miles away - at least furlongs away - in another cloud of fog - while you are sitting by a comfortable fire in the land of Goshen where probably there is no fog or if any, it is rendered invisible by flow of soul. If we get to you we shall never get back, for the atmosphere thickens every moment.

Will come some day nevertheless. Kind regards to Mrs Gosse from

Yours, much disappointed

T.H.

7 JANUARY

The Letter

Published 1919

Little cramped words scrawling all over the paper
Like draggled fly's legs,
What can you tell of the flaring moon
Through the oak leaves?
Or of my uncertain window and the bare floor
Spattered with moonlight?
Your silly quirks and twists have nothing in them
Of blossoming hawthorns,
And this paper is dull, crisp, smooth, virgin of loveliness
Beneath my hand.

I am tired, Beloved, of chafing my heart against
The want of you;
Of squeezing it into little inkdrops,
And posting it.
And I scald alone, here, under the fire
Of the great moon.

Amy Lowell

The pen makes distance, presence

Samuel Richardson to Sophia Westcomb

1746

This correspondence is the cement of friendship: it is friendship avowed under hand and seal: more pure, yet more ardent, and less broken in upon, than personal conversation can be even amongst the most pure, because of the deliberation it allows, from the very preparation to, and action of writing.

A proof of this appears in the letter before me! – Every line of it flowing with that artless freedom, that noble consciousness of honourable meaning, which shines in every feature, in every sentiment, in every expression of the fair writer!

While I read it, I have you before me in person: I converse with you, and your dear Anna, as arm-in-arm you traverse the happy terrace: kept myself at humble distance – I see you, I sit with you, I talk with you, I read to you, I stop to hear your sentiments, in the summerhouse: your smiling obligingness, your polite and easy expression, even your undue diffidence, are all in my eye and my ear as I read. – Who then shall decline the converse of the pen? The pen that makes distance, presence; and brings back to sweet remembrance all the delights of presence; which makes even presence but body, while absence becomes the soul; and leaves no room for the intrusion of breakfast-calls, or dinner or supper direction, which often broke in upon us.

A pseudonym

Eric Blair to Leonard Moore; Eric Blair (pseudonym George Orwell) published his first work *Down and Out in Paris and London* on this day in 1933

Dear Mr Moore

Many thanks for your letter. I sent off the proof with the printer's queries on it yesterday. I made a few alterations & added one or two footnotes. I will send on the other proof as soon as possible.

As to a pseudonym, the name I always use when tramping etc. is P. S. Burton, but if you don't think this sounds a probable kind of name, what about

Kenneth Miles,
George Orwell,
H. Lewis Allways.

I rather favour George Orwell.

Yours sincerely
Eric A. Blair

P.S. As to the title of the book. Would *The Confessions of a Dishwasher* do as well? I would rather answer to 'dishwasher' than 'down and out', but if you and Mr. G think the present title best for selling purposes, then it is better to stick to it.

I love your verses with all my heart – and I love you too

Robert Browning to Elizabeth Barrett

New Cross, Hatcham, Surrey, 10 January 1845

I love your verses with all my heart, dear Miss Barrett, – and this is no off-hand complimentary letter that I shall write, – whatever else, no prompt matter-of-course recognition of your genius, and there a graceful and natural end of the thing. Since the day last week when I first read your poems, I quite laugh to remember how I have been turning and turning again in my mind what I should be able to tell you of their effect upon me, for in the first flush of delight I thought I would this once get out of my habit of purely passive enjoyment, when I do really enjoy, and thoroughly justify my admiration – perhaps even, as a loyal fellow-craftsman should, try and find fault and do you some little good to be proud of hereafter – but nothing comes of it all – so into me has it gone, and part of me has it become, this great living poetry of yours, not a flower of which but took root and grew – Oh, how different that is from lying to be dried and pressed flat and prized highly, and put in a book with a proper account at top and bottom, and shut up and put away ... and the book called a 'Flora', besides.

After all, I need not give up the thought of doing that, in time; because even now, talking with whoever is worthy, I can give a reason for my faith in one and another excellence, the fresh strange music, the affluent language, the exquisite pathos and true new brave thought; but in this addressing myself to you – your own self, and for the first time, my feeling rises altogether.

I do, as I say, love these with all my heart – and I love you too. Do you know I was once not very far from seeing you? Mr Kenyon said to me one morning, 'Would you like to see Miss Barrett?' then he went to announce me, – then he returned ... you were too unwell, and now it is years ago, and I feel as at some untoward passage in my travels, as if I had been close, so close, to some world's-wonder in chapel or crypt, only a screen to push and I might have entered, but there was some slight, so it now seems, slight and just sufficient bar to admission, and the half-opened door shut, and I went home my thousands of miles, and the sight was never to be?

Well, these Poems were to be, and this true thankful joy and pride with which I feel myself,

Yours ever faithfully,
Robert Browning

11 JANUARY

I thank you, dear Mr Browning

Elizabeth Barrett to Robert Browning

50 Wimple Street, London, 11 January 1845

I thank you, dear Mr Browning, from the bottom of my heart. You meant to give me pleasure by your letter – and even if the object had not been answered, I ought still to thank you. But it is thoroughly answered. Such a letter from such a hand! Sympathy is dear – very dear to me: but the sympathy of a poet, and of such a poet, is the quintessence of sympathy of me! Will you take back my gratitude for it? – agreeing, too, that of all the commerce done in the world, from Tyre to Carthage, the exchange of sympathy for gratitude is the most princely thing!

For the rest you draw me on with your kindness. It is difficult to get rid of when you once have given them too much pleasure – that is a fact, and we will not stop for the moral of it. What I was going to say – after a little natural hesitation – is, that if ever you emerge without inconvenient effort from your 'passive state', and will tell me of such faults as rise to the surface and strike you as important in my poems (for of course, I do not think of troubling you with criticism in detail) you will confer a lasting obligation on me, and one which I shall value so much, that I covet it at a distance.

...

Is it indeed true that I was so near to the pleasure and honour of making your acquaintance? and can it be true that you look upon the lost opportunity with any regret? But – you know – if you had entered the 'crypt,' you might have caught cold, or been tired to death, and wished yourself 'a thousand miles off'; which would have been worse than travelling them. It is not my interest, however, to put such thoughts in your head about its being 'all for the best' and I would rather hope (as I do) that what I lost by one chance I may recover by some future one. Winters shut me up as they do dormouse's eyes; in the spring, we shall see: and I am so much better that I seem turning round to the outward world again. And in the meantime I have learnt to know your voice, not merely from the poetry but from the kindness in it.

I am writing too much, and - notwithstanding that I am writing too much, I will write of one thing more. I will say that I am your debtor, not only for this cordial letter and for all the pleasure which came with it, but in other ways, and those the highest: and I will say that while I live to follow this divine art of poetry, in proportion to my love for it and my devotion to it, I must be a devout admirer and student of your works. This is in my heart to say to you - and I say it.

And for the rest, I am proud to remain,

Your obliged and faithful Elizabeth B. Barrett

12 JANUARY

A bucket of Greek sun

Dylan Thomas to Lawrence Durrell

Ringwood, Hampshire, c.1938

I think England is the very place for a fluent and fiery writer. The highest hymns of the sun are written in the dark. I like the grey country. A bucket of Greek sun would drown in one colour the crowds of colours I like trying to mix for myself out a grey flat insular mud. If I went to the sun I'd just sit in the sun; that would be very pleasant but I'm not doing it, and the only necessary things I do are the thing I am doing.

13 JANUARY

This is a grey, grim, pavement of a day

Katherine Mansfield to Lady Ottoline Morrell

London, 1918

I feel that winter, cruel forbidding winter is content to leave nothing unfrozen – not one heart or one bud of a soul to escape! If only one did not feel that it is all so wrong – so wrong. It would be much happier if one could feel – like M. – mankind is born to suffer. But I do feel that is so wrong – so wrong. It is like saying: mankind is born to walk about in goloshes under an umbrella. Oh dear – I should like to put a great notice over England, closed during the winter months. Perhaps if everybody were shipped off to blue skies and big bright flowers they would change. But I don't know. The miracle is that one goes on hoping and believing through it all just as passionately as ever one did –

This is a grey, grim, pavement of a day, with slow dropping rain.

14 JANUARY

A splendid frog

Christina Rossetti to her brother William Michael Rossetti
Longleat, Wiltshire, 14 January 1850

My dear William

The other day I met a splendid frog. He was of a sort of sere yellow spotted with black, and very large. Were you in this lovely country, you could hardly fail to gush poetry; with me the case is altogether different. The trees, the deer, the scenery, and indeed everything here, seems to influence me but little, with two exceptions, the cold, and the frog. The cold can never fail to interest a well brought-up Englishwoman; and the frog every claim on my sympathy. He appeared to be leading a calm and secluded life.

Sick of writing nonsense (can you echo this with the alteration of one word?), with Aunt Charlotte's love, I remain

Dear William
Ever your affect. sister,
Christina G. Rossetti

Might I ask after the cat?

Lord Alfred Tennyson to Matilda Jessei

January 1849

My dear Matty

Write 'as long' letters as you like. I always like receiving letters with a bit of news. My fault is that I do not often answer - indeed just now I have rather a press of business in that way, such a heap of correspondence has accumulated at Moxon's while I have been away. I have just despatched a note to Lord Monteagle, a very obstinate one in return for an invitation to dine. I will not dine out if by any means I can avoid so doing. I am here in a pretty fix. The room smokes like the vestibule of ovens, the laundress is a Roman Catholic and has gone to her chapel and will not be here till night. The lock of the door is spoilt, so that I cannot fasten it up when I go out, and I couldn't leave open chambers in London. So here I am hungry too and want my dinner and shall want till night. I wish you were here with your rosy face and nice kittenish ways sitting opposite, but I am alone, the rain falls, the bells are tolling. O me. Goodbye, dear.

P.S. I know you are fond of your relations - might I ask after the cat? Love to mother, ev[angelical] poet, Richard, etc. etc, dogs, monkeys, etc. etc.

No moment must be lost when a heart is breaking

Emily Dickinson to Mary Bowles; sent after the death of Samuel, Mary's husband

16 January 1878

I hasten to you, Mary, because no moment must be lost when a heart is breaking, for though it broke so long, each time is newer than the last, if it broke truly. To be willing that I should speak to you was so generous, dear.

Sorrow almost resents love, it is so inflamed.

I am glad if the broken words helped you. I had not hoped so much, I felt so faint in uttering them, thinking of your great pain. Love makes us 'heavenly' without our trying in the least. 'Tis easier than a Saviour – it does not stay on high and call us to its distance; its low 'Come unto me' begins in every place. It makes but one mistake, it tells us it is 'rest' – perhaps its toil is rest, but what we have not known we shall know again, that divine 'again' for which we are all breathless.

I am glad you 'work.' Work is a bleak redeemer, but it does redeem; it tires the flesh so that can't tease the spirit.

Dear 'Mr Sam' is very near, these midwinter days. When purples come on Pelham, in the afternoon, we say 'Mr Bowles's colors'. I spoke to him once of his Gem chapter, and the beautiful eyes rose till they were out of reach of mine, in some hallowed fathom.

Not that he goes – we love him more
Who led us while he stayed.
Beyond earth's trafficking frontier,
For what he moved, he made.

Mother is timid and feeble, but we keep her with us. She thanks you for remembering her, and never forgets you ... Your sweet 'and left me all alone,' consecrates your lips.

Emily

17 JANUARY

My thoughts are all aqueous

George Eliot to Sara Hennell

January 1849

I think of you perpetually, but my thoughts are all aqueous;
they will not crystallize – they are as fleeting as ripples on the sea.
I am suffering perhaps as acutely as ever I did in my life.
Breathe a wish that I may gather strength
– the fragrance of your wish will reach me somehow.

Deprived of the power to read and write

Frederick Douglass to Thomas Auld, the slave owner from whom Douglass escaped

Published in the abolitionist newspaper *The Liberator*, 1848

At this moment, you are probably the guilty holder of at least three of my own dear sisters, and my only brother in bondage. These you regard as your property. They are recorded on your ledger, or perhaps have been sold to human flesh mongers, with a view to filling your own ever-hungry purse.

Sir, I desire to know how and where these dear sisters are. Have you sold them? Or are they still in your possession? What has become of them? Are they living or dead? And my dear old grandmother, whom you turned out like an old horse, to die in the woods - is she still alive?

Write and let me know all about them. Oh! she was to me a mother, and a father. Send me my grandmother! that I may watch over and take care of her in her old age.

And my sisters, let me know all about them. I would write to them, and learn all I want to know of them, without disturbing you in any way, but that, through your unrighteous conduct, they have been entirely deprived of the power to read and write. You have kept them in utter ignorance, and have therefore robbed them of the sweet enjoyments of writing or receiving letters from absent friends and relatives. Your wickedness and cruelty committed in this respect on your fellow-creatures, are greater than all the stripes you have laid upon my back, or theirs. It is an outrage upon the soul - a war upon the immortal spirit.

19 JANUARY

Under a hedge, or at the side of a pond

William Cowper to Samuel Rose

Weston Lodge, Buckinghamshire, 19 January 1789

My dear Sir – I have taken, since you went away, many of the walks which we have taken together; and none of them, I believe, without thoughts of you. I have, though not a good memory in general, yet a good local memory, and can recollect, by the help of a tree or stile, what you said on that particular spot. For this reason I purpose, when the summer is come, to walk with a book in my pocket; what I read at my fireside I forget, but what I read under a hedge, or at the side of a pond, that pond and that hedge will always bring to my remembrance; and this is a sort of *memoria technica* which I would recommend to you if I did not know that you have no occasion for it.

20 JANUARY

Time cures at last

Voltaire to a friend in bereavement
England, 1728

The squaring of the circle and perpetual motion are simple discoveries in comparison to the secret of bringing peace to a soul distraught by passionate grief. It is only magicians who pretend to calm storms with words. If an injured man, with a deep, gaping wound, begs his surgeon to close that wound so that only a slight scar shall remain, the surgeon replies: 'That must be done by a greater physician than I am: only Time can mend what has been torn in a moment. I can amputate, cut out, destroy; Time alone can repair.'

So is it with the wounds of the soul: the would-be comforter inflames and excites them: or, at tempting to comfort, moves to fresh tears: but Time cures at last.

Translated from the French by S. G. Tallentyre

21 JANUARY

I am a kind of hobgoblin clouted and bagged up

Samuel Taylor Coleridge to Mrs Evans

1793

This is the third day of my resurrection from the couch, or rather, the sofa of sickness. About a fortnight ago, a quantity of matter took it into its head to form in my left gum, and was attended with such violent pain, inflammation and swelling, that it threw me into a fever. However, God be praised, my gum has at last been opened, a villainous tooth extracted, and all is well. I am still very weak, as well I may, since for seven days together I was incapable of swallowing anything but spoon meat, so that in point of spirits I am but the dregs of my former self – a decaying flame agonizing in the snuff of a tallow candle – a kind of hobgoblin, clouted and bagged up in the most contemptible shreds, rags and yellow relics of threadbare mortality.

22 JANUARY

Care took wing

Mary Wollstonecraft to Gilbert Imlay

Scandanavia, January 1796

Rocks were piled on rocks, forming a suitable bulwark to the ocean. 'Come no further,' they emphatically said, turning their dark sides to the waves to augment the idle roar. The view was sterile; still little patches of earth of the most exquisite verdure, enamelled with the sweetest wild flowers, seemed to promise the goats and a few straggling cows luxurious herbage. How silent and peaceful was the scene!

I gazed around with rapture, and felt more of that spontaneous pleasure which gives credibility to our expectation of happiness than I had for a long, long time before. I forgot the horrors I had witnessed in France*, which had cast a gloom over all nature, and suffering the enthusiasm of my character - too often, gracious God! damped by the tears of disappointed affection - to be lighted up afresh, care took wing while simple fellow-feeling expanded my heart.

**during the French Revolution*

I don't much care if I never see a mountain in my life

Charles Lamb to William Wordsworth

January 1801

I don't much care if I never see a mountain in my life. I have passed all my days in London, until I have formed as many and intense local attachments as any of you mountaineers can have done with dead Nature. The lighted shops of the Strand and Fleet Street; the innumerable trades, tradesmen and customers, coaches, waggons, playhouses; all the bustle and wickedness round about Covent Garden; the very women of the Town; the watchmen, drunken scenes, rattles; life awake, if you awake, at all hours of the night; the impossibility of being dull in Fleet Street; the crowds, the very dirt and mud, the sun shining upon houses and pavements, the print shops, the old bookstalls, parsons cheapening books, coffee-houses, steams of soups from kitchens, the pantomimes - London itself a pantomime and a masquerade - all these things work themselves into my mind, and feed me, without a power of satiating me. The wonder of these sights impels me into nightwalks about her crowded streets, and I often shed tears in the motley Strand from fullness of joy at so much life. All these emotions must be strange to you; so are your rural emotions to me.

My attachments are all local, purely local, I have no passion (or have had none since I was in love, and then it was the spurious engendering of poetry and books) for groves and valleys. The rooms where I was born, the furniture which has been before my eyes all my life, a bookcase which has followed me about like a faithful dog (only exceeding him in knowledge), wherever I have moved, old chairs, old tables, streets, squares, where I have sunned myself, my old school - these are my mistresses. Have I not enough, without your mountains? I do not envy you. I should pity you, did I not know that the mind will make friends of anything. Your sun, and moon, and skies, and hills, and lakes, affect me no more, or scarcely come to me in more venerable characters, than as a gilded room with tapestry and tapers, where I might live with handsome visible objects. I consider the clouds above me but as a roof beautifully painted, but unable to satisfy the mind: and at last, like the pictures of the apartment of a connoisseur, unable to afford him any longer a pleasure. So fading upon me, from disuse, have been the beauties of Nature, as they have been confinedly called; so ever fresh, and green, and warm are all the inventions of men, and assemblies of men in this great city.

C. L.

24 JANUARY

We thought we had got into fairyland

Charles Lamb to Thomas Manning

London, 1802

And my final resolve was, a tour to the Lakes. I set out with Mary* to Keswick, without giving Coleridge any notice, for my time, being precious, did not admit of it. He received us with all the hospitality in the world, and gave up his time to show us all the wonders of the country. He dwells upon a small hill by the side of Keswick, in a comfortable house, quite enveloped on all sides by a net of mountains: great floundering bears and monsters they seemed, all couchant and asleep. We got in in the evening, travelling in a post-chaise from Penrith, in the midst of a gorgeous sunshine, which transmuted all the mountains into colours, purple, etc. etc. We thought we had got into fairyland. But that went off (as it never came again; while we stayed we had no more fine sunsets), and we entered Coleridge's comfortable study just in the dusk, when the mountains were all dark with clouds upon their heads. Such an impression I never received from objects of sight before, nor do I suppose I can ever again.

**Charles's sister, the writer Mary Lamb*

A little wounded hare

Robert Burns to Alexander Cunningham

Ellisland, Scotland, 1789

My dear Sir

- I have just put the last hand to a little Poem, which I think will be something to your taste - One morning lately as I was out pretty early in the fields sowing some grass-seeds, I heard the burst of a shot from a neighbouring Plantation, & presently a little wounded hare came crippling by me. - You will guess my indignation at the inhuman fellow, who could shoot a hare at this season when they all of them have young ones; & it gave me no little gloomy satisfaction to see the poor injured creature escape him. - Indeed there is something in all that multiform business of destroying for our sport individuals in the animal creation that do not injure us materially, that I could never reconcile to my ideas of native Virtue & eternal Right -

> On Seeing a Fellow Sound a Hare with a Shot -
> April - 1789
> Inhuman man! curse on thy barb'rous art

If I lived in the golden age of English letter writing

Philip Larkin to Monica Jones

Hull, 1967

Oh dear. I don't seem to be able to write you the interesting sort of letter I should like to – if I lived in the golden age of English letter writing, and had nothing to do but snuff the candles, draw the curtains, and lodge the kettle on the fire, I'm sure I could do much better. 'Past Turvey's Mill on my walk, dyd see a Hare,' etc. A pity we can't live in our imaginations! My kitchen wireless has gone wrong, so I eat my meals in silence – having heard *The Archers* in the sitting room. All well, I shall see you next weekend. I don't know whether I shall appear by six – I'll let you know.

27 JANUARY

Monday was the great and glossy day

Marianne Moore to Mary and John Warner Moore

New York, 1909

Dear Family

I have passed through the multimum of strange adventures, this past week. [...]

Monday was the great and glossy day – I thrived then, most. [...]

The shops are beau.ti-ful – with natural polished wood backgrounds and panne velvet draperies, a few pieces, of lace or of diamonds or vases, or what not according to the store – we went to Tiffany's to order cards for Hilda. The place is a marvel, obsequious lacqueys at the door – and a maze of jewels and necklaces, vases, and silverware to beat Aladdin – inside a very beautiful display of Favrile glass in one case. Two pieces were dull iridescent blue with silver twisted stripes about them, squat like jars that [I] liked excellently, but some of the pieces are hideous and I think don't pretend to be pretty. The uncut stones and jewel flowers entertained me – a whole carnation, crusted with topaz (pink not very pretty) but the ancient dull gold chains and twisted pearl short necklaces and the lapis lazuli and crystal turned me sea green, and the plain gold hair brushes and belt buckles and shoe buckles and the stained glass lamp shades.

The unfortunate transcriber

Lady Mary Wortley Montagu to her daughter, the Countess of Bute

Louvere, Italy, 28 January 1733

Many a young damsel has been ruined by a fine copy of verses, which she would have laughed at if she had known it had been stolen from Mr Waller*. I remember, when I was a girl, I saved one of my companions from destruction, who communicated to me an epistle she was quite charmed with. As she had naturally a good taste, she observed the lines were not so smooth as Prior's or Pope's, but had more thought and spirit than any of theirs. She was wonderfully delighted with such a demonstration of her lover's sense and passion, and not a little pleased with her own charms, that had force enough to inspire such elegancies. In the midst of this triumph I shewed her, that they were taken from Randolph's** poems, and the unfortunate transcriber was dismissed with the scorn he deserved. To say truth, the poor plagiary was very unlucky to fall into my hands; that author being no longer in fashion, would have escaped any one of less universal reading than myself.

**the poet Edmund Waller (1606-1687)*

***the poet Thomas Randolph (1605-1635)*

29 JANUARY

You are the best woman in the world

Entries in Louisa May Alcott's journal

January 1845

MY DEAREST LOUY, – I often peep into your diary, hoping to see some record of more happy days. Hope, and keep busy, dear daughter, and in all perplexity or trouble come freely to your
MOTHER.

DEAR MOTHER, – You shall see more happy days, and I will come to you with my worries, for you are the best woman in the world.

L.M.A.

I am a half mad melancholly dog in this moozy misty country

John Clare to John Taylor

January 1821

Dear Taylor

I am writing 'Winter' a half salve as it were but as true as the gospel & why is not a man to tell truth & shame the devil in these devilish comical times – when that's finished I shall have 'Days gone bye' & then the 'Loves of Jockey & Jinney'. I have something I think that will struggle and hobble out of me better than I have yet done only tell me my faults in long poems of the Ways in a village you last got & I shall know how to escape shipwreck for the future with your Compass I cannot feel satisfied without leading strings yet tho I think I want them less then before

Give my respects to Keats & tell him I am a half mad melancholly dog in this moozy misty country he has lately cast behind him but I feel somthing better at least I fancy which I believe to tell truth is the whole of my complaint which I am so fussy over bytimes

I cannot write sense this Morning

John Keats to John Hamilton Reynolds

Hampstead, 31 January 1818

My dear Reynolds ... the fact is, I cannot write sense this Morning – however you shall have some – I will copy out my last Sonnet.

When I have fears that I may cease to be
Before my pen has glean'd my teeming brain,
Before high piled Books in charactery,
Hold like rich garners the full ripen'd grain –
When I behold, upon the night's starr'd face,
Huge cloudy symbols of a high romance,
And think that I may never live to trace
Their shadows, with the magic hand of chance;
And when I feel, fair creature of an hour,
That I shall never look upon thee more,
Never have relish in the faery power
Of unreflecting Love; – then on the shore
Of the wide world I stand alone, and think
Till Love and Fame to nothingness do sink.

--

Your sincere friend
John Keats

FEBRUARY

1 FEBRUARY

A horror of letter writing

Jane Carlyle to John Sterling

1 February 1837

The fact is, since I became so sick and dispirited I have contracted a horror of letter-writing, almost equal to the hydrophobia horror for cold water. I would write anything under heaven – fairytales, or advertisements for Warren's Blacking even – rather than a letter! A letter behoves to tell about oneself, and when oneself is disagreeable to oneself, one would rather tell about anything else; for, alas! one does not find the same gratification in dwelling upon one's own sin and misery, as in showing up the sin and misery of one's neighbour.

2 FEBRUARY

I have no sweet sunset to gild a page for you

Emily Dickinson to Susan Huntington Dickinson

February 1852

And thank you for my dear letter, which came on Saturday night, when all the world was still; thank you for the love it bore me, and for it's golden thoughts, and feelings so like gems, that I was sure I gathered them in whole baskets of pearls! I mourn this morning, Susie, that I have no sweet sunset to gild a page for you, nor any bay so blue - not even a little chamber way up in the sky, as your's is, to give me thoughts of heaven, which I would give to you. You know how I must write you, down, down, in the terrestrial - no sunset here, no stars; not even a bit of twilight which I may poetize - and send you! Yet Susie, there will be romance in the letter's ride to you - think of the hills and the dales, and the rivers it will pass over, and the drivers and conductors who will hurry it on to you; and wont that make a poem such as can ne'er be written?

3 FEBRUARY

Send me a blotted thought

Elizabeth Barrett to Robert Browning

50 Wimpole Street, London, 3 February 1845

Why how could I hate to write to you, dear Mr Browning? Could you believe in such a thing? If nobody likes writing to everybody (except such professional letter writers as you and I are *not*), yet everybody likes writing to somebody, and it would be strange and contradictory if I were not always delighted both to hear from *you* and to write to *you*, this talking upon paper being as good a social pleasure as another, when our means are somewhat straitened. As for me, I have done most of my talking by post of late years – as people shut up in dungeons take up with scrawling mottoes on the walls.

I write this to you to show how I can have pleasure in letters, and never think them too long, nor too frequent, nor too illegible from being written in little 'pet hands'. I can read any MS except the writing on the pyramids. And if you will only promise to treat me *en bon camarade*, without reference to the conventionalities of 'ladies and gentlemen', taking no thought for your sentences (nor for mine), nor for your blots (nor for mine), nor for your blunt speaking (nor for mine), nor for your badd speling (nor for mine), and if you agree to send me a blotted thought whenever you are in the mind for it, and with as little ceremony and less legibility than you would think it necessary to employ towards your printer – why, *then*, I am ready to sign and seal the contract, and to rejoice in being 'articled' as your correspondent. Only *don't* let us have any constraint, any ceremony! *Don't* be civil to me when you feel rude, – nor loquacious when you incline to silence, – nor yielding in the manners when you are perverse in the mind.

4 FEBRUARY

Now the babies are crying, I must take them out to tea

Sylvia Plath to her US psychiatrist Dr Ruth Tiffany Barnhouse Beuscher; Plath took her own life a week later

London, 4 February 1963

What appals me is the return of my madness, my paralysis, my fear & vision of the worst – cowardly withdrawal, a mental hospital, lobotomies. Perhaps this is accentuated by my seeing Ted once a week when he comes to see Frieda – seeing how happy & whole & independent he is now, how much more I admire him like this, & what good friends we could be if I could manage to grow up too. He is gaga over this ad-agency girl who has gone back to live with her third husband to keep the passion hot, although she did live for three weeks with Ted & flew to Spain for a holiday with him. If I were simply jealous about this it would be okay. But I know Spain and lovemaking would do me no good now, not until I find myself again. I feel I need a ritual for survival from day to day until I begin to grow out of this death & found Fromm's recommendation* for concentration, patience & faith gave me a kind of peace, but that I keep slipping into this pit of panic & deepfreeze, with my mother's horrible example of fearful anxiety & 'unselfishness' on one side & the beauties of my two little children on the other. I am living on sleeping pills & nerve tonic & have managed a few commissions for a magazine & the BBC and poems very good but, I feel written on the edge of madness. The publicity of Ted's leaving is universal & I was taking it all with dignity & verve at first – people were buying poems & putting BBC work in my way & I am scared to death I shall just pull up the psychic shroud & give up. A poet, a writer, I am I think very narcissistic & the despair at being 30 & having let myself slide, studied nothing for years, having mastered no body of objective knowledge is on me like a cold, accusing wind. Just now it is torture to me to dress, plan meals, put one foot in front of the other. Ironically my novel about my first breakdown is getting rave reviews over here. I feel a simple act of will would make the world steady & solidify. No one can save me but myself, but I need help & my doctor is referring me to a woman psychiatrist. Living on my wits, my writing – even partially, is very hard at this time, it is so subjective & dependent on objectivity. I am, for the first time since my marriage, relating to people without Ted, but my own lack of center, of mature identity, is a great torment. I am aware of a cowardice in myself, a wanting to give up. If I could study, read, enjoy people on my own Ted's leaving would be hard, but manageable.

But there is this damned, self-induced freeze. I am suddenly in agony, desperate, thinking, 'Yes, let him take over the house, the children, let me just die & be done with it.' How can I get out of this ghastly defeatist cycle & grow up. I am only too aware that love and a husband are impossibles to me at this time, I am incapable of being myself & loving myself. Now the babies are crying, I must take them out to tea.

With love,
Sylvia

*The Art of Loving *(1956) by Erich Fromm*

What am I thinking about? you ask. So help me God, of immortality

John Milton to Charles Diodati

London, 1637

Cæterum jam curiositati tuæ vis esse satisfactum scio. Multa solicite quæris, etiam quid cogitem. Audi, Theodote, verum in aurem ut ne rubeam, & sinito paulisper apud te grandia loquar; quid cogitem quæris; ita me bonus Deus, immortalitatem. Quid agam vero? πτεροφυ˜ω, & volare meditor: sed tenellis admodum adhuc pennis evehit se noster Pegasus, humile sapiamus.

I know it is time to satisfy your curiosity. You make many eager enquiries, even asking about my thoughts. I will tell you, Diodati, but let me whisper it in your ear, to spare my blushes, and allow me for a moment to speak to you in a boastful strain. 'What am I thinking about?' you ask. So help me God, of immortality. What am I doing? Growing wings and learning to fly; but my Pegasus can only rise on tender pinions as yet, so let my new wisdom be humble.

Translated from the Latin by Phyllis B. Tillyard

Not all is completely well with us

Anton Chekhov to Alexander Chekhov

Melikhovo, Russia, 6 February 1893

Not all is completely well with us. I'll itemize the matters point by point:
1) Father is ill. He has severe pain in his spine and numbness in his fingers. Neither condition is permanent but comes and goes, like angina pectoris. Both symptoms are clearly manifestations of old age. He ought to have treatment, but the lord and master continues to insist on eating all the wrong things and refuses to cut down on anything: pancakes for lunch, hot gruel for supper and all kinds of rubbishy snacks. He says of himself: 'I'm a martyr to paralysis' but won't take any advice.
2) Masha is ill. She has been in bed with a high temperature for a week, and we thought it must be typhoid. She is getting better now.
3) I am ill with influenza. I can't do anything and am irritable.
4) The pure-bred calf's ears have got frostbite.
5) The geese have chewed off the cockerel's comb.
6) Guests come all the time and stay the night.
7) The zemstvo management committee wants a medical report from me.
8) The house is subsiding in places and some of the doors won't shut.
9) The icy weather continues.
10) The sparrows are already copulating.
Actually, you may ignore the last point if you wish.
There is a distinctly hospital-like atmosphere in the house.
Be well.

Your
A. Chekhov

Translated from the Russian by Rosamund Bartlett and Antony Phillips

Your letter was a soothing gift

Dorothy Wordsworth to Mrs J Marshall; Dorothy's brother John, a sea captain, was drowned in a shipwreck

Grasmere, The Lake District, 1805

I cannot rest till I have written, so I choose a time in which my thoughts are calm and settled, and I will endeavour to keep in the grief which gushes out of me so many times in the day. I will tell you wherein my consolation is, and all that I can to comfort your tender heart. My good and dear Friend, your letter was a soothing gift, it drew a flood of tears from us, while we sate round our melancholy fire, and after they had passed away, we were in some sort cheared by your sympathy – it does me good to weep for him: it does me good to find that others weep, and I bless them for it. Enough of this, it is not now the time, if I go on I shall do no better than before.

I can turn to no object that does not remind me of our loss. I see nothing that he would not have loved with me and enjoyed had he been by my side; and indeed, indeed my consolations rather come to me in gusts of feeling, than are the quiet growth of my Mind. I know it will not always be so – the time will come when the light of the setting sun upon these mountain tops will be as heretofore a pure joy – not the same *gladness*, that can never be – but yet a joy even more tender. It will soothe me to know how happy *he* would have been could he have seen the same beautiful spectacle. I shall have him with me, and yet shall know that he is out of the reach of all sorrow and pain, can never mourn for us – his tender soul was awake to all our feeling – his wishes were intimately connected with our happiness.

... he loved solitude and he rejoiced in society – he would wander alone among these hills with his fishing-rod, or led on merely by the pleasure of walking, for many hours – or he would walk with William or me, or both of us, and was continually pointing out with a gladness which is seldom seen but in very young people something which perhaps would have escaped our observation, for he had so fine an eye that no distinction was unnoticed by him, and so tender a feeling that he never noticed any thing in vain. Many a time has he called me out in an evening to look at the moon or stars, or a cloudy sky, or this vale in the quiet moonlight but the stars and moon were his chief delight - he made of them his companions when he was at Sea, and was never tired of those thoughts which the silence of the night fed in him - then he was so happy by the fire-side, any little business of the house interested him, he loved our cottage, he helped us to furnish it, and to make the gardens - trees are growing now which he planted. Oh! my dear Jane!

8 FEBRUARY

William Blake lives in a world of his own

Crabb Robinson to Dorothy Wordsworth

February 1826

[William Blake] lives in a world of his own, enjoying constant intercourse with the world of spirits. He receives visits from Shakespeare, Milton, Dante, Voltaire, etc. etc. etc., and has given me repeatedly their very words in their conversations. His paintings are copies of what he saw in his Visions. His books are dictations from the spirits. He told me yesterday that when he writes it is for the spirits only; he sees the words fly about the room the moment he has put them on paper, and his book is then published. A man so favoured, of course, has sources of wisdom and truth peculiar to himself.

9 FEBRUARY

This World Is a World of imagination & Vision

William Blake to Dr. Trusler

1799

Fun I love, but too much Fun is of all things the most loathsome. Mirth is better than Fun, & Happiness is better than Mirth. I feel that a Man may be happy in This World. And I know that This World Is a World of imagination & Vision. I see Every thing I paint In This World, but Every body does not see alike. To the Eyes of a Miser a Guinea is more beautiful than the Sun, & a bag worn with the use of Money has more beautiful proportions than a Vine filled with Grapes. The tree which moves some to tears of joy is in the Eyes of others only a Green thing that stands in the way. Some see Nature all Ridicule & Deformity & by these I shall not regulate my proportions & Some Scarce see Nature at all. But to the Eyes of the Man of Imagination, Nature is Imagination itself. As a man is, So he Sees. As the Eye is formed, such are its Powers. You certainly Mistake, when you say that the Visions of Fancy are not to be found in This World. To Me This World is all One continued Vision of Fancy or Imagination, & I feel Flatter'd when I am told so. What is it sets Homer, Virgil & Milton in so high a rank of Art? Why is the Bible more Entertaining & Instructive than any other book? Is it not because they are addressed to the Imagination, which is Spiritual Sensation, & but mediately to the Understanding or Reason? Such is True Painting, and such was alone valued by the Greeks & the best modern Artists.

But I am happy to find a Great Majority of Fellow Mortals who can Elucidate My Visions, & Particularly they have been Elucidated by Children, who have taken a greater delight in contemplating my Pictures than I even hoped. Neither Youth nor Childhood is Folly or Incapacity. Some Children are Fools & so are some Old Men. But There is a vast Majority on the side of Imagination or Spiritual Sensation.

Two lonely cross-roads

Robert Frost to Susan Hayes Ward; describing the winter walk that inspired Frost's poem 'The Road Not Taken'

Plymouth, New Hampshire, 10 February 1912

Dear Miss Ward

Two lonely crossroads that themselves cross each other I have walked several times this winter without meeting or overtaking so much as a single person on foot or on runners. The practically unbroken condition of both for several days after a snow or a blow proves that neither is much travelled. Judge then how surprised I was the other evening to see a man, who to my own unfamiliar eyes and in the dusk looked for all the world like myself, coming down the other, his approach to the point where our paths must intersect being so timed that unless one of us pulled up we must inevitably collide. I felt as if I was going to meet my own image in a slanting mirror. Or say I felt as we slowly converged on the same point with the same noiseless yet laborious strides as if we were two images about to float together with the uncrossing of someone's eyes. I verily expected to take up or absorb this other self and feel the stronger by the addition for the three-mile journey home. But I didn't go forward to the touch. I stood still in wonderment and let him pass by; and that, too, with the fatal omission of not trying to find out by a comparison of lives and immediate and remote interests what could have brought us by crossing paths to the same point in the wilderness at the same moment of nightfall. Some purpose I doubt not, if we could but have made it out. I like a coincidence almost as well as an incongruity.

Nonsensically yours
Robert Frost

11 FEBRUARY

I threw the pearl of my soul into a cup of wine

Oscar Wilde to Lord Alfred Douglas; from *De Profundis*, unsent but later published on this day in 1905

HM Prison, Reading, 1897

Dear Bosie

I must learn how to be happy. Once I knew it, or thought I knew it, by instinct. It was always springtime once in my heart. My temperament was akin to joy. I filled my life to the very brim with pleasure, as one might fill a cup to the very brim with wine. Now I am approaching life from a completely new standpoint, and even to conceive happiness is often extremely difficult for me. I remember during my first term at Oxford reading in Pater's *Renaissance* – that book which has had such strange influence over my life – how Dante places low in the Inferno those who wilfully live in sadness; and going to the college library and turning to the passage in the *Divine Comedy* where beneath the dreary marsh lie those who were 'sullen in the sweet air,' saying for ever and ever through their sighs –

Tristi fummo
*Nell aer dolce che dal sol s'allegra.**

I knew the church condemned accidia**, but the whole idea seemed to me quite fantastic, just the sort of sin, I fancied, a priest who knew nothing about real life would invent. Nor could I understand how Dante, who says that 'sorrow remarries us to God', could have been so harsh to those who were enamoured of melancholy, if any such there really were. I had no idea that some day this would become to me one of the greatest temptations of my life.

--

I don't regret for a single moment having lived for pleasure. I did it to the full, as one should do everything that one does. There was no pleasure I did not experience. I threw the pearl of my soul into a cup of wine. I went down the primrose path to the sound of flutes. I lived on honeycomb.

Your affectionate friend

* *We once were sullen,*
In the sweet air, made gladsome by the sun.
***listlessness*

12 FEBRUARY

I want to live by the spirit of Love

Katherine Mansfield to Richard Murry

February 1920

Life is a mystery to me. It is made up of Love and pains. One loves and one suffers, one suffers and one has to love. I feel (for myself individually) that I want to live by the spirit of Love - love all things. See into things so deeply and truly that one loves. That does not rule out hate, far from it. I mean it doesn't rule out anger. But I confess I only feel that I am doing right when I am living by love. I don't mean a personal love - you know - but - the big thing. Why should one love? No reason; it's just a mystery. But it is like light. I can only truly see things in its rays.

My dear mother's letters

Elizabeth Gaskell to George Hope
13 February 1849

I will not let an hour pass, my dear sir, without acknowledging your kindness in sending me my dear mother's letters, the only relics of her that I have, and of more value to me than I can express, for I have so often longed for some little thing that had once been hers or been touched by her. I think no one but one so unfortunate as to be early motherless* can enter into the craving one has after the lost mother.

It never entered my head to imagine you wished to see me for any other reason than as the daughter of old friends. You cannot think how it gratified one to be sought out for their sakes, – a gratification I should certainly have been very far from feeling if I had for a moment suspected you of coming from mere curiosity. I have been brought up away from all those who knew my parents, and therefore those who come to me with a remembrance of them as an introduction seem to have a holy claim on my regard.

**Elizabeth was 13 months old when her mother died*

My letters are written from my spirit to your spirit

Nathaniel Hawthorne to Sophia Peabody

Boston, 1839

Mine own Dove,

I have been sitting by my fireside ever since teatime, till now it is past eight o'clock: and have been musing and dreaming about a thousand things, with every one of which, I do believe, some nearer or remoter thought of you was intermingled. I should have begun this letter earlier in the evening, but was afraid that some intrusive idler would thrust himself between us and so the sacredness of my letter would be partly lost - for I feel as if my letters were sacred, because they are written from my spirit to your spirit. I wish it were possible to convey them to you by other than earthly messengers - to convey them directly into your heart, with the warmth of mine still lingering in them. When we shall be endowed with our spiritual bodies, I think they will be so constituted, that we may send thoughts and feelings any distance, in no time at all, and transfuse them warm and fresh into the consciousness of those whom we love. Oh what a bliss it would be, at this moment; if I could be conscious of some purer feeling, some more delicate sentiment, some lovelier fantasy, than could possibly have had its birth in my own nature, and therefore be aware that my Dove was thinking through my mind and feeling through my heart! Try - some evening when you are alone and happy, and when you are most conscious of loving me and being loved by me - and see if you do not possess this power already. But, after all, perhaps it is not wise to intermix fantastic ideas with the reality of our affection. Let us content ourselves to be earthly creatures, and hold communion of spirit in such modes as are ordained to us - by letters (dipping our pens as deep as may be into our hearts) by heartfelt words, when they can be audible; by glances - through which medium spirits do really seem to talk in their own language - and by holy kisses, which I do think have something supernatural in them.

And now good night, my beautiful Dove. I do not write any more at present, because there are three more whole days before this letter will visit you; and I desire to talk with you, each of those three days. Your letter did not come today.

Inscape

Gerard Manley Hopkins to Robert Bridges

St. Giles's, Oxford, 15 February 1879

Dearest Bridges

When I say that I do not mean to publish I speak the truth.

If some one in authority knew of my having some poems printable and suggested my doing it I should not refuse, I should be partly, though not altogether, glad. But that is very unlikely. All therefore that I think of doing is to keep my verses together in one place - at present I have not even correct copies - , that, if anyone should like, they might be published after my death. And that again is unlikely, as well as remote. I could add other considerations, as that if I meant to publish at all it ought to be more or ought at least to be followed up, and how can that be? I cannot in conscience spend time on poetry, neither have I the inducements and inspirations that make others compose. Feeling, love in particular, is the great moving power and spring of verse and the only person that I am in love with seldom, especially now, stirs my heart sensibly and when he does I cannot always 'make capital' of it, it would be a sacrilege to do so. Then again I have of myself made verse so laborious.

No doubt my poetry errs on the side of oddness. I hope in time to have a more balanced and Miltonic style. But as air, melody, is what strikes me most of all in music and design in painting, so design, pattern or what I am in the habit of calling 'inscape' is what I above all aim at in poetry. Now it is the virtue of design, pattern or inscape to be distinctive and it is the vice of distinctiveness to become queer. This vice I cannot have escaped.

16 FEBRUARY

The inward light of poetry

George Eliot to the Hon. Mrs Ponsonby

February 1875

Do send me the papers you have written – I mean as a help and instruction to me. I need very much to know how ideas lie in other minds than my own, that I may not miss their difficulties while I am urging only what satisfies myself. I shall be deeply interested in knowing exactly what you wrote at that particular stage. Please remember that I don't consider myself a teacher, but a companion in the struggle of thought. What can consulting physicians do without pathological knowledge? And the more they have of it, the less absolute – the more tentative – are their procedures.

...

Consider what the human mind en masse would have been if there had been no such combination of elements in it as has produced poets. All the philosophers and savants would not have sufficed to supply that deficiency. And how can the life of nations be understood without the inward light of poetry – that is, of emotion blending with thought?

But the beginning and object of my letter must be the end – please send me your papers.

Hiding the ravages of care with a sickly mask of mirth

From Chapter 17 of Charles Dickens's novel *David Copperfield* (1850). David describes a dinner with the Micawbers after which he receives a letter from Mr Micawber. It is by no means the last letter which David receives from him.

We had a beautiful little dinner. Quite an elegant dish of fish; the kidney-end of a loin of veal, roasted; fried sausage-meat; a partridge, and a pudding. There was wine, and there was strong ale; and after dinner Mrs Micawber made us a bowl of hot punch with her own hands.

Mr Micawber was uncommonly convivial. I never saw him such good company. He made his face shine with the punch, so that it looked as if it had been varnished all over. He got cheerfully sentimental about the town, and proposed success to it; observing that Mrs Micawber and himself had been made extremely snug and comfortable there and that he never should forget the agreeable hours they had passed in Canterbury. He proposed me afterwards; and he, and Mrs Micawber, and I, took a review of our past acquaintance. Then I proposed Mrs Micawber or, at least, said, modestly, 'If you'll allow me, Mrs Micawber, I shall now have the pleasure of drinking your health, ma'am.' [...]

As the punch disappeared, Mr Micawber became still more friendly and convivial. Mrs Micawber's spirits becoming elevated, too, we sang 'Auld Lang Syne'. When we came to 'Here's a hand, my trusty frere', we all joined hands round the table; and when we declared we would 'take a right gude Willie Waught', and hadn't the least idea what it meant, we were really affected.

In a word, I never saw anybody so thoroughly jovial as Mr Micawber was, down to the very last moment of the evening, when I took a hearty farewell of himself and his amiable wife. Consequently, I was not prepared, at seven o'clock next morning, to receive the following communication, dated half past nine in the evening; a quarter of an hour after I had left him: -

'My DEAR YOUNG FRIEND,

'The die is cast - all is over. Hiding the ravages of care with a sickly mask of mirth, I have not informed you, this evening, that there is no hope of the remittance! Under these circumstances, alike humiliating to endure, humiliating to contemplate and humiliating to relate, I have discharged the pecuniary liability contracted at this establishment, by giving a note of hand, made payable fourteen days after date, at my residence, Pentonville, London. When it becomes due, it will not be taken up. The result is destruction. The bolt is Impending, and the tree must fall.

'Let the wretched man who now addresses you, my dear Copperfield, be a beacon to you through life. He writes with that intention, and in that hope. If he could think himself of so much use, one gleam of day might, by possibility, penetrate into the cheerless dungeon of his remaining existence - though his longevity is, at present (to say the least of it), extremely problematical.

'This is the last communication, my dear Copperfield, you will ever receive

'From

'The

'Beggared Outcast,

'WILKINS MICAWBER.'

18 FEBRUARY

Everything unnatural, broken, blasted

Wilfred Owen to his mother; from the Front in the First World War
Advanced Horse Transport Depot, France, 1917

My own dear Mother

I have no mind to describe all the horrors of this last Tour. But it was almost worse than the first, because in this place my Platoon had no Dug-Outs, but had to lie in the snow under the deadly wind. By day it was impossible to stand up or even to crawl about because we were behind only a little up ridge screening us from the Boches' periscope.

We had five Tommy's cookers between the Platoon, but they did not suffice to melt the ice in the water-cans. So we suffered cruelly from thirst.

The marvel is that we did not all die of cold. As a matter of fact, only one of my party actually froze to death before he got back, but I am not able to tell how many have ended in hospital. I had no real casualties from shelling, though for ten minutes every hour whizz-bangs fell a few yards short of us. Showers of soil rained on us, but no fragments of shell could find us.

I had lost my gloves in a dug-out, but I found one mitten on the Field; I had my Trench Coat (without lining but with a Jerkin underneath). My feet ached until they could ache no more, and so they temporarily died. I was kept warm by the ardour of life within me. I forgot hunger in the hunger for Life. The intensity of your Love reached me and kept me living. I thought of you and Mary without break all the time. I cannot say I felt any fear. We were all half crazed by the buffeting of the High Explosives. I think the most unpleasant reflection that weighed on me was the impossibility of getting back any wounded, a total impossibility. All day impossible, and frightfully difficult by night.

We were marooned on a frozen desert.

There is not a sign of life on the horizon and a thousand signs of death.

Not a blade of grass, not an insect; once or twice a day the shadow of a big hawk scenting carrion.

By degrees, day-by-day, we worked back through the reserve, & support lines. At last I got to the village, and found all your dear precious letters.

Your own Wilfred x

P.S. I suppose I can endure cold, and fatigue, and the face-to-face death, as well as another; but extra for me there is the universal pervasion of *Ugliness*. Hideous landscapes, vile noises, foul language, and nothing but foul even from one's own mouth (for all are devil ridden), everything unnatural, broken, blasted; the distortion of the dead, whose unburiable bodies sit outside the dug-outs all day, all night, the most execrable sights on earth. In poetry we call them the most glorious. But to sit with them all day, all night ... and a week later to come back and find them still sitting there in motionless groups THAT is what saps the 'soldierly spirit'.

This sparing touch of noble Books

John Keats to John Hamilton Reynolds
Hampstead, 19 February 1818

My dear Reynolds

I had an idea that a Man might pass a very pleasant life in this manner – Let him on a certain day read a certain page of full Poesy or distilled Prose, and let him wander with it, and muse upon it, and reflect from it, and bring home to it, and prophesy upon it, and dream upon it: until it becomes stale – But when will it do so? Never – When Man has arrived at a certain ripeness in intellect any one grand and spiritual passage serves him as a starting-post towards all 'the two-and-thirty Palaces'.

How happy is such a voyage of conception, what delicious diligent indolence! A doze upon a sofa does not hinder it, and a nap upon Clover engenders ethereal finger-pointings – the prattle of a child gives it wings, and the converse of middle-age a strength to beat them – a strain of music conducts to 'an odd angle of the Isle', and when the leaves whisper it puts a girdle round the earth. – Nor will this sparing touch of noble Books be any irreverence to their Writers – for perhaps the honors paid by Man to Man are trifles in comparison to the benefit done by great works to the 'spirit and pulse of good' by their mere passive existence.

20 FEBRUARY

After the time of leaving you

Mary Lamb To Sarah Stoddart

February 1806

My dear Sarah,

I am going to make a sort of promise to myself and to you, that I will write you kind of journal-like letters of the daily what-we-do matters, as they occur. This day seems to me a kind of new era in our time. It is not a birthday, nor a new-year's day, nor a leave-off-smoking day; but it is about an hour after the time of leaving you; and I am holding a solitary consultation with myself as to the how I shall employ myself.

Writing plays, novels, poems and all manner of such-like vapouring and vapourish schemes are floating in my head, which at the same time aches with the thought of parting from you, and is perplext at the idea of I-cannot-tell-what-about notion that I have not made you half so comfortable as I ought to have done, and a melancholy sense of the dull prospect you have before you on your return home. Then I think I will make my new gown; and now I consider the white petticoat will be better candle-light worth; and then I look at the fire, and think, if the irons was but down, I would iron my Gowns.

21 FEBRUARY

Your Bible

Edna St Vincent Millay to her mother Cora B. Millay

Vassar College, New York, February 1914

Dear Mother, -

Will you lend me, and send to me, your Bible - I think I am old enough now to read it; too grown-up to be any longer bitter and scoffing and sceptical about it all, and so lose all the loveliness there is in it. - No, I've not 'got religion', and I don't have much time to read, goodness knows, but it really is, isn't it, sort of heathenish, with all the books I have, not to have a Bible? - You know it by heart, so you don't need it. But I really do need it, Mother dear, and want it a whole lot, and especially your own Bible, if I may borrow it. - Moral support perhaps. Anyway I want it in my room.

I have two sonnets soaking

Gerard Manley Hopkins to Robert Bridges
Oxford, 22 February 1879

I have two sonnets soaking, which if they should come to anything you shall have, and something, if I could only seize it, on the decline of wild nature, beginning somehow like this –

O where is it, the wilderness.
The wildness of the wilderness?
Where is it, the wilderness?

and ending –

And wander in the wilderness;
In the weedy wilderness,
Wander in the wilderness.

23 FEBRUARY

Beating about in the tempest of his mind

Joseph Severn to Charles Armitage Brown, written shortly before John Keats's death on this day in 1821

Rome, Italy, February 1821

– Little or no change has taken place, accepting this beautiful one, that [Keats's] mind is growing to great quietness and peace. I find this change has to do with the increasing weakness of his body, but to me it seems like a delightful sleep; I have been beating about in the tempest of his mind so long. Tonight he has talked very much, but so cozily, that he fell at last into a pleasant sleep. He seems to have happy dreams. This will bring on some change – it cannot be worse – it may be better. Among the many things he has requested of me tonight, this is the principal – that on his grave-stone shall be this inscription:

'HERE LIES ONE WHOSE NAME WAS WRIT IN WATER.'

You will understand this so well that I need not say a word about it.

On the Sale by Auction of Keats' Love-Letters

Oscar Wilde wrote this sonnet the day before the auction of John Keats' love letters to Fanny Brawne at Sotheby's in London, 1885. He bid for some of the letters.

These are the letters which Endymion wrote
    To one he loved in secret, and apart,
    And now the brawlers of the auction mart
Bargain and bid for each poor blotted note,
Ay, for each separate pulse of passion quote
    The latest price – I think they love not Art
    Who break the crystal of a poet's heart
That small and sickly eyes may glare or gloat.

Is it not said, that many years ago
    In a far Eastern Town some soldiers ran
    With torches through the midnight, and began
To wrangle for mean raiment, and to throw
    Dice for the garments of a wretched man,
Not knowing the Gods wonder or his woe?

Oscar Wilde

25 FEBRUARY

Good bye, my love, my dear love, my beauty

John Keats to Fanny Brawne

Wentworth Place, London, 25 February 1820

My dearest Fanny,

I have been turning over two volumes of Letters written between Rousseau and two Ladies in the perplexed strain of mingled finesse and sentiment in which the Ladies and gentlemen of those days were so clever, and which is still prevalent among Ladies of this Country who live in a state of reasoning romance. The likeness however only extends to the mannerism, not to the dexterity. What would Rousseau have said at seeing our little correspondence! What would his Ladies have said! I don't care much – I would sooner have Shakespeare's opinion about the matter.

Thank God I am born in England with our own great Men before my eyes. Thank God that you are fair and can love me without being Letter-written and sentimentaliz'd into it. –
Good bye, my love, my dear love, my beauty –

love me for ever.
J. K.

26 FEBRUARY

The sad work of reading old letters

From Chapter 5, 'Old Letters', of Elizabeth Gaskell's novel *Cranford* (1853)

All through tea-time [Miss Matty's] talk ran upon the days of her childhood and youth. Perhaps this reminded her of the desirableness of looking over all the old family letters, and destroying such as ought not to be allowed to fall into the hands of strangers; for she had often spoken of the necessity of this task, but had always shrunk from it, with a timid dread of something painful. Tonight, however, she rose up after tea and went for them – in the dark; for she piqued herself on the precise neatness of all her chamber arrangements, and used to look uneasily at me when I lighted a bed-candle to go to another room for anything. When she returned there was a faint, pleasant smell of Tonquin beans in the room. I had always noticed this scent about any of the things which had belonged to her mother; and many of the letters were addressed to her – yellow bundles of love-letters, sixty or seventy years old.

Miss Matty undid the packet with a sigh; but she stifled it directly, as if it were hardly right to regret the flight of time, or of life either. We agreed to look them over separately, each taking a different letter out of the same bundle and describing its contents to the other before destroying it. I never knew what sad work the reading of old letters was before that evening, though I could hardly tell why. The letters were as happy as letters could be – at least those early letters were. There was in them a vivid and intense sense of the present time, which seemed so strong and full, as if it could never pass away, and as if the warm, living hearts that so expressed themselves could never die, and be as nothing to the sunny earth. I should have felt less melancholy, I believe, if the letters had been more so. I saw the tears stealing down the well-worn furrows of Miss Matty's cheeks, and her spectacles often wanted wiping. I trusted at last that she would light the other candle, for my own eyes were rather dim, and I wanted more light to see the pale, faded ink; but no, even through her tears, she saw and remembered her little economical ways.

...

'We must burn them, I think,' said Miss Matty, looking doubtfully at me. 'No one will care for them when I am gone.' And one by one she dropped them into the middle of the fire, watching each blaze up, die out, and rise away, in faint, white, ghostly semblance, up the chimney, before she gave another to the same fate. The room was light enough now; but I, like her, was fascinated into watching the destruction of those letters, into which the honest warmth of a manly heart had been poured forth.

27 FEBRUARY

An infallible little rule for verse

Voltaire to M. Helvétius

Cirey, France, 27 February 1739

Shall I give you an infallible little rule for verse? Here it is. When a thought is just and noble, something still remains to be done with it: see if the way you have expressed it in verse would be effective in prose: and if your verse, without the swing of the rhyme, seems to you to have a word too many – if there is the least defect in the construction – if a conjunction is forgotten – if, in brief, the right word is not used, or not used in the right place, you must then conclude that the jewel of your thought is not well set. Be quite sure that lines which have any one of these faults will never be learnt by heart, and never re-read: and the only good verses are those which one re-reads and remembers, in spite of oneself.

Translated from the French by S. G. Tallentyre

28 FEBRUARY

Thoughts and feelings heaped up and clotted together

Edward FitzGerald to John Allen

Manchester, February 1833

Dear Allen

... I am fearful to boast, lest I should lose what I boast of: but I think I have achieved a victory over my evil spirits here: for they have full opportunity to come, and I often observe their approaches, but hitherto I have managed to keep them off. Lord Bacon's *Essay on Friendship* is wonderful for its truth: and I often feel its truth. He says that with a Friend 'a man tosseth his thoughts', an admirable saying, which one can understand, but not express otherwise. But I feel that, being alone, one's thoughts and feelings, from want of communication, become heaped up and clotted together, as it were: and so lie like undigested food heavy upon the mind: but with a friend one tosseth them about, so that the air gets between them, and keeps them fresh and sweet.

'A head overworked, and a heart over-loaded'

Madame d'Arblay (Fanny Burney) to Mrs. Burney

29 February 1823

I have been suddenly taken, in the middle of the night, with a seizure as if a hundred windmills were turning round in my head: in short, - I had now recourse to serious medical help, ... and, to come to the sum total, I am now so much better that I believe myself to be merely in the common road of such gentle, gradual decay as, I humbly trust, I have been prepared to meet with highest hope, though with deepest awe - for now many years back.

The chief changes, or reforms, from which I reap benefit are first. Totally renouncing for the evenings all revision or indulgence in poring over those letters and papers whose contents come nearest to my heart, and work upon its bleeding regrets. Next, transferring to the evening, as far as is in my power, all of sociality, with Alex, or my few remaining friends, or the few he will present to me of new ones. Third, constantly going out every day - either in brisk walks in the morning, or in brisk jumbles in the carriage of one of my three friends who send for me, to a *tête-a-tête* tea-converse. Fourth, strict attention to diet.

I ought to have told you the medical sentence upon which I act. These were the words - 'You have a head overworked, and a heart over-loaded.' This produces a disposition to fulness in both that causes stagnation and so on, with a consequent want of circulation at the extremities, that keeps them cold and aching.

The worst of all is, that I have lost, totally lost, my pleasure in reading! except when Alex is my lecturer, for whose sake my faculties are still alive to what - erst! gave them their greatest delight. But alone, I have no longer that resource! I have scarcely looked over a single sentence, but some word of it brings to my mind some mournful recollection, or acute regret, and takes from me all attention – my eyes thence glance vainly over pages that awaken no ideas. – This is melancholy in the extreme; yet I have tried every species of writing and writer – but all pass by me mechanically, instead of instructing or entertaining me intellectually. But for this sad deprivation of my original taste, my evenings might always be pleasing and reviving – but alas!

MARCH

1 MARCH

Epistle To A Young Friend

1786

I Lang hae thought, my youthfu' friend,
A something to have sent you,
Tho' it should serve nae ither end
Than just a kind memento:
But how the subject-theme may gang,
Let time and chance determine;
Perhaps it may turn out a sang:
Perhaps turn out a sermon.

To catch dame Fortune's golden smile,
Assiduous wait upon her;
And gather gear by ev'ry wile
That's justified by honour;
Not for to hide it in a hedge,
Nor for a train attendant;
But for the glorious privilege
Of being independent.

Adieu, dear, amiable youth!
Your heart can ne'er be wanting!
May prudence, fortitude, and truth,
Erect your brow undaunting!
In ploughman phrase, 'God send you speed,'
Still daily to grow wiser;
And may ye better reck the rede,
Then ever did th' adviser!

Robert Burns

2 MARCH

A sealed letter

Jane Carlyle to her husband Thomas

Chelsea, London, 1852

Last Sunday I thought I had got a letter! Oh, worth all the letters that this earth could have given me! I was tumbling two boxfuls of my papers into one large box, when the desire took me to look into my father's day-book, which I had never opened since it came to me, wrapt in newspaper, and sealed. I removed the cover and opened it; and fancy my feelings on seeing a large letter lying inside, addressed 'Mrs Carlyle', in my mother's handwriting, with three unbroken seals of her ring! I sat with it in my hands, staring at it, with my heart beating and my head quite dizzy. Here was at last the letter I had hoped would be found after her death – now, after so many years, after so much sorrow! I am sure I sat ten minutes before I could open it, and when I did open it I could not see to read anything. Alas! It was not that wished-for letter of farewell; still it was something. The deed was there, making over my property to her, and written inside the envelope were a few words: 'When this comes into your possession, my dearest child, do not forget my sister. –'

Beside the deed lay my letter, which accompanied it, and a long, long letter, also mine, most sad to read, about my marriage, some copies of letters also in my father's writing, and a black profile of him. On the whole I felt to have found a treasure, though I was dreadfully disappointed too, and could do nothing all the day after but cry.

A curse on my pen! It twing-twangs away but my heart is heavy

Katherine Mansfield to Lady Ottoline Morrell

France, March 1918

A curse on my pen! It twing-twangs away but my heart is heavy. Why aren't I true as steel - firm as rock? I am - I am - but in my way, Ottoline - in my way.

I wish you were here. Dark England is so far and this room smells spicy and sweet from the carnations - pink and red and wonderful yellow. The hyacinths, in a big jar are put on the window sill for the night for my little maid says they give you not only sore throats but dreams as well! It is very quiet. I can just hear the sea breathe - a fine warm night after a hot day.

Spring, this year, is so beautiful, that watching it unfold one is filled with a sort of anguish. Why - O Lord, why? I have spent days just walking about or sitting on a stone in the sun and listening to the bees in the almond trees and the wild pear bushes and coming home in the evening with rosemary on my fingers and wild thyme on my toes - tired out with the loveliness of the world.

It has made the war so awfully real, and not only the war - Ah, Ottoline - it has made me realize so deeply and finally the corruption of the world. I have such a horror of the present day men and women that I mean never to go among them again. They are thieves, spies, jongleurs all - and the only possible life is remote - remote - with books - with all the poets and a large garden full of flowers and fruits - and a cow (kept for butter only!).

What have you been reading lately? Shelley? Have you read 'The Question'* lately?

I dreamed that as I wandered by the way
    Bare winter suddenly was changed to spring.

    Oh, do read it – this moment – it's so marvellous –

**a poem by Percy Bysshe Shelley*

4 MARCH

The overflowings of a mind

Percy Bysshe Shelley to Mary Wollstonecraft Shelley

Ravenna, Italy, 1821

My greatest content would be utterly to desert all human society. I would retire with you and our child to a solitary island in the sea, would build a boat, and shut upon my retreat the flood-gates of the world. I would read no reviews and talk with no authors. If I dared trust my imagination, it would tell me that there are one or two chosen companions besides yourself whom I should desire. But to this I would not listen. Where two or three are gathered together the devil is among them, and good far more than evil impulses, love far more than hatred, has been to me, except as you have been its object, the source of all sorts of mischief. So on this plan I would be *alone*, and would devote either to oblivion or to future generations the overflowings of a mind which, timely withdrawn from the contagion, should be kept fit for no baser object.

5 MARCH

Did I ever grow great, this letter would figure in my life

Robert Louis Stevenson to Bob Stevenson; Stevenson wrote this letter when he was 18 years old

New Harbour Hotel, Wick, Caithnesshire, Scotland, 1868

Monmouth [a play] is finished. A spasmodic effort, not a sustained and completed work. There are pieces in it which I think decent enough, some little touches of nature and an end sufficiently sensational to satisfy all lovers of poetic justice, of which I am one. But the play has somehow *crined in* – to use our Scotch expression. The characters do not come forth on the stage: they are only seen peeping out of a window. They are not developed, they are merely roughly and hastily sketched. With the versification, except in some parts, I am tolerably pleased; and the little touches of description also give me satisfaction. You see I am frank and praise myself: did I ever grow great, this letter would figure in my life.

Strange how my mind runs on this idea. Becoming great, becoming great, becoming great. A heart burned out with the lust of this world's approbation: a hideous disease to have, even though shielded, as it is in my case, with a certain imperturbable something – self-consciousness or common sense, I cannot tell which – that would prevent me poisoning myself like Chatterton or drinking like Burns on the failure of my ambitious hopes. My nature is at once sanguine and ambitious; but I do not think I am so great a fool as to become my own dupe. Even in my vilest and most shameful thoughts – and who suffers more from such? – there is a something nobler intermixed [...] At least, it is the only thing in my nature that gives me hope, the only thing that I see and cannot trace back to absolute self-love and bald, unholy self-seeking. And yet what is it, merely the returning pang of conscience that bids me communicate my own fears to those who ought to share them. Would God it were more!

6 MARCH

Writing letters: an intercourse with ghosts

Franz Kafka to Milena Jesenská

Prague, March 1922

All my misfortune in life - I don't want to complain, just make a generally instructive observation - derives, one might say, from letters or from the possibility of writing letters.

People have hardly ever deceived me, but letters always have, and as a matter of fact not those of other people, but my own. [...] The easy possibility of writing letters - from a purely theoretical point of view - must have brought wrack and ruin to the souls of the world.

Writing letters is actually an intercourse with ghosts and by no means just with the ghost of the addressee but also with one's own ghost, which secretly evolves inside the letter one is writing or even in a whole series of letters, where one letter corroborates another and can refer to it as witness. How did people ever get the idea they could communicate with one another by letter! One can think about someone far away and one can hold on to someone nearby; everything else is beyond human power. Writing letters, on the other hand, means exposing oneself to the ghosts, who are greedily waiting precisely for that. Written kisses never arrive at their destination; the ghosts drink them up along the way. It is this ample nourishment which enables them to multiply so enormously. People sense this and struggle against it; in order to eliminate as much of the ghosts' power as possible and to attain a natural intercourse, a tranquility of soul, they have invented trains, cars, aeroplanes - but nothing helps anymore; after the postal system, the ghosts invented the telegraph, the telephone, the wireless. They will not starve, but we will perish.

Translated by Philip Boehm

7 MARCH

It begins to look like a jolly voyage

P G Wodehouse to his step-daughter Leonora

SS Adriatic, Southampton, March 1921

Darling precious angel Snorklet,

I think the jolly old boat is just starting. I shall mail this at Cherbourg. It begins to look like a jolly voyage, if we don't cop any rough weather. This cabin is a snorter. About the size of my den, with a lounge, a chair, two windows, and a closet and a chest of drawers. In fact, if only there was that bit of lawn and shrubbery we discussed the other day, I would settle down here for life and grow honey-coloured whiskers. As it is, I shall probably keep fowls during the voyage.

Only blot is, the table they have given me is one of those ones that sway in the breeze and wobble violently if you touch them. What it will be like out in the open ocean heaven knows. If all goes well, I ought to be able to do quite a chunk of work.

We had a very jolly journey down, talking of this and that. (First this, then that.) Thompson is going to be a very cheery old bean to have around on the trip, and altogether everything looks pretty well all right.

The engines have just started going pretty hard, so I can now tell what it will be like trying to work during the voyage. All right, I think.

I'll write and tell you how New York looks. Goodbye, my queen of all possible Snorkles.

Lots of love
Your
Plummie

Looking is such a marvellous thing

Rainer Maria Rilke to his wife Clara

Capri, Italy, 8 March 1907

Go on collecting impressions; don't think of letters which have to be informative and comprehensible; take in this and that with quick snatching-gestures: passing thoughts, ideas, fancies that suddenly flare up in you and last only a second under the influence of some occurrence; all those unimportant things that often become significant through a fleeting intensity of vision or because they take place on a spot where they are absolute in their irrelevance, unceasingly valid and profoundly meaningful for any personal insight which, rising up in us at the same moment, coincides pregnantly with that image.

Looking is such a marvellous thing, of which we know but little; through it, we are turned absolutely towards the Outside, but when we are most of all so, things happen in us that have waited longingly to be observed, and while they reach completion in us, intact and curiously anonymous, *without our aid* – their significance grows up in the object outside: a powerful, persuasive name, the only name these inner events could possibly have, a name in which we joyfully and reverently recognize the happenings within us, a name we ourselves do not touch, only apprehending it very gently, from a distance, under the similitude of a thing that, a moment ago, was strange to us, and the next moment will be estranged anew.

Well then, once again, make many notes, don't even read them through (for in the revision one is often unfair and much that is strictly necessary appears impossible), and if you can, make such sketches as the above with the sheer immediacy of the instantaneous stroke. All of it only as material which we can view here, discuss and piece together at the natural breaks. You will see how it all fits. Only, there must be a lot of it, so that you can really shake it out before you and plunge your hands in. The more the better. Write little, and be greedy of your notes and sketches. (Looking into the interior of a house as into the flesh of a fruit is an experience I have had somewhere. In Rome?) Look, look, look all you can.

Translated from the German by R.F.C. Hull

Please give me some good advice in your next letter. I promise not to follow it

Edna St Vincent Millay to Arthur Davison Ficke

New York City, March 1913

Dear Mr Ficke

I think you are very, very nice.

And I wish very much that you were here in New York and that some of the people who are here were out in Iowa.

I am not being a Bohemian. I am not so Bohemian by half as I was when I came. You see, here one has to be one thing or the other, whereas at home one could be a little of both. And whereas heretofore I have amused myself in idle moments by the diffusing of indiscreet letters which I would now give the half of my kingdom to recall, I am at present (unless indeed that confession has made this letter also indiscreet) prudent to the point of Jane Austen. I left all my bad habits at home, - bridge-pad, cigarette-case, and cocktail-shaker. I brought with me all my good habits, - diary, rubbers, and darning-cotton.

This is not intended to be humourous. So please believe that this whole page is true, and take it seriously.

I am quite settled down. I run in my rut now like a well-directed wheel. Sometimes, it is true, I feel that I am exceeding the speed-limit. But I seldom skid, and when I do there is very little splash.

Please give me some good advice in your next letter. I promise not to follow it.

Very sincerely,
Vincent Millay

10 MARCH

Letter To N.Y.

For Louise Crane

Published 1955

In your next letter I wish you'd say
where you are going and what you are doing;
how are the plays and after the plays
what other pleasures you're pursuing:

taking cabs in the middle of the night,
driving as if to save your soul
where the road goes round and round the park
and the meter glares like a moral owl,

and the trees look so queer and green
standing alone in big black caves
and suddenly you're in a different place
where everything seems to happen in waves,

and most of the jokes you just can't catch,
like dirty words rubbed off a slate,
and the songs are loud but somehow dim
and it gets so terribly late,

and coming out of the brownstone house
to the gray sidewalk, the watered street,
one side of the buildings rises with the sun
like a glistening field of wheat.

– Wheat, not oats, dear. I'm afraid
if it's wheat it's none of your sowing,
nevertheless I'd like to know
what you are doing and where you are going.

Elizabeth Bishop

11 MARCH

Your letters are my spiritual food

Nathaniel Hawthorne to Sophia Peabody

March 1839

My dear Sophie, your letters are no small portion of my spiritual food, and help to keep my soul alive, when otherwise it might languish unto death, or else become hardened and earth-encrusted, as seems to be the case with almost all the souls with whom I am in daily intercourse. They never interfere with my worldly business – neither the reading nor the answering them – (I am speaking of your letters, not of those 'earth-encrusted' souls) – for I keep them to be the treasure of my still and secret hours, such hours as pious people spend in prayer; and the communion which my spirit then holds with yours has some thing of religion in it. The charm of your letters does not depend upon their intellectual value, though that is great, but on the spirit of which they are the utterance, and which is a spirit of wonderful efficacy. No one, whom you would deem worthy of your friendship, could enjoy so large a share of it as I do, without feeling the influence of your character throughout his own – purifying his aims and desires, enabling him to realise that this is a truer world than the feverish one around us, and teaching him how to gain daily entrance into that better world. Such, so far as I have been able to profit by it, has been your ministration to me. Did you dream what an angelic guardianship was entrusted to you?

12 MARCH

As reassuring to me as geology is to architecture

Seamus Heaney to John Hewitt

Belfast, Northern Ireland, 1969

A couple of days ago I read Hawthorne's introduction to *The Scarlet Letter* where he talks of authors who 'indulge themselves in such confidential depths of revelation as could fittingly be addressed only and exclusively, to the one heart and mind of perfect sympathy as if the printed book, thrown at large on the wide world, were certain to find out the divided segment of the writer's own nature and complete his circle of existence by bringing him into communion with it'.

I think Hawthorne was a bit sceptical about the possibility, but after your two letters, first after the television programme which I should have replied to long since, and now, about the book, I am convinced I am one of the lucky authors who has found an ideal audience. The sincerity and solidity of the Hewitts' response and the kindness that is, we feel, parental (our parents cannot say what they feel about literature) – these things are as reassuring to me as geology is to architecture.

I always know that your praise is not a compliment but a communication and am sensible that a gracious patter of gratitude to you only scratches the surface of what I feel. My good luck in all spheres of life makes my Irish Catholic consciousness apprehensive that, as my mother would say, 'something is going to happen', but all that occurs is the returning tide of kindness which no one could predict for himself. The calm rooting of your friendship has been one of the bonuses of declaring for poetry. I'll write again – I'm up to the oxters (how *do* you spell it?) in exams just now.

13 MARCH

The joy of my heart

Madame de Sévigné to her daughter Madame de Grignan

Paris, France, 13 March 1671

To the joy of my heart, I am alone in my own apartment, and writing quietly to you - nothing is more agreeable to me than this.

All the world was at the sermon, and the sermon was worthy of the audience. I thought of you twenty times, and wished as often that you were with me: you would have been delighted to hear it, and I should have been still more delighted to have seen you listening to it.

Here is a budget full of nonsense, but not a syllable yet from you: you may suppose that I can guess at what you are doing; but the state of your health and your mind is too precious for me to rest satisfied with mere conjecture. The most trifling circumstances that relate to those we love are as dear to us as the concerns of others about whom we are indifferent are troublesome.

14 MARCH

Chuckstones of granite & slate

Ralph Waldo Emerson to Margaret Fuller

Concord, Massachusetts, 14 March 1841

But how to reply to your fine eastern pearls with chuckstones of granite & slate. There is nothing for it but to pay you the grand compliment which you deserve, if we can pay it, of speaking the truth.

Even Prose I honour in myself & others very often as an awkward worship of truth – it is the plashing & struggling in the water of one who would learn to swim & though not half so graceful as to stand erect on the shore, yet more brave, & leads to something. He who swum by nature that is, the poet, and he who has learned to swim, that is, the cultivated, will see that this floundering results from genuine admiration & is the straight road to the Fortunate Isles.–

15 MARCH

The only rift opening on the outside world

Vita Sackville-West to Virginia Woolf

Teheran, Iran (then Persia), 15 March 1926

There are days of going into the mountains, and eating sandwiches beside a stream, and picking wild almonds, and of coming home by incredible sunsets across the plain. And every morning at seven we ride, and the freshness and beauty of the morning are inconceivable.

Then once a fortnight the muddy car comes in, and there are letters: the only rift opening on the outside world.

...

Now this letter is long if apparently un-loving, but a lot of love gets spilt over them, like sand to dry the ink, of which no trace remains when the letter arrives, but which nevertheless was there, an important ingredient.

The little owls are hooting, and the bag leaves tomorrow on its long journey. You can write me only one more letter after you get this, for I shall be starting home.

Your letters are always a shock to me, for you typewrite the envelope, and they look like a bill, and then I see your writing. A system I rather like, for the various stabs it affords me.

Now this letter is really getting disproportionately long, and you will be bored. It leaves such chasms of non-information, too; regular continents of unwrapped territory.

What fun it will be to sit on your floor again and stick on stamps. And to carry you off in the little blue motor. If you knew what you meant to me, you might be pleased.

Your
V.

A thoughtful, reading, feeling being

Charlotte Brontë to W. S. Williams; Brontë writes of a local man's reaction to her novel *Jane Eyre* (1847)

Haworth, Yorkshire, 1850

I enclose for your perusal a scrap of paper which came into my hands without the knowledge of the writer. He is a poor working man of this village – a thoughtful, reading, feeling being, whose mind is too keen for his frame, and wears it out. I have not spoken to him above thrice in my life, for he is a Dissenter, and has rarely come in my way. The document is a sort of record of his feelings, after the perusal of *Jane Eyre*; it is artless and earnest; genuine and generous. You must return it to me, for I value it more than testimonies from higher sources. He said, 'Miss Brontë, if she knew he had written it, would scorn him', but, indeed, Miss Brontë does not scorn him; she only grieves that a mind of which this is the emanation, should be kept crushed by the leaden hand of poverty – by the trials of uncertain health, and the claims of a large family.

17 MARCH

I Shake Hands with Misfortune & Wear Through the Storm

John Clare to his wife Patty; Clare was admitted to an asylum in Essex. A few months after writing this he left and walked 80 miles back home

Leppits Hill, 17 March 1841

My Dear wife Patty

It Makes Me More Than Happy To Hear That You & My Dear Family Are All Well - And You Will Be As well Pleased To Hear That I Have Been So Long In Good Health & Spirits As To Have Forgotten That I Ever Was Any Otherwise - My Situation Here Has Been Even From The Beginning More Than Irksome But I Shake Hands With Misfortune & Wear Through The Storm - The Spring Smiles & So Shall I - But Not While I Am Here - I Am Very Happy To Hear My Dear Boy Mention His Brothers & Sisters So Kindly As I Feel Assured That They Love One Another As They Ever Have Done - It Was My Lot To Seem As Living Without Friends Until I Met With You & Though We Are Now Parted My Affection Is Unaltered & We Shall Meet Again I Would Sooner Wear The Trouble's Of Life Away Single Handed Than Share Them With Others - As Soon As I Get Relieved On Duty Here I Shall Be In Northamptonshire - Though Essex Is A Very Pleasant County Yet To Me 'There Is No Place Like Home' - As My Children Are All Well - To Keep Them So Be Sure & Keep Them In Good Company & Then They Will Be Not Only Well But Happy - For What Reason They Keep Me Here I Cannot Tell For I Have Been No Otherwise Than Well A Couple Of Year's At The Least & Never Was Very Ill Only Harrassed By Perpetual Bother - & It Would Seem By Keeping Me Here One Year After Another I Was Destined For The Same Fate Again & I Would Sooner Be Packed On A Slave Ship For Africa Than Belong To The Destiny Of Mock Friends & Real Enemies

- Honest Men & Modest Women Are My Friend -

Give My Best Love to My Dear Children & Kiss The Little Ones For Me Good Bye & God Be With You All For Ever

I Had Three Seperate Dreams About Three Of Your Boys Frederick John & William - Not Any Ways Remarkable Only I Was In A Wreck With The Latter - Such Things Never Trouble Me Now In Fact Nothing Troubles Me & Thank God It Is so - I Hope The Time Is Not Long Ere I Shall see You All By Your Own Fireside Though Every Day In Abscence Seems To Me Longer Than Years

I Am My Dear Wife Your Affectionate Husband
JOHN CLARE

18 MARCH

I smoked a pipe with Carlyle yesterday

Edward FitzGerald to Bernard Barton

Charlotte Street, London, 1844

Dear Barton,

I smoked a pipe with Carlyle* yesterday. We ascended from his dining room carrying pipes and tobacco up through two stories of his house, and got into a little dressing room near the roof: there we sat down: the window was open and looked out on nursery gardens, their almond trees in blossom, and beyond, bare walls of houses, and over these, roofs and chimneys, and roofs and chimneys, and here and there a steeple, and whole London crowned with darkness gathering behind like the illimitable resources of a dream. I tried to persuade him to leave the accursed den, and he wished - but - but - perhaps he didn't wish on the whole.

**Thomas Carlyle, essayist and historian*

'Do you mind if I smoke?'

Edna St Vincent Millay to the Millay Family

New York City, March 1913

Dear Family, -

Yes, I have seen and talked with Witter Bynner*. He has said to me 'Do you mind if I smoke?' and I have said to him, 'Not in the least.'

He has proffered me his cigarette case and I have said, 'No, thank you.' He has raised his eyebrows and said, 'O, you don't smoke?' And I have replied, 'Not here, certainly.'

He. - Then you have no prejudice against it.

I. - None whatever.

He. - I'm glad of that. My sister used to think it dreadful, but now she smokes more than I do.

(Did you ever think of Witter Bynner as having a sister? - I never did.)

We talked a long time. And later in the evening he read 'Renascence'** aloud. He has a beautiful voice, and he reads beautifully. It was truly wonderful to hear it like that. He's crazy about it anyway.

**a poet*

***Millay's poem which was first published in 1912 when she was nineteen*

20 MARCH

The almost breathing creations of genius

Percy Bysshe Shelley to Thomas Love Peacock

Rome, Italy, March 1819

And what shall I say to you of Rome? If I speak of the inanimate ruins, the rude stones piled upon stones, which are the sepulchres of the fame of those who once arrayed them with the beauty which has faded, will you believe me insensible to the vital, the almost breathing creations of genius yet subsisting in their perfection? What has become, you will ask, of the Apollo, the Gladiator, the Venus of the Capitol? What of the Apollo di Belvedere, the Laocoon? What of Raffael and Guido? These things are best spoken of when the mind has drunk in the spirit of their forms; and little indeed can I, who must devote no more than a few months to the contemplation of them, hope to know or feel of their profound beauty.

21 MARCH

The presence of decay

Thomas Hardy to Edmund Gosse

Rome, Italy, March 1887

My dear Gosse,

We have been pottering on from city to city – & have now been here about a week. I am so overpowered by the presence of *decay* in Ancient Rome that I feel it like a nightmare in my sleep. Modern Rome is full of building energy – but how any community can go on building in the face of the 'Vanitas vanitatum' reiterated by the ruins is quite marvellous. For my part if I were going to erect a mere shed I shd say Is it worth while?

From this you will gather that we are mostly confining our attention to the older section of the city. This morning we drove to the English Cemetery, to the graves of Keats & Shelley – I send you a violet or two which I gathered from Keats's – he is covered with violets in full bloom just now, & thousands of daisies stud the grass around. The whole place is indeed quite lovely at this time with the greenery of spring.

Believe me
Always yours sincerely
Thomas Hardy

My Dear Friend

Alexander Pope to Jonathan Swift

Duke Street, London, 22 March 1740

My Dear Friend, When the Heart is full of Tenderness, it must be full of Concern at the absolute Impotency of all Words to come up to it. You are the only Man now in the world, who cost me a Sigh every day of my Life, and the Man it troubles me most, altho' I most wish, to write to ... I value and enjoy more, the memory of the Pleasures & Endearing Obligations I have formerly received from you, than the present Possession of any other.

A poet in whom live all the poets of the past

Virginia Woolf to John Lehman

From *A Letter to a Young Poet* (1932)

... once you begin to take yourself seriously as a leader or as a follower, as a modern or as a conservative, then you become a self-conscious, biting and scratching little animal whose work is not of the slightest value or importance to anybody. Think of yourself rather as something much humbler and less spectacular, but to my mind, far more interesting – a poet in whom live all the poets of the past, from whom all poets in time to come will spring. You have a touch of Chaucer in you, and something of Shakespeare; Dryden, Pope, Tennyson – to mention only the respectable among your ancestors – stir in your blood and sometimes move your pen a little to the right or to the left. In short you are an immensely ancient, complex and continuous character, for which reason please treat yourself with respect.

24 MARCH

My friends are my estate

Emily Dickinson to Samuel Bowles

Amherst, Massachusetts, 1858

I hope your cups are full.

I hope your vintage is untouched. In such a porcelain life one likes to be sure that all is well lest one stumble upon one's hopes in a pile of broken crockery.

My friends are my estate. Forgive me then the avarice to hoard them! They tell me those were poor early have different views of gold. I don't know how that is.

25 MARCH

Renewal of toil

Madame d'Arblay (Fanny Burney) to her father Dr. Burney

West Hamble, Hampshire, March 1800

M. d'Arblay has worked most laboriously in his garden; but his misfortunes there, during our absence, might melt a heart of stone. The horses of our next neighbouring farmer broke through our hedges, and have made a kind of bog of our meadow, by scampering in it during the wet; the sheep followed, who have eaten up all our greens, every sprout and cabbage - and lettuce destined for the winter; while the horses dug up our turnips and carrots; and the swine, pursuing such examples, have trod down all the young plants, besides devouring whatever the others left of vegetables. Our potatoes, left, from our abrupt departure, in the ground, are all rotten or frostbitten, and utterly spoilt; and not a single thing has our whole ground produced us since we came home. A few dried carrots, which remain from the indoors collection, are all we have to temper our viands.

What think you of this for people who make it a rule to owe a third of their sustenance to the garden? Poor M. d'A.'s renewal of toil, to supply future times, is exemplary to behold, after such discouragement. But he works as if nothing had failed.

Hamlet's letter to Ophelia

From *Hamlet*, Act 2, Scene 2

To the celestial and my soul's idol, the most
beautified Ophelia,-

Doubt thou the stars are fire,
Doubt that the sun doth move,
Doubt truth to be a liar,
    But never doubt I love.

O dear Ophelia, I am ill at these numbers. I have not art to reckon my groans, but that I love thee best, oh, most best, believe it. Adieu.

Thine evermore, most dear lady,
whilst this machine is to him,
    Hamlet.

William Shakespeare

27 MARCH

Love me and use me well

Lady Mary Pierrepont to Edward Wortley Montagu; written a few days before their elopement

1712

I tremble for what we are doing. – Are you sure you will love me for ever? Shall we never repent? I fear and I hope. I forsee all that will happen on this occasion. I shall incense my family in the highest degree. The generality of the world will blame my conduct, and the relations and friends of (----) will invent a thousand stories of me; yet, 'tis possible, you may recompense everything to me. In this letter, which I am fond of, you promise me all that I wish. Since I writ so far, I received your Friday letter. I will be only yours, and I will do what you please.

You shall hear from me again tomorrow, not to contradict, but to give some directions. My resolution is taken. Love me and use me well.

28 MARCH

Everything has gone from me but the certainty of your goodness

Virginia Woolf to her husband Leonard Woolf; written shortly before her death on 28 March 1941

Dearest,

I feel certain that I am going
mad again: I feel we cant go
through another of those terrible times.
And I shant recover this time. I begin
to hear voices, and I cant concentrate.
So I am doing what seems the best thing to do. You have
given me
the greatest possible happiness. You
have been in every way all that anyone
could be. I dont think two
people could have been happier till
this terrible disease came. I cant
fight any longer. I know that I am
spoiling your life that without me you
could work. And you will I know.
You see I cant even write this properly. I
cant read. What I want to say is that
I owe all the happiness of my life to you.
You have been entirely patient with me &
incredibly good. I want to say that –
everybody knows it. If anybody could
have saved me it would have been you.

Everything has gone from me but the
certainty of your goodness. I
can't go on spoiling your life any longer. I don't think two
people
could have been happier than we have been.

V.

Curse on the mechanical, icy medium of pen & paper

William Godwin to Mary Wollstonecraft; they married a year later

1796

By way of discharging a debt, an obligation, what shall I say, I take up the pen.

'Oh No!' exclaimeth Mary, 'it is a mere task then, is it?'

Now, I take all my Gods to witness - do you know how many they are - but I obtest & obsecrate them all - that your company infinitely delights me, that I love your imagination, your delicate epicurism, the malicious leer of your eye, in short every thing that constitutes the bewitching tout ensemble of the celebrated Mary. But to write!

Alas, I have no talent, for I have no subject. Shall I write a love letter? May Lucifer fly away with me, if I do! No, when I make love, it shall be with the eloquent tones of my voice, with dying accents, with speaking glances (through the glass of my spectacles) with all the witching of that irresistible, universal passion. Curse on the mechanical, icy medium of pen & paper. When I make love, it shall be in a storm, as Jupiter made love to Semele, & turned her at once to a cinder. Do not these menaces terrify you?

Well then, what shall be my subject. Shall I send you an eulogium of your beauty, your talents & your virtues? Ah! that is an old subject: beside, if I were to begin, instead of a sheet of paper, I should want a ream.

30 MARCH

Like flights of hummingbirds

Edward Thomas to his wife Helen; written from the Front in the First World War

France, March 1917

The worst moment is when you find you have survived and that all your fear was useless. You screw yourself up to beat anything and nothing comes – except a curious disappointment which, I suppose, is also relief. Sometimes at night I have been in in this state a hundred times, but partly through inexperience, not knowing what might mean harm. Still, I shall never like the shell that flaps as it falls, or the one that suddenly bounces into hearing and in a second is bursting far off – no sooner does it open the gate than it is right in the door, or even the small one that complains and whimpers and is called a 'pipqueak' or a 'whizz-bang,' and flies into that ghastly village all night long like flights of hummingbirds.

31 MARCH

The last of your kisses was ever the sweetest

John Keats to Fanny Brawne

Wentworth Place, London, March 1820

Sweetest Fanny,

You fear, sometimes, I do not love you so much as you wish? My dear Girl I love you ever and ever and without reserve. The more I have known you the more have I lov'd. In every way - even my jealousies have been agonies of Love, in the hottest fit I ever had I would have died for you. I have vex'd you too much. But for Love! Can I help it? You are always new. The last of your kisses was ever the sweetest; the last smile the brightest; the last movement the gracefullest.

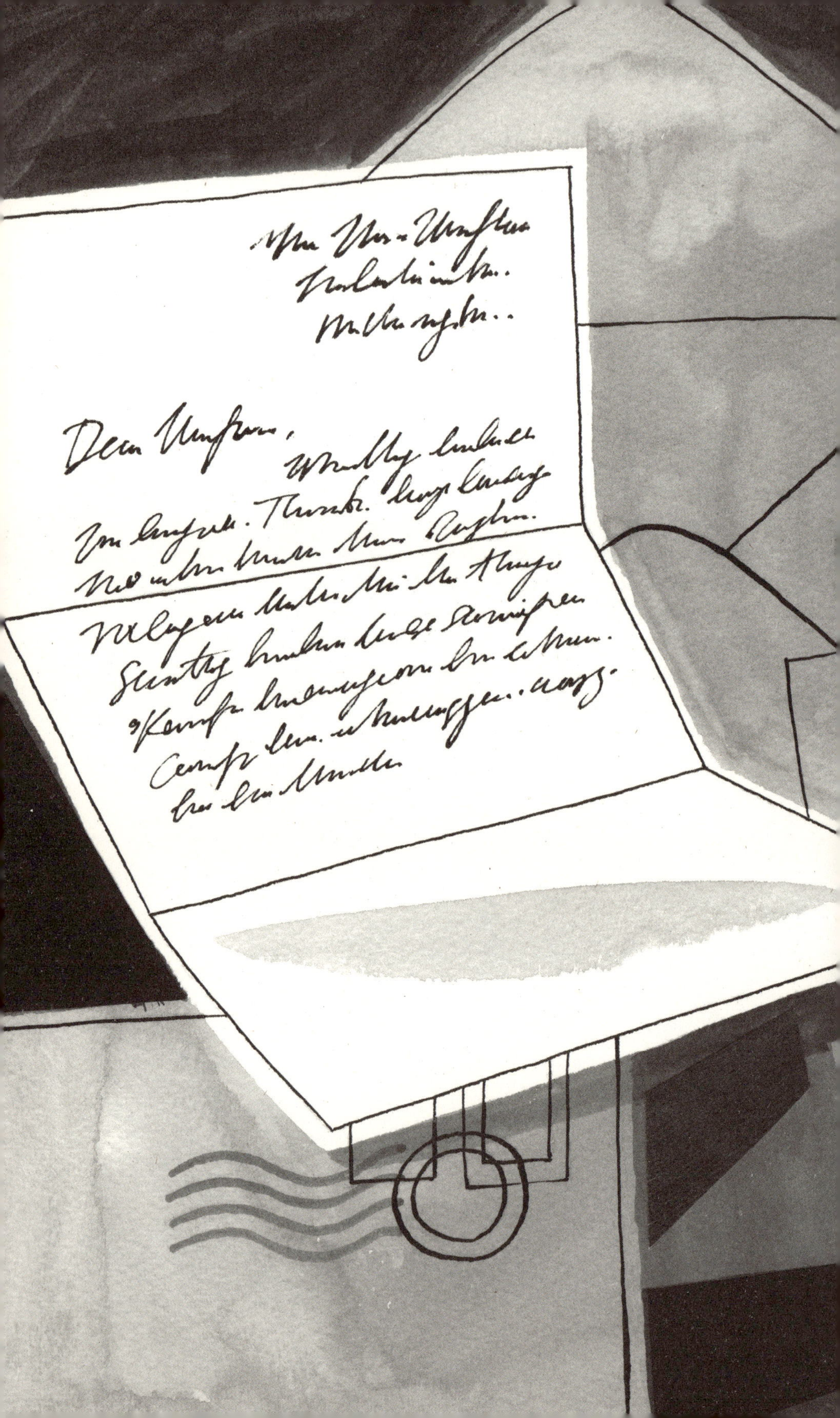

APRIL

1 APRIL

The little celandine

Dorothy Wordsworth to Lady Beaumont

Grasmere, The Lake District, 1806

I am seated in a *shady* corner of the moss hut (for it fronts the west and towards evening the sun shines full into it) and but that Mr Crump's ruinous mansion (has my Brother told you that one third of it is fallen down?) stares me in the face whenever I look up there is not any object that is not chearful and in harmony with the sheltering mountains and quiet vale. The lake is perfectly calm, two or three ploughs are at work, the fields scattered over with sheep and lambs. Within three days the flowers have sprung up by thousands. William's favourite, the little celandine, glitters upon every bank, the fields are becoming green, the buds bursting; and but three days ago scarcely a trace of spring was to be seen. We have had two days and nights of gentle rain with a South wind; and now that the sun shines again the change seems almost miraculous. We are so proud of it that we have scarcely been in the house ten minutes together the whole day.

O Frugality!

Robert Burns to Peter Hill, an Edinburgh bookseller; Burns, working as an exciseman, seems to be making use of his workplace stationery

Ellisland, Scotland, 2 April 1789

I will make no excuses, my dear Bibliopolus, (God forgive me for murdering language) that I have sat down to write you on this vile paper, stained with the sanguinary scores of 'thae curst horse leeches o' th' Excise'. – It is economy. Sir; it is that cardinal virtue. Prudence.

O Frugality! thou mother of ten thousand blessings! Thou Cook of fat beef & dainty greens! Thou Manufacturer of warm Shetland hose & comfortable surtouts! Thou old Housewife, darning thy decayed stockings, with thy ancient spectacles on thy aged nose!!! Lead me, hand me in thy clutching, palsied fist, up those heights & through those thickets hitherto inaccessible & impervious to my anxious, weary feet – not those damned Parnassian Crags, bleak & barren, where the hungry worshippers of Fame are, breathless, clambering, hanging between heaven & hell: but these glittering cliffs of Potosi where the all-sufficient, all-powerful deity, WEALTH, holds his immediate court of joys & pleasures; where the sunny exposure of Plenty & the hot-walls of profusion produce those blissful fruits of LUXURY, exotics in this world and natives of Paradise!!!

But to descend from heroics – what, in the name of all the devils at once, have you done with my trunk?

3 APRIL

I have rummaged every Stationer's shop in Dumfries

Robert Burns to Frances Dunlop

Ellisland, Scotland, 1789

I have rummaged every Stationer's shop in Dumfries, for a long and broad, ample and capacious-sized sheet of writing paper, just to keep by me for epistles to you; and you see, dear Madam, by this honest-looking page, that I have succeeded to a miracle. - I own indeed you deserve a jolly letter-

There is a small river, Afton, that falls into Nith, near New-Cumnock, which has some charming, wild, romantic scenery on its banks. - I have a particular pleasure in those little pieces of poetry such as our Scots songs, where the names and landskip-features of rivers, lakes or woodlands, that one knows, are introduced. I attempted a compliment of that kind, to Afton, as follows: I mean it for Johnson's Musical Museum*.

Flow gently, clear Afton, among thy green braes**.

**a collection of traditional folk music of Scotland published from 1787 to 1803 to which Burns contributed many songs*

***banks*

4 APRIL

A little praise now and then

William Cowper to the Rev. W. Unwin

Weston Lodge, Buckinghamshire, 1786

The dew of your intelligence has refreshed my poetical laurels. A little praise now and then is very good for your hard-working poet, who is apt to grow languid and perhaps careless without it. Praise, I find, affects us as money does. The more a man gets of it, with the more vigilance he watches over and preserves it. Such, at least is its effect on me, and you may assure yourself that I will never lose a mite of it for want of care.

5 APRIL

I am ripples of waves on silver seas

Maya Angelou, writing to a fictional daughter

From *Letter to My Daughter* (2009)

At [a] reading, the other students, who were all white, the teacher, and I sat in a circle. Mr Wilkerson asked me to read a section, which ended with the words, 'God loves me'. I read the piece and closed the book. The teacher said, 'Read it again.' I pointedly opened the book, and a bit sarcastically read, 'God loves me.' Mr Wilkerson said, 'Again.' I wondered if I was being set up to be laughed at by the professional, older, all-white company? After about the seventh repetition I became nervous and thought that there might be a little truth in the statement. There was a possibility that God really did love me, me Maya Angelou. I suddenly began to cry at the gravity and grandeur of it all. I knew that if God loved me then I could do wonderful things, I could try great things, learn anything, achieve anything. For what could stand against me, since one person, with God, constitutes the majority?

That knowledge humbles me today, melts my bones, closes my ears, and makes my teeth rock loosely in my gums. And it also liberates me. I am a big bird winging over high mountains, down into serene valleys. I am ripples of waves on silver seas. I'm a spring leaf trembling in anticipation of full growth.

6 APRIL

Literary Immortality

Sir Walter Scott to Anna Seward

1808

... those that have really attained literary immortality have gained it under very hard conditions. To some it has not attached till after death ... To others it has been the means of handing down personal vices and follies which had otherwise been unremembered in their epitaphs. And all enjoy this same immortality under a condition similar to that of Noureddin in an Eastern tale. Noureddin you remember was to enjoy the gift of immortality, but with this qualification, that he was subjected to long naps of forty, fifty, or an hundred years at a time. Even so Homer and Virgil slumbered through whole centuries. To be sure these were the dark ages, and therefore proper for repose.

Shakespeare himself enjoyed undisturbed sleep from the age of Charles I until Garrick waked [him]. Dryden's fame has nodded, that of Pope begins to be drowsy; Chaucer is as sound as a top, and Spenser is snoring in the midst of his commentators. Milton indeed is quite awake, but observe he was at his very outset refreshed with a nap of half a century; and in the midst of all this we sons of degeneracy talk of immortality. Let me please my own generation, and let those that come after us judge of their taste and my performances as they please, the anticipation of their neglect or censure will affect me very little.

7 APRIL

The sun shone and larks and partridges and magpies made love

Edward Thomas to his wife Helen; Thomas was killed two days after this, his last letter

France, 7 April 1917

Here I am in my valise on the floor of my dug-out writing before sleeping. The artillery is like a stormy tide on the shores of the full moon that rides high and clear among white cirrus clouds. It has been a day of cold feet in the O.P. [observation post] I had to go unexpectedly. When I posted my letter in the morning I thought it would be a bad day, but we did all the shelling. Hardly anything came near the O.P. or even the village. I simply watched the shells changing the landscape. The village among trees that I first saw two weeks ago is now just ruins among violated stark tree-trunks.

But the sun shone and larks and partridges and magpies made love and the trench was being made passable for the wounded that will be harvested in a day or two. Either the Boche is beaten or he is going to surprise us. The air was full of fights and I saw one enemy fall in fire and one of ours into the enemy's wire. I am tired but resting. Yesterday afternoon was more exciting. Our billet was shelled. The shells fell all around and you should have seen Horton and me dodging them. It was quite fun for me, though he was genuinely alarmed, being more experienced. None of us was injured, and our home escaped. Then we went off in the car, in the rain, to buy things.

Sunday. I slept fairly well and now it is sunshine and wind and we are in for a long day and I must post this when I can.

8 APRIL

A clock ticking

J M Barrie to Mrs Raymond Asquith

Adelphi Terrace House, London, 8 April 1928

I am the only man in London, quite a common experience of mine at Easter. There are it is true a few visitors wandering the streets and longing wearily for the trains that will take them back to their homes.

The silence is so great that all sorts of sounds become audible that are not heard at normal times, such as a stick falling in the fire or a dog pattering along a distant street or a clock (or a heart) ticking. If the postman had knocked on Good Friday how we should all have jumped. There has been a church bell at long intervals which made me stare at your cathedral (of which though you may not know it there is a fine view from some of my windows); I felt it was calling to me but I didn't go, I don't know why or perhaps I do.

I hope you pray for me still.

9 APRIL

To establish one's own religion in one's heart

D H Lawrence to his sister Ada

Croydon, South London, 9 April 1911

I am sorry more than I can tell to find you going through the torment of religious unbelief: it is so hard to bear, especially now.

When we die, like raindrops falling back again into the sea, we fall back into the big, shimmering sea of unorganized life which we call God. We are lost as individuals, yet we count in the whole. It requires a lot of pain and courage to come to discover one's own creed, and quite as much to continue in lonely faith. Would you like a book or two of philosophy? Or will you merely battle out your own ideas? I would still go to chapel if it did me any good. I shall go myself, when I am married.

It is a fine thing to establish one's own religion in one's heart, not to be dependent on tradition and second-hand ideals. Life will seem to you, later, not a lesser, but a greater thing. This which is a great torment now will be a noble thing to you later on. Let us talk, if you feel like it, when I come home.

10 APRIL

A pessimist & a pagan

Thomas Hardy to John Addington Symonds

Near Dorchester, 10 April 1889

Dear Mr Symonds,

I get smart raps sometimes from critics who appear to think that to call me a pessimist & a pagan is to say all that is necessary for my condemnation.

I often begin a story with the intention of making it brighter & gayer than usual; but the question of conscience soon comes in; & it does not seem right, even in novels, to wilfully belie one's own views. All comedy, is tragedy, if you only look deep enough into it. A question which used to trouble me was whether we ought to write sad stories, considering how much sadness there is in the world already. But of late I have come to the conclusion that, the first step towards cure of, or even relief from, any disease being to understand it, the study of tragedy in fiction may possibly here & there be the means of showing how to escape the worst forms of it, at least, in real life.

I, too, am in a sense exiled. I was obliged to leave Town after a severe illness some years ago - & the spot on which I live here is very lonely. However I think that, though one does get a little rusty by living in remote places, one gains, on the other hand, freedom from those temporary currents of opinion by which town people are caught up & distracted out of their true courses.

11 APRIL

Bettering my Blue Devils

Edward FitzGerald to John Allen

London 1832

My dear Allen

I have been poring over Wordsworth lately: which has had much effect in bettering my Blue Devils: for his philosophy does not abjure melancholy, but puts a pleasant countenance upon it, and connects it with humanity. It is very well, if the sensibility that makes us fearful of ourselves is diverted to become a cause of sympathy and interest with Nature and mankind: and this I think Wordsworth tends to do. I think I told you of Shakespeare's sonnets before: I cannot tell you what sweetness I find in them.

So by Shakespeare's Sonnets roasted, and Wordsworth's poems basted.
My heart will be well toasted, and excellently tasted.

Today I have bought a little terrier to keep me company. You will think this is from my reading of Wordsworth: but if that were my cue, I should go no further than keeping a primrose in a pot for society. Farewell, dear Allen. I am astonished to find myself writing a very long letter once a week to you: but it is next to talking to you: and after having seen you so much this summer, I cannot break off suddenly.

I am your most affectionate friend, E. F. G.

12 APRIL

My stock of poetry

William Wordsworth to Joseph Cottle, publisher
Alfoxden, Somerset, 12 April 1798

My Dear Cottle –

You will be pleased to hear that I have gone on very rapidly adding to my stock of poetry*. Do come and let me read it to you under the old trees in the park. We have a little more than two months to stay in this place. Within these four days the season has advanced with greater rapidity than I ever remember, and the country become almost every hour more lovely.

God bless you.

**Wordsworth and Coleridge's* Lyrical Ballads *was published by Cottle six months later*

13 APRIL

My scribbling pen

E Nesbit to Ada Breakell

13 April 1884

I am all alone in the house, 'alone' that is, as a far as grown-ups are concerned – for the bunnies are here. I have just got Iris to sleep, and laid her down and Paul is standing watching my scribbling pen – his quietness will not last long, so I will provide him with a box of bricks and then go on with this. It is so quiet – the peculiar stillness attaching only to Sunday afternoons. Especially from two to four. The maid has gone out for the day and I have just washed up the dinner things, and am sitting in the kitchen. The kettle is singing on the fire and the kitten purring before it. I sit here in my 'deck' chair, and my blue dress – and write to you. Charming domestic picture, isn't it. Paul and his bricks make a feature in it. His continual 'look, mother, look' only emphasizes the silence – like the hum of bees and the stirring of trees, leaves undisturbed the silence of a June day in the country. The country – ah! I was there yesterday. Hubert and I went to Halstead, and had a long delicious time among the woods and primroses and dog-violets. But though Spring is well awake in these same woods, they are not green, only grey. The dead grass is grey – the birch stems are grey – the hazel stems where the light catches them are grey. The pale green of the budding leaves blends in a curious way with the brown twigs, so that the trees look grey too – at a little distance, and the windflowers and wood sorrel are thick enough to make the ground look white, as with frost or snow. We had a delightful day – and brought home no end of primroses. I got dreadfully sunburnt and am no end tired – but it was worth it. Where we used to picnic, in the old days. I seem to have lived three or four lives right through since those old times – I wonder if your life seems as long to you as mine does to me.

14 APRIL

Our little baby is dead

Charles Dickens to his wife Catherine; eight-month-old Dora was the couple's ninth child

Devonshire Terrace, London, 14 April 1851

My Dearest Kate,

Now observe, you must read this letter very slowly and carefully. If you have hurried on thus far without quite understanding (apprehending some bad news) I rely on your turning back and read again.

Little Dora, without being in the least pain, is suddenly stricken ill. She awoke out of a sleep, and was seen in one moment to be very ill. Mind! I will not deceive you. I think her 'very' ill.

There is nothing in her appearance but perfect rest. You would suppose her quietly asleep. But I am sure she is very ill, and I cannot encourage myself with much hope of her recovery. I do not - and why should I say I do to you, my dear? - I do not think her recovery at all likely. ... You will not like to be away, I know, and I cannot reconcile it to myself to keep you away. Forster, with his usual affection for us, comes down to bring you this letter and to bring you home, but I cannot close it without putting the strongest entreaty and injunction upon you to come with perfect composure - to remember what I have often told you, that we never can expect to be exempt, as to our many children, from the afflictions of other parents, and that if - if - when you come, I should even have to say to you, 'Our little baby is dead,' you are to do your duty to the rest, and to shew yourself worthy of the great trust you hold in them.

If you will read this steadily I have a perfect confidence in your doing what is right.

Ever affectionately, Charles Dickens

15 APRIL

The dachshunds

Anton Chekhov to Nikolay Leikin

Melikhovo, Russia, April 1893

My dear Nikolay Alexandrovich,

The dachshunds finally arrived yesterday. They had got cold and hungry and tired on the way from the station, and were fantastically happy to be here. They raced round all the rooms jumping up affectionately on to everyone and barking at the servants. As soon as they had been fed, they felt completely at home. During the night they dug up all the soil from the window boxes, complete with the seeds that had been sown in them, and distributed the galoshes from the front porch through all the rooms in the house. In the morning, when I was taking them for a walk in the garden, they caused panic in the breasts of our yard dogs, who had never in all their lives seen such monstrous creatures. The bitch is prettier than the dog. There is something not quite right, not only with his face, but also with his hind legs and rump. But both of them have such kind and grateful eyes. What have you been feeding them on, and how often? How do I train them not to answer calls of nature inside the house, and so on? Everybody has fallen for the dachshunds; they are now the main topic of conversation. My most grateful thanks for them.

Translated from the Russian by Rosamund Bartlett and Antony Phillips

16 APRIL

Is My Verse Alive?

Emily Dickinson to Thomas Wentworth Higginson

16 April 1862

MR HIGGINSON, -

Are you too deeply occupied to say if my verse is alive?

The mind is so near itself it cannot see distinctly, and I have none to ask.

Should you think it breathed, and had you the leisure to tell me, I should feel quick gratitude.

If I make the mistake, that you dared to tell me would give me sincerer honour toward you.

I enclose my name, asking you, if you please, sir, to tell me what is true?

That you will not betray me it is needless to ask, since honour is its own pawn.

17 APRIL

A great morning

Rainer Maria Rilke to his wife Clara

Capri, Italy, 1907

So completely was the spring all at once there and so significant, it seemed, was my penetration into its depths that my conscience remained easy although I used up very many hours, nearly all my mornings.

But being in the sun and breathing the spring sky and listening to the birds' voices – which are so perfectly distributed that you feel there is one in every tract of air that can carry – and the sense of belonging that all these things reinforce in you, – surely this can lead to no loss or omission. And however many reasons I may have to constrain myself to my writing desk, I always sally forth again when the morning suddenly calls outside, making you surmise the presence of another morning, a great morning, the morning of seagulls and island-birds, the morning of hills and unattainable flowers, that unchanging, eternal morning which need take no account as yet of the people who blink at it dubiously and surlily and critically before breakfast.

And you have only to walk for half an hour with those light, rapid steps that carry you so inconceivably far, in order to have it really environing you, the sea-morning, which is confident that everything is for it and nothing against it, which reiterates its gesture of opening a thousand thousand times until it gradually slows down in the smallest flowers and is wholly comprised there.

Translated from the German by R.F.C. Hull

News! News!

Dorothy Wordsworth to her niece; Dorothy's last surviving letter. She was ill, and possibly had dementia, in her final years

Spring 1838

My dearest Dora

They say I must write a letter - and what shall it be? News - news I must seek for news. My own thoughts are a wilderness - 'not pierceable by power of any star'* - news then is my resting-place - News! news!

Poor Peggy Benson lies in Grasmere Churchyard beside her once beautiful Mother. Fanny Haigh is gone to a better world. My Friend Mrs Rawson has ended her ninety and two years pilgrimage and *I* have fought and fretted and striven - and am here beside the fire. The Doves behind me at the small window - the laburnum with its naked seedpods shivers before my window and the pine trees rock from their base. - More I cannot write so farewell! And may God bless you and your kind good Friend Miss Fenwick, to whom I send love and all the best of wishes.

Yours
evermore
Dorothy Wordsworth

**Edmund Spenser,* The Fairie Queene *(1590)*

19 APRIL

The pleasantnesse of the season displeases me

John Donne to Sir Henry Goodyer

Micham, Surrey, 1608

Because I am in a place and season where I see everything bud forth, I must do so too, and vent some of my meditations to you; the rather because all other buds being yet without taste or virtue, my Letters may be like them. The pleasantnesse of the season displeases me. Every thing refreshes, and I wither, and I grow older and not better, my strength diminishes, and my load growes, and being to passe more and more stormes, I finde that I have not only cast out all my ballast which nature and time gives, Reason and discretion, and so am as empty and light as Vanity can make me; but I have over fraught my self with Vice, and so am riddingly subject to two contrary wrackes, Sinking and Oversetting, and under the iniquity of such a disease as inforces the patient when he is almost starved, not only to fast, but to purge. For I have much to take in, and much to cast out; sometimes I thinke it easier to discharge myself of vice then of vanity, as one may sooner carry the fire out of a room then the smoake: and then I see it was a new vanity to think so. And when I think sometimes that vanity, because it is thinne and airie, may be expelled with virtue or businesse, or substantiall vice; I finde that I give entrance thereby to new vices.

Advice on my granddaughter's education

Lady Mary Wortley Montagu to her daughter, the Countess of Bute

Louvere, Italy, 1733

You should encourage your daughter to talk over with you what she reads; and take care she does not mistake pert folly for wit and humour, or rhyme for poetry, which are the common errors of young people, and have a train of ill consequences. The second caution to be given her (and which is most absolutely necessary) is to conceal whatever learning she attains, with as much solicitude as she would hide crookedness or lameness; the parade of it can only serve to draw on her the envy, and consequently the most inveterate hatred, of all he and she fools, which will certainly be at least three parts in four of her acquaintance. The use of knowledge in our sex, beside the amusement of solitude, is to moderate the passions, and learn to be contented with a small expense, which are the certain effects of a studious life; and it may be preferable even to that fame which men have engrossed to themselves, and will not suffer us to share. You will tell me I have not observed this rule myself; but you are mistaken: it is only inevitable accident that has given me any reputation that way. I have always carefully avoided it, and ever thought it a misfortune.

If she has the same inclination (I should say passion) for learning that I was born with, history, geography and philosophy will furnish her with materials to pass away cheerfully a longer life than is allotted to mortals. I believe there are few heads capable of making Sir Isaac Newton's calculations, but the result of them is not difficult to be understood by a moderate capacity.

A governess's work

Charlotte Brontë to her friend Ellen Nussey; Brontë, born on this day in 1816, used her experiences as a governess in her novels

Upperwood House, Rawdon, West Yorkshire, 1841

My pupils are two in number, a girl of eight, and a boy of six. As to my employers, you will not expect me to say much about their characters when I tell you that I only arrived here yesterday. I have not the faculty of telling an individual's disposition at first sight. Before I can venture to pronounce on a character, I must see it first under various lights and from various points of view. All I can say therefore is, both Mr and Mrs ---- seem to me good sort of people. I have as yet had no cause to complain of want of considerateness or civility.

My pupils are wild and unbroken, but apparently well-disposed. I wish I may be able to say as much next time I write to you. My earnest wish and endeavour will be to please them. If I can but feel that I am giving satisfaction, and if at the same time I can keep my health, I shall, I hope, be moderately happy.

But no one but myself can tell how hard a governess's work is to me – for no one but myself is aware how utterly averse my whole mind and nature are for the employment. Do not think that I fail to blame myself for this, or that I leave any means unemployed to conquer this feeling. Some of my greatest difficulties lie in things that would appear to you comparatively trivial. I find it so hard to repel the rude familiarity of children. I find it so difficult to ask either servants or mistress for anything I want, however much I want it. It is less pain for me to endure the greatest inconvenience than to go into the kitchen to request its removal. I am a fool. Heaven knows I cannot help it!

22 APRIL

My mind – a stratum of conglomerated fragments

George Eliot to Maria Lewis

1839

My mind, never of the most highly organized genus, is more than usually chaotic, or, rather, it is like a stratum of conglomerated fragments, that shows here a jaw and rib of some ponderous quadruped, there a delicate alto-relievo of some fern-like plant, tiny shells and mysterious nondescripts incrusted and united with some unvaried and uninteresting but useful stone. My mind presents just such an assemblage of disjointed specimens of history, ancient and modern; scraps of poetry picked up from Shakespeare, Cowper, Wordsworth and Milton; newspaper topics; morsels of Addison and Bacon, Latin verbs, geometry, entomology and chemistry; reviews and metaphysics – all arrested and petrified and smothered by the fast-thickening everyday accession of actual events, relative anxieties and household cares and vexations.

How deplorably and unaccountably evanescent are our frames of mind, as various as the forms and hues of the summer clouds!

A single word is sometimes enough to give an entirely new mould to our thoughts – at least, I find myself so constituted; and therefore to me it is pre-eminently important to be anchored within the veil, so that outward things may be unable to send me adrift.

Write to me as soon as you can.

I ne'er found so many beauties in the Sonnets

John Keats to John Hamilton Reynolds

Fox and Hounds Inn, Surrey, 1817

I like this place very much. There is Hill & Dale and a little River - I went up Box hill this Evening after the Moon - you a' seen the Moon - came down - and wrote some lines. Whenever I am separated from you, and not engaged in a continued Poem - every Letter shall bring you a lyric - but I am too anxious for you to enjoy the whole, to send you a particle. One of the three Books I have with me is Shakespear's Poems: I ne'er found so many beauties in the Sonnets - they seem to be full of fine things said unintentionally - in the intensity of working out conceits. Is this to be borne? Hark ye!

> When lofty trees I see barren of leaves
> Which erst from heat did canopy the herd,
> And Summer's green all girded up in sheaves,
> Borne on the bier with white and bristly beard*.

Your affectionate friend
John Keats

**Shakespeare's 'Sonnet 12'*

24 APRIL

The first violet

Robert Louis Stevenson to Frances Sitwell

Mentone, France, 1873

The first violet. There is more secret trouble for the heart in the breath of this small flower, than in all the wines of all the vineyards of Europe. I cannot contain myself. I do not think so small a thing has ever given me such a princely festival of pleasure. I am quite drunken at heart, and you do not know how the scent of this flower strikes in me the same thought, as I think almost all things will do now; everything beautiful to me brings back the thought of what is most beautiful to me. My little violet, if you could speak I know what you would say! I feel as if my heart were a little bunch of violets in my bosom; and my brain is pleasantly intoxicated with the wonderful odour. I suppose I am writing nonsense but it does not seem nonsense to me. Is it not a wonderful odour; is it not something incredibly subtle and perishable? The first breath, veiled and timid as it seems, maddens and transfigures and transports you out of yourself; and yet if you seek to breathe it again, it is gone. - It is like a wind blowing to one out of fairy land. - No one need tell me that the phrase is exaggerated if I say that this violet sings; it sings with the same voice as the March blackbird; and the same adorable tremor goes through one's soul at the hearing of it. I am writing much about my little violet; and yet you know how much I am keeping back. It is [one] of these delicate penetrating sensations that passes, like a two-edged sword, through your heart; it presents itself in the holy of holies; it is there a sweet incense before the little image that one cherishes most secretly. This violet has known all my past and in a moment in the twinkling of an eye, showed me all that was beautiful and lovable in my bygone life.

Monday

All yesterday, I was under the influence of opium; I had been rather seedy during the night and took a dose in the morning and, for the first time in my life it took effect upon me. I had a day of extraordinary happiness; and when I went to bed, there was something almost terrifying in the pleasures that besieged me in the darkness. Wonderful tremors filled me; my head swam in the most delirious but enjoyable manner; and the bed softly oscillated with me, like a boat in a very gentle ripple. It does not make me write a good style apparently, which is just as well lest I should be tempted to renew the experiment; and some verses, which I wrote turn out, on inspection, to be not quite equal to 'Kubla Khan'. However I was happy; and the recollection is not troubled by any reaction this morning.

25 APRIL

A spot of enchantment

Samuel Taylor Coleridge to the Rev. George Coleridge; Coleridge's *Kubla Khan* (1816) may have been written under the influence of laudanum

April 1798

My dear brother,

An illness, which confined me to my bed, prevented me from returning an immediate answer to your kind and interesting letter ... Laudanum gave me repose, not sleep; but you, I believe, know how divine that repose is, what a spot of enchantment, a green spot of fountain and flowers and trees in the very heart of a waste of sands! God be praised, I am now recovering apace, and enjoy that newness of sensation from the fields, the air and the sun which makes convalescence almost repay one for disease.

26 APRIL

I can feel a sunshine stealing into my soul

Emily Dickinson to Susan Huntington Dickinson

April 1852

I have thought of [your letter] all day, Susie, and I fear of but little and when I was gone to meeting it filled my mind so full, I could not find a chink to put the worthy pastor; when he said, 'Our Heavenly Father,' I said 'Oh Darling Sue'; when he read the 100th Psalm, I kept saying your precious letter all over to myself, and Susie, when they sang - it would have made you laugh to hear one little voice, piping to the departed. I made up words and kept singing how I loved you, and you had gone, while all the rest of the choir were singing Hallelujahs. I presume nobody heard me, because I sang so small, but it was a kind of a comfort to think I might put them out, singing of you. I a'nt there this afternoon, tho', because I am here, writing a little letter to my dear Sue, and I am very happy. I think of ten weeks - Dear One, and I think of love, and you, and my heart grows full and warm, and my breath stands still. The sun does'nt shine at all, but I can feel a sunshine stealing into my soul and making it all summer, and every thorn, a rose. And I pray that such summer's sun shine on my Absent One, and cause her bird to sing!

I gathered antique stones, and your little flowers of moss opened their lips and spoke to me, so I was not alone. I gathered something for you, because you were not there, an acorn, and some moss blossoms, and a little shell of a snail, so whitened by the snow you would think 'twas a cunning artist had carved it from alabaster - then I tied them all up in a leaf with some last summer's grass I found by a brookside, and I'm keeping them all for you.

27 APRIL

A funny mixture all this

Edward FitzGerald to John Allen

Geldestone Hall, Beccles, Norfolk, April 1839

Here is a glorious sunshiny day: all the morning I read about Nero in Tacitus lying at full length on a bench in the garden: a nightingale singing and some red anemones eyeing the sun manfully not far off. A funny mixture all this: Nero and the delicacy of Spring: all very human however.

Then at half past one lunch on Cambridge cream cheese: then a ride over hill and dale: then spudding up some weeds from the grass: and then coming in, I sit down to write to you, my sister winding red worsted from the back of a chair, and the most delightful little girl in the world chattering incessantly. So runs the world away.

You think I live in Epicurean ease: but this happens to be a jolly day: one isn't always well, or tolerably good, the weather is not always clear, nor nightingales singing, nor Tacitus full of pleasant atrocity. But such as life is, I believe I have got hold of a good end of it ...

Fill your paper with the breathings of your heart

William Wordsworth to his wife Mary; the couple had been married nearly ten years when this was written

Grosvenor Square, London, April 1812

I have infinite pleasure in the thought of seeing thee again in Wales; and travelling with thee. - I long for the day. Love me and think of me & wish for me, and be assured that I am repaying thee in the same coin. - [...}

Write to me frequently & the longest Letters possible; never mind whether you have facts or no to communicate; fill your paper with the breathings of your heart most tenderly your friend & Husband W.W. Love to every one.

O My William!

Mary Wordsworth to William Wordsworth

Grasmere, The Lake District, 1810

O My William!
it is not in my power to tell thee how I have been affected by this dearest of all letters – it was so unexpected – so new a thing to see the breathing of thy inmost heart upon paper that I was quite overpowered, & now that I sit down to answer thee in the loneliness and depth of that love which unites us & which cannot be felt but by ourselves, I am so agitated & my eyes are so bedimmed that I scarcely know how to proceed.

30 APRIL

Every day every hour every moment

William Wordsworth to his wife Mary

Hindwell, near Radnor, Wales, 1810

O my blessing, how happy was I in learning that my Letter had moved thee so deeply, and thy delight in reading had if possible been more exquisite than mine in writing. [...] I was sure that you would be most happy in receiving from me such a gift from the whole undivided heart for your whole & sole possession; and the Letter in answer which I have received from you today I will entrust to your keeping when I return, and they shall be deposited side by side as a bequest for the survivor of us. Every day every hour every moment makes me feel more deeply how blessed we are in each other. How purely how faithfully how ardently, and how tenderly we love each other; I put this last word last because, though I am persuaded that a deep affection is not uncommon in married life, yet I am confident that a lively, gushing, thought-employing, spirit-stirring, passion of love, is very rare even among good people. I will say more upon this when we meet, grounded upon recent observation of the condition of others. We have been parted my sweet Mary too long, but we have not been parted in vain, for wherever I go I am admonished how blessed, and almost peculiar a lot mine is. –

MAY

1 MAY

My Building rises

Alexander Pope to Robert Digby; on the building of Pope's Villa at Twickenham by the River Thames

1 May 1720

Our River glitters beneath an unclouded Sun, at the same time that its Banks retain the Verdure of Showers: Our Gardens are offering their first Nosegays; our Trees, like new Acquaintance brought happily together, are stretching their Arms to meet each other, and growing nearer and nearer every Hour: The Birds are paying their thanksgiving Songs for the new Habitations I have made 'em: My Building rises high enough to attract the eye and curiosity of the Passenger from the River, where, upon beholding a Mixture of Beauty and Ruin, he enquires what House is falling, or what Church is rising?

2 MAY

Human nature in a different light

Robert Burns to his tutor John Murdoch

1783

– I seem to be one sent into the world, to see, and observe; and I very easily compound with the knave who tricks me of my money, if there be any thing original about him which shews me human nature in a different light from any thing I have seen before. In short, the joy of my heart is to 'Study men, their manners, and their ways'*; and for this darling subject, I cheerfully sacrifice every other consideration: I am quite indolent about those great concerns that set the bustling, busy Sons of Care agog.

I am a poor, insignifant [sic] devil, unoticed [sic] and unknown, stalking up and down fairs and markets when I happen to be in them, reading a page or two of mankind, and 'catching the manners living as they rise'**, whilst the men of business jostle me on every side, as an idle encumbrance in their way.

**Alexander Pope 'January and May'*

***Alexander Pope's* Essay on Man, *Epistle 1*

3 MAY

To That Man Robert Burns

Woody Guthrie to (posthumously) Robert Burns

1947

Dear Robert Burns,

You skipped the big town streets just like I done, you ducked the crosstown cop just like I ducked, you dodged behind a beanpole to beat the bigtime dick and you very seldom stopped off in any big city where the rigged corn wasn't drying nor the hot vine didn't help you do your talking.

Your talking was factual figures of the biggest sort, though. Your talking had the graphboard and the chart and had something else most singers seem to miss, the very kiss of warm dew on the stalk.

Your words turned into songs and floated upstream and then turned into rains and drifted down and lodged and swung and clung to drifts of driftwood to warm and heat and fertilize new seeds. Your words were of the upheath and the down, your words were more from heather than from town. Your thoughts came more from weather than from schoolroom and more from shifting vines than from the book.

I bought your little four-inch square book when I was a torpedoed seaman walking around over your clods and sods of Glasgow and the little book says on the outer cover, *Fifty Songs of Burns*, the price 4d, and I read from page to page and found you covered a woman on every page.

Well, Rob, it's awfully rainy here in Coney today. Been drizzling like this now for several days to make some folks happy and some folks sad. I like it and love it for several reasons, like you'd love it, to see our new seeds grow in this old trashy back yard, and to see these green shoots, roots, limbs and leaves start dancing. And because Marjorie just painted some flowers of a wild and jumpy colour on the pink wall of the baby's room so when he does squirm his way out he'll see some twisting flowers like you seen all around your rock hearths and heatherhills there all over your Scotland. This rain is making the grass and flowers spud out, the roots to crawl like guerrillas, and the house to take a better shape.

Cherry trees

Anton Chekhov to Alexey Suvorin

Sumy, Ukraine, 4 May 1889

I'm writing to you, dear Alexey Sergeyevich, having just returned from catching crayfish. Everything is in song, in bloom and ablaze with beauty. The garden is already quite green; even the oak trees are in leaf. The trunks of the apple, pear, cherry and plum trees are painted white to protect them from worms, and in combination with their white blossom they look strikingly like brides at a wedding: white dresses, white garlands and an air of innocence as though they feel ashamed to be looked at. Nightingales, bitterns, cuckoos and other denizens of the feathered kingdom never cease their racket for a moment day and night, to the accompaniment of the frogs. Every hour of the day and night has its own characteristic sound, so for instance at nine o'clock in the evening the cockchafers start up literally with a roar. The nights are moonlit and the days are bright with sunshine. The result of all this is that my mood is splendid, and if only it were not for the artist coughing all the time, and the mosquitoes, who seem to be immune even to Elpe's prescription, I'd be a complete Potemkin.

Nature is an excellent tranquillizer. It calms one, that is makes one indifferent to one's fate. And in this world one must be indifferent to one's fate. You can only see things as they truly are and be capable of working if you don't care about what lies in store for you – of course I'm speaking of intelligent people with noble natures; those who are egotistical and vacuous are quite indifferent enough as it is.

Translated from the Russian by Rosamund Bartlett and Antony Phillips

5 MAY

P.S. I am poor

Edgar Allan Poe to Joseph T. and Edwin Buckingham

Baltimore, Maryland, May 1833

Gentlemen,

I send you an original tale in hope of your accepting it for the *N. E. Magazine*. It is one of a number of similar pieces which I have contemplated publishing under the title of *Eleven Tales of the Arabesque*. They are supposed to be read at table by the eleven members of a literary club, and are followed by the remarks of the company upon each. These remarks are intended as a burlesque upon criticism. In the whole, originality more than any thing else has been attempted. I have said this much with a view of offering you the entire manuscript.

Edgar Allan Poe

P.S. I am poor.

6 MAY

Every Mortal loss is an Immortal Gain

William Blake to William Hayley; sent following the death of Hayley's two-year-old son

Lambeth, London, 6 May 1800

Dear Sir,

I am very sorry for your immense loss, which is a repetition of what all feel in this valley of misery & happiness mixed. I send the Shadow of the departed Angel: hope the likeness is improved. The lip I have again lessened as you advised & done a good many other softenings to the whole. I know that our deceased friends are more really with us than when they were apparent to our mortal part. Thirteen years ago I lost a brother & with his spirit I converse daily & hourly in the Spirit & see him in my remembrance in the regions of my Imagination. I hear his advice & even now write from his Dictate.

Forgive me for Expressing to you my Enthusiasm which I wish all to partake of since it is to me a Source of Immortal Joy: even in this world by it I am the companion of Angels. May you continue to be so more & more & to be more & more persuaded that every Mortal loss is an Immortal Gain. The Ruins of Time builds Mansions in Eternity.

I have also sent A Proof of Pericles for your Remarks, thanking you for the Kindness with which you Express them & feeling heartily your Grief with a brother's Sympathy.

I remain, Dear Sir, Your humble Servant
William Blake

The night grows old and tomorrow's duties are to be faced

Alice Ruth Moore to Paul Laurence Dunbar; the couple married in 1898

New Orleans, 7 May 1895

Dear Sir: -

Your letter was handed me at a singularly inopportune moment - the house was on fire. So I laid it down, not knowing what it was and I must confess not caring very much. After the house was declared safe and the excitement had somewhat subsided I found it laid in my desk and read it somewhere about ten days later. Strange combination of circumstances though it was, I was not to blame, being partially blind and suffering from a bad hand burned in the fire. But I enjoyed it nevertheless when I did read it, and those dainty little verses have been ringing in my head ever since I read them.

I must thank you ever so much and though I don't like to appear greedy, still if you have any more like them, please send them down this way. Your name is quite familiar to me from seeing your poems in different papers. I always enjoyed them very much.

I am sorry to say I have done very little. It seems I cannot possibly find time to write when I want. My regular everyday duties are so voluminous, so to speak. That I have no moments at all left for that which I love above all ... when I start a story I always think of my folk characters as simple human beings, not of types of a race or an idea, and I seem to be on more friendly terms with them. I have a little collection of short stories - a small book - in press now. I must not write more as the night grows old and tomorrow's duties are to be faced.
I shall be pleased to hear from you soon and often.

Yours Very Truly,
Alice Ruth Moore

8 MAY

Trees of centuries growth

Dorothy Wordsworth to Thomas de Quincey

Grasmere, The Lake District, May 1809

It is quite a pleasure to us to go down to the old spot and linger about. Yesterday I sat half an hour musing by myself in the moss-hut. The little birds, our old companions, I could have half fancied were glad that we were come back again, for it seemed I had never before seen them so joyous on the branches of the naked apple trees. Pleasant indeed it is to think of that little orchard, undisturbed by the woodman's ax. There is no other spot which we may have prized year after year that we can ever look upon without apprehension that next year, next month, or even tomorrow it may be deformed and ravaged.

You have walked to Rydale under Nab Scar? There is not anywhere in this country such a scene of ancient trees and Rocks - trees of centuries growth inrooted among and overhanging the mighty crags. These trees you would have thought could have had no enemy to contend with but the mountain winds, for they seemed to set all human avarice at defiance; and indeed if the owners had had no other passion but avarice they might have remained till the last stump was mouldered away, but *malice* has done the work, and the trees are levelled.

A hundred labourers more or less have been employed for more than a week in hewing, peeling bark, gathering sticks, etc. and the mountain echoes with the riotous sound of their voices.

Oh, my dear Friend! I cannot express how deeply we have been affected by the loss of the trees.

I prefer tree-like people to flower-like people

C S Lewis to Mrs Edward A. Allen

Magdalen College, Oxford, 1954

Thank you for your nice woody and earthy (almost like Thoreau or Dorothy Wordsworth) letter of the sixth. I think I go with you in preferring trees to flowers in the sense that if I had to live in a world without one or the other I'd choose to keep the trees. I certainly prefer tree-like people to flower-like people – the staunch and knotty and storm-enduring kind to the frilly and fragrant and easily withered ...

I think what makes even beautiful country (in the long run) so unsatisfactory when seen from a train or a car is that it whirls each tree, brook, or haystack close up into the foreground, soliciting individual attention but vanishing before you can give it ... Didn't someone give a similar explanation of the weariness we feel in a crowd where we can't help seeing individual faces but can do no more than see them so that (he said) 'it is like being forced to read the first page, but no more, of 100 books in succession'?

Have you heard about the Toad?

Kenneth Grahame to his son Alastair; one of Grahame's letters containing the story that was to become *Wind in the Willows* (1908)

Durham Villas, London, 10 May 1907

MY DARLING Mouse, -

This is a birthday letter to wish you very many happy returns of the day. I wish we could have been all together, but we shall meet again soon and then we will have treats. I have sent you two picture books, one about Brer Rabbit, from Daddy, and one about some other animals, from Mummy. And we have sent you a boat, painted red, with mast and sails to sail in the round pond by the windmill - and Mummy has sent you a boat-hook to catch it when it comes ashore. Also Mummy has sent you some sand toys to play in the sand with, and a card game.

Have you heard about the Toad? He was never taken prisoner by brigands at all. It was all a horrid low trick of his. He wrote that letter himself - the letter saying that a hundred pounds must be put in the hollow tree. And he got out of the window early one morning and went off to a town called Buggleton and went to the Red Lion Hotel and there he found a party that had just motored down from London and while they were having breakfast he went into the stable-yard and found their motor car and went off in it without even saying Poop-poop! And now he has vanished and every one is looking for him, including the police. I fear he is a bad low animal.

Good-bye, from
Your loving DADDY

11 MAY

If I could destroy every letter I have ever written in my life I would do so

T S Eliot to his brother Henry

May 1930

And I am glad to have the letters to make ashes of. I should never have wanted to read them again, with all the folly and selfishness; and I dont want anyone else ever to read them and possibly print them; and if I could destroy every letter I have ever written in my life I would do so before I die. I should like to leave as little biography as possible. So that's done and done with.

12 MAY

Oven-cakes and fresh butter

Elizabeth Gaskell to her sister-in-law Eliza; written from her grandparents' home near Knutsford, the model for the farm in *Cousin Phyllis* (1864)

Sandlebridge, Cheshire, 12 May 1836

My dearest Lizzy,

I wish I could paint my present situation to you. Fancy me sitting in an old fashioned parlour, 'doors & windows opened wide', with casement window opening into a sunny court all filled with flowers which scent the air with their fragrance in the very depth of the country – five miles from the least approach to a town – the song of birds, the hum of insects the lowing of cattle the only sounds – and such pretty fields & woods all round – here are Baby, Betsy, Mama & Bessy Holland – and indeed at this present moment here is Sue, who has ridden over, to bring us news of the civilized world – in the shape of letters and so forth. One from Aunt Lumb enclosing yours, & so full of gratitude about the rasberry wine, & so over-flowing with thanks to you and your mother, that I fear there is little chance of my coming in for any of it. I shall try & put an affront into her head I can assure you, but I fear she will 'wallow' the affront. She begs her kind regards to your mother, & that I will say how *very* kind she thought it of her, & how much she shall enjoy getting tipsy – it *was* very kind of you to think of it, & you are a nice creature, & every body has so liked you, & I do so wish you were here to revel in flowers, & such thorough country.

We are up with the birds, and sitting out on the old flag steps in the very middle of fragrance – 'far from the busy hum of men', but not far from the busy hum of bees. Here is a sort of little standard library kept – Spenser, Shakspeare, Wordsworth & a few foreign books, & we sit & read & dream our time away – except at meals when we *don't* dream over cream that your spoon stands upright in, & such sweet (not sentimental but literal) oven-cakes, and fresh butter.

Baby is at the very tip-top of bliss; & gives a happy prospect of what she will be at your Aunt Holbrook. There are chickens, & little childish pigs, & cows & calves & horses, & *baby horses*, & fish in the pond, & ducks in the lane, & the mill & the smithy, & sheep & baby sheep, & flowers – oh! you would laugh to see her going about, with a great big nosegay in each hand, & wanting to be bathed in the golden bushes of wall-flowers – she is absolutely fatter since she came here, & is I'm sure stronger. I suspect I'm writing a queer medley, for I have had a walk in the heat, & my hand trembles & I think my brain trembles too – I ramble so. I was so sorry to miss you, and for James going when there was no need whatever for you to go. I rode above 18 miles that day, & lunched at Mr Davenport's at Capesthorne – such a beautiful place, not the house which is rather shabby; but the views from the park – the next day William and I had a ride, Mr Deane mounting & accompanying us both – nearly to Bowden. Saturday & Monday I rode again, & came here on Tuesday, having my choice, between coming here, & another 18 mile ride with Mr Deane – but I longed to see the old familiar place. The house & walls are over-run with roses, honeysuckles & vines – not quite in flower, *but all but* – Betsy is quite in her element, and teaches baby to call the pigs, & grunt just like any old sow.

13 MAY

A cloud wreath

Amy Lowell to Grace Conkling
1922

A cloud wreath. A dryad. Wind through beeches. Little waves over glittering sand. An unhappy woman tinged by time, grievous with memories, impatient at the world's dust, seeking a home for those thoughts which will in no wise contented if caged.

14 MAY

I find myself in my element

Walt Whitman to Hugo Fritsch

Washington, 1863

Dear comrade,

I still live here as a hospital missionary after my own style, & on my own hook – I go every day or night without fail to some of the great government hospitals – O the sad scenes I witness – scenes of death, anguish, the fevers, amputations, friendlessness, of hungering & thirsting young hearts, for some loving presence – such noble young men as some of these wounded are – such endurance, such native decorum, such candor – I will confess to you, dear Hugo, that in some respects I find myself in my element amid these scenes – shall I not say to you that I find I supply often to some of these dear suffering in my presence & magnetism that which nor doctors nor medicines nor skill nor any routine assistance can give?

I am excellent well. I have cut my beard short, & hair ditto (all my acquaintances are in anger & despair & go about wringing their hands). My face is all tanned & red. If the weather is moist or has been lately, or looks as if it thought of going to be, I perambulate this land in big army boots outside & up to my knees. Then around my majestic brow, around my well-brimmed felt hat – a black & gold cord with acorns. Altogether the effect is satisfactory. The guards as I enter or pass places often salute me – all of which I tell, as you will of course take pride in your friend's special & expanding glory.

15 MAY

Read with your ears

Gerard Manley Hopkins to Robert Bridges

May 1878

Please remember me very kindly to your mother.

To do the Eurydice any kind of justice you must not slovenly read it with the eyes but with your ears, as if the paper were declaiming it at you. For instance the line 'she had come from a cruise training seamen' read without stress and declaim is mere Lloyd's Shipping Intelligence; properly read it is quite a different thing. Stress is the life of it.

16 MAY

We bring reprieve of roses!

Emily Dickinson to Samuel Bowles

1863

Dear Friend,

We hope our joy to see you gave of its own degree to you. We pray for your new health, the prayer that goes not down when they shut the church. We offer you our cups – stintless, as
to the bee, – the lily, her new liquor.
Would you like summer? Taste of ours.
Spices? Buy here !
Ill ! We have berries, for the parching !
Weary ! Furloughs of down !
Perplexed ! Estates of violet trouble ne'er looked on !
Captive ! We bring reprieve of roses !
Fainting ! Flasks of air !
Even for Death, a fairy medicine.
But, which is it, sir?

EMILY

I'll send the feather from my hat !
Who knows but at the sight of that
My sovereign will relent?
As trinket, worn by faded child,
Confronting eyes long comforted
Blisters the adamant !

EMILY

17 MAY

Extreme quiet with few incidents

Christina Rossetti to Amelia Barnard Heimann

Tunbridge Wells, May 1867

My dear Mrs Heimann

Here comes my traditional out-of-town letter. We are getting on here very nicely in extreme quiet, with few incidents, and those not very exciting ones. Who is to fill a letter with trees in leaf and blossom, gardens in gradations of beauty, green slopes, rocky interruptions, gorse-clad common and cloudy sky? The local dogs are interesting and varied, but it passes my descriptive faculty to bring before your absent eyes their expressive countenances and also expressive tails. We have had no drives as yet, a supplementary winter having come to pass: but perhaps we may yet enjoy some before returning home next Friday.

Your always affectionate Christina G. Rossetti.

18 MAY

I could not bear my sufferings to be without meaning

Oscar Wilde to Lord Alfred Douglas; Wilde was released from Reading Gaol on this day in 1897

From *De Profundis* (1905)

I have lain in prison for nearly two years. Out of my nature has come wild despair; an abandonment to grief that was piteous even to look at; terrible and impotent rage; bitterness and scorn; anguish that wept aloud; misery that could find no voice; sorrow that was dumb. I have passed through every possible mood of suffering. Better than Wordsworth himself I know what Wordsworth meant when he said –

'Suffering is permanent, obscure, and dark
And has the nature of infinity.'

But while there were times when I rejoiced in the idea that my sufferings were to be endless, I could not bear them to be without meaning. Now I find hidden somewhere away in my nature something that tells me that nothing in the whole world is meaningless, and suffering least of all. That something hidden away in my nature, like a treasure in a field, is Humility.

It is the last thing left in me, and the best: the ultimate discovery at which I have arrived, the starting-point for a fresh development. It has come to me right out of myself, so I know that it has come at the proper time. It could not have come before, nor later. Had any one told me of it, I would have rejected it. Had it been brought to me, I would have refused it. As I found it, I want to keep it. I must do so. It is the one thing that has in it the elements of life, of a new life, *Vita Nuova* for me. Of all things it is the strangest. One cannot acquire it, except by surrendering everything that one has. It is only when one has lost all things, that one knows that one possesses it.

Now I have realized that it is in me, I see quite clearly what I ought to do; in fact, must do. And when I use such a phrase as that, I need not say that I am not alluding to any external sanction or command. I admit none. I am far more of an individualist than I ever was.

Nothing seems to me of the smallest value except what one gets out of oneself. My nature is seeking a fresh mode of self-realisation. That is all I am concerned with. And the first thing that I have got to do is to free myself from any possible bitterness of feeling against the world.

As globule of dew on a rose-leaf

George Eliot to Caroline Bray
19 May 1854

When I spoke of myself as an island, I did not mean that I was so exceptionally. We are all islands -

'Each in his hidden sphere of joy or woe,
Our hermit spirits dwell and roam apart' -*

and this seclusion is sometimes the most intensely felt at the very moment your friend is caressing you or consoling you. But this gradually becomes a source of satisfaction instead of repining. When we are young we think our troubles a mighty business - that the world is spread out expressly as a stage for the particular drama of our lives and that we have a right to rant and foam at the mouth if we are crossed. I had done enough of that in my time. But we begin to understand that these things are important only to one's own consciousness, which is but as a globule of dew on a rose-leaf that at mid-day there will be no trace of. This is no high-flown sentimentality, but a simple reflection which I find useful to me every day ...

**from John Keble's* The Christian Year *(1827)*

20 MAY

The three rules of life

Wilkie Collins to Holman Hunt

Portman Square, London, 1885

My dear Hunt

The three rules of life that I find the right ones, by experience, in the matter of health are:

1. As much fresh air as possible (I don't get as much as I ought).
2. Live well - eat light and nourishing food, eggs, birds, fish, sweetbreads - no heavy chops or joints. And find out the wine that agrees with you, and don't be afraid of it (here, I set an excellent example!)
3. Empty your mind of your work before you go to bed - and don't let the work get in again until after breakfast the next morning (this is a serious struggle - many defeats must be encountered - but the victory may be won at last, as I can personally certify).

One last word - and I have done preaching. If you don't find that you make better progress, under your present medical guidance, try my old friend, F. Carr Beard, 44 Welbeck Street, Cavendish Square. He kept Dickens alive, he kept Fechter alive, he is keeping me alive. The most capable, and the most honest, doctor I have ever known.

Always affectionately yours
Wilkie Collins

21 MAY

I'll take care of you

Edna St Vincent Millay to her mother Cora B. Millay

Vassar College, New York, 21 May 1915

Beloved, beautiful, sad, sick Mother, -

I love you, I love you. Don't be sad any more. I'll take care of you, way from here. I remember how you used to rock me and sing to me when I was sick and sad. And now I'm going to make you better by telling you some lovely things all about yourself.

First: - Of all the songs I sing, - and I sing often now to crowds of people who love my little songs - the one they seem to love best is your beautiful 'I may not dream again'. Miss Landon, the Spoken English teacher, is just mad about it. She appreciates every little lovely thing about it.

Second: I'm just beginning to really appreciate at last the 25 red books full of knowledge that you gave me once. Now I'm really reading them a lot. Elaine has found that some of them are just what she needs for her biology courses and is using them, too. She said, 'Who gave them to you?' and I said, 'My mother.' And she said, 'That's what I call a present. That's a wonderful present to give.'

I'll save other nice things to tell you in another letter, dear.

Give my love to my sisters, my mother.

Your daughter,
Vincent

The post office man is sorting the letters by the light of his lamp

Robert Louis Stevenson to Frances Sitwell

17 Heriot Row, Edinburgh, 1873

I must write you a little word again before I go to bed; although my last is not yet many miles on its southward journey. Blessings on the trains that go all night, through rain and moon-glimpse, over the sleeping country, to bring people so near together. The post office man is just now sorting the letters by the light of his lamp, as the whole thundering train goes swaying round the angles of the line; and some time soon, my letter will slip through his fingers and be thrown on the right heap to get safely to its happy destination: I wish I could go with it.

I want to say so many things to you, that I find it impossible to begin. I want to tell you how any little detail of your life makes absence a mere dream; but on that head, dear, you know already all that I feel. And I want to tell you what I hope to do and of what I fear to fail in the accomplishment. And again, I want to tell you all manner of small things out of my own life, all sorts of infinitesimal joys and sorrows and disappointments and happy surprises, that I desire to share with my dearest of all friends; and yet these and many other things (do you understand me?) it seems a sort of insincerity to write about between us two, as when people talk of the weather for a long while, warily avoiding something of superlative interest to both. Let us talk of the weather, however. And, at least, dear, I hope the weather is now warmer with you: it would be a real gladness to me to think of you in warm sunshine, and I should not feel so cold myself up here, if I could believe so.

I know a great many secrets not to be got out of books

Mark Twain to ----

1891

I confined myself to the boy-life out on the Mississippi because that had a peculiar charm for me, and not because I was not familiar with other phases of life. I was a soldier two weeks once in the beginning of the war, and was hunted like a rat the whole time. Familiar? My splendid Kipling himself hasn't a more burnt-in, hard-baked and unforgetable familiarity with that death-on-the-pale-horse-with-hell-following-after, which is a raw soldier's first fortnight in the field - and which, without any doubt, is the most tremendous fortnight and the vividest he is ever going to see.

Yes, and I have shoveled silver tailings in a quartz-mill a couple of weeks, and acquired the last possibilities of culture in that direction. And I've done 'pocket-mining' during three months in the one little patch of ground in the whole globe where Nature conceals gold in pockets - or did before we robbed all of those pockets and exhausted, obliterated, annihilated the most curious freak Nature ever indulged in. There are not 30 men left alive who, being told there was a pocket hidden on the broad slope of a mountain, would know how to go and find it, or have even the faintest idea of how to set about it; but I am one of the possible 20 or 30 who possess the secret, and I could go and put my hand on that hidden treasure with a most deadly precision.

And I've been a prospector, and know pay rock from poor when I find it - just with a touch of the tongue. And I've been a silver miner and know how to dig and shovel and drill and put in a blast.

And I was a newspaper reporter four years in cities, and so saw the inside of many things; and was reporter in a legislature two sessions and the same in Congress one session, and thus learned to know personally three sample bodies of the smallest minds and the selfishest souls and the cowardliest hearts that God makes.

And I was some years a Mississippi pilot, and familiarly knew all the different kinds of steam-boatmen - a race apart, and not like other folk.

And I was a lecturer on the public platform a number of seasons and was a responder to toasts at all the different kinds of banquets - and so I know a great many secrets about audiences - secrets not to be got out of books, but only acquirable by experience.

And I watched over one dear project of mine for years, spent a fortune on it, and failed to make it go - and the history of that would make a large book in which a million men would see themselves as in a mirror; and they would testify and say, 'Verily, this is not imagination; this fellow has been there' - and after would cast dust upon their heads, cursing and blaspheming.

And I am a publisher, and did pay to one author's widow (General Grant's) the largest copyright checks this world has seen - aggregating more than $80,000 in the first year.

And I have been an author for 20 years and an ass for 55.

Now then; as the most valuable capital or culture or education usable in the building of novels is personal experience I ought to be well equipped for that trade.

I surely have the equipment, a wide culture, and all of it real, none of it artificial, for I don't know anything about books.

24 MAY

The heart of England beating healthily

Edward FitzGerald to Frederic Tennyson

Woodbridge, Suffolk, 24 May 1844

My Dear Frederic

London melts away all individuality into a common lump of cleverness. I am amazed at the humour and worth and noble feeling in the country, however much railroads have mixed us up with metropolitan civilization. I can still find the heart of England beating healthily down here, though no one will believe it.

You know my way of life so well that I need not describe it to you, as it has undergone no change since I saw you. I read of mornings; the same old books over and over again, having no command of new ones; walk with my great black dog of an afternoon, and at evening sit with open windows, up to which China roses climb, with my pipe, while the blackbirds and thrushes begin to rustle bedwards in the garden, and the nightingale to have the neighbourhood to herself. We have had such a spring (bating the last ten days) as would have satisfied even you with warmth. And such verdure! White clouds moving over the newfledged tops of oak trees, and acres of grass striving with buttercups. How old to tell of, how new to see!

25 MAY

Omniscient, omnipresent

Charles Dickens to John Forster; the concept of *Household Worlds*, Dickens's weekly magazine

Broadstairs, Kent, 1849

I want to suppose a certain SHADOW, which may go into any place, by sunlight, moonlight, starlight, firelight, candlelight and be in all homes, and all nooks and corners, and be supposed to be cognisant of everything, and go everywhere, without the least difficulty. Which may be in the Theatre, the Palace, the House of Commons, the Prisons, the Unions, the Churches, on the Railroad, on the Sea, abroad and at home: a kind of semi-omniscient, omnipresent, intangible creature. I want him to loom as a fanciful thing all over London; and to get up a general notion of 'What will the Shadow say about this, I wonder? What will the Shadow say about that? Is the Shadow here?' and so forth ... it presents an odd, unsubstantial, whimsical, new thing: a sort of previously unthought-of Power going about ... in which people will be perfectly willing to believe, and which is just mysterious and quaint enough to have a sort of charm for their imagination, while it will represent common-sense and humanity. I want to express in the title, and in the grasp of the idea to express also, that it is the Thing at everybody's elbow, and in everybody's footsteps. At the window, by the fire, in the street, in the house, from infancy to old age, everyone's inseparable companion ...

26 MAY

Forsake, namesake, keepsake

Gerard Manley Hopkins to Robert Bridges

Oxford, 26 May 1879

Dearest Bridges,

Sake is a word I find it convenient to use: I did not know when I did so first that it is common in German, in the form *sach*. It is the *sake* of 'for the sake of', *forsake, namesake, keepsake*. I mean by it the being a thing has outside itself, as a voice by its echo, a face by its reflection, a body by its shadow, a man by his name, fame, or memory, *and also* that in the thing by virtue of which especially it has this being abroad, and that is something distinctive, marked, specifically or individually speaking, as for a voice and echo clearness; for a reflected image light, brightness; for a shadow-casting body bulk; for a man genius, great achievements, amiability and so on. In this case it is, as the sonnet says, distinctive quality in genius.

27 MAY

The little girl

Mary Wollstonecraft to Gilbert Imlay; Mary writes about their four-month old daughter Fanny

Paris, 1794

I have been playing and laughing with the little girl so long, that I cannot take up my pen to address you without emotion. Pressing her to my bosom, she looked so like you (*entre nous*, your best looks, for I do not admire your commercial face) every nerve seemed to vibrate to the touch, and I began to think that there was something in the assertion of man and wife being one - for you seemed to pervade my whole frame, quickening the beat of my heart, and lending me the sympathetic tears you excited.

Have I anything more to say to you? No; not for the present - the rest is all flown away; and, indulging tenderness for you, I cannot now complain of some people here, who have ruffled my temper for two or three days past.

28 MAY

I have no horror of death

Anne Brontë to Ellen Nussey; written shortly before Anne's death, on this day in 1849

Haworth, Yorkshire, 1849

I have no horror of death: if I thought it inevitable I think I could quietly resign myself to the prospect, in the hope that you, dear Miss Nussey, would give as much of your company as you possibly could to Charlotte and be a sister to her in my stead. But I wish it would please God to spare me not only for Papa's and Charlotte's sakes, but because I long to do some good in the world before I leave it. I have many schemes in my head for future practise - humble and limited indeed - but still I should not like them all to come to nothing, and myself to have lived to so little purpose. But God's will be done.

I go out on the moors alone

Charlotte Brontë to James Taylor; sisters Emily and Anne had died within six months of each other

Haworth, Yorkshire, May 1850

I am free to walk on the moors; but when I go out there alone, everything reminds me of the times when others were with me, and then the moors seem a wilderness, featureless, solitary, saddening. My sister Emily had a particular love for them, and there is not a knoll of heather, not a branch of fern, not a young bilberry leaf, not a fluttering lark or linnet, but reminds me of her. The distant prospects were Anne's delight, and when I look round, she is in the blue tints, the pale mists, the waves and shadows of the horizon. In the hill-country silence, their poetry comes by lines and stanzas into my mind: once I loved it; now I dare not read it, and am driven often to wish I could taste one draught of oblivion, and forget much that, while mind remains, I never shall forget. Many people seem to recall their departed relatives with a sort of melancholy complacency, but I think these have not watched them through lingering sickness, nor witnessed their last moments: it is these reminiscences that stand by your bedside at night, and rise at your pillow in the morning. At the end of all, however, exists the Great Hope. Eternal Life is theirs now.

'Good news! good news! Anna has a fine boy!'

Louisa May Alcott to her sister Anna Pratt; Anna had just had a baby boy

1863

We were all sitting deep in a novel, not expecting Father home owing to the snowstorm, when the door burst open, and in he came, all wet and white, waving his bag, and calling out, 'Good news! good news! Anna has a fine boy!'

With one accord we opened our mouths and screamed for about two minutes. Then Mother began to cry; I began to laugh; and May to pour out questions; while Papa beamed upon us all, - red, damp, and shiny, the picture of a proud old Grandpa. Such a funny evening as we had! Mother kept breaking down, and each time emerged from her handkerchief saying solemnly, 'I must go right down and see that baby!' Father had told every one he met, from Mr Emerson to the coach driver, and went about the house saying, 'Anna's boy! Yes, yes, Anna's boy!' in a mild state of satisfaction.

May and I at once taxed our brains for a name, and decided upon 'Amos Minot Bridge Bronson May Sewall Alcott Pratt', so that all the families would be suited.

Grandma and Grandpa Pratt came to hear the great news; but we could only inform them of the one tremendous fact, that Pratt, Jr., had condescended to arrive. Now tell us his weight, inches, colour, etc.

I know I shall fall down and adore when I see that mite.

Now get up quickly, and be a happy mamma. Of course John does *not* consider his son as *the* most amazing product of the nineteenth century.

Bless the baby!

Ever your admiring
Lu.

Poetry is with me an impulse and a reality

Christina Rossetti to William Edmonstoune Aytou; Rossetti went on to publish over nine hundred poems

London, 1854

As an unknown and unpublished writer, I beg leave to bespeak your indulgence for laying before you the enclosed verses. I am not unaware, Sir, that the editor of a magazine looks with dread and contempt upon the offerings of a nameless rhymester – and that the feeling is in nineteen cases out of twenty, a just and salutary one. It certainly is not for me to affirm that I am the one twentieth in question: but, speaking as I am to a poet, I hope that I shall not be misunderstood as guilty of egotism or foolish vanity, when I say that my love for what is good in the works of others teaches me that there is something above the despicable in mine; that poetry is with me, not a mechanism but an impulse and a reality; and that I know my aims in writing to be pure, and directed to that which is true and right.

I do not blush to confess that, with these feelings and beliefs, it would afford me some gratification to place my productions before others, and ascertain how far what I do is expressive of mere individualism, and how far it is capable of approving itself to the general sense. It would be a personal favour to me if you would look into the enclosed with an eye not inevitably to the waste paper basket; and a further obligation if, whatever be the result, you would vouchsafe me a few words as to the fate of the verses: I am quite conscious that volunteer contributors have no right to expect this of an editor; I ask it simply as a courtesy. It is mortifying to have done something sincerely, offer it in faith, and be treated as 'non avenue'.

JUNE

1 JUNE

A Pitchy Blackness

Mary Wollstonecraft Shelley to ---- ; *Frankenstein* (1818) was conceived during a rainy weekend shortly after Mary wrote this letter

Near Coligny, Switzerland, 1 June 1816

We now inhabit a little cottage on the opposite shore of the lake, and have exchanged the view of Mont Blanc and her snowy *aiguilles* for the dark frowning Jura, behind whose range we every evening see the sun sink, and darkness approaches our valley from behind the Alps, which are then tinged by that glowing rose-like hue which is observed in England to attend on the clouds of an autumnal sky when day-light is almost gone.

The lake is at our feet, and a little harbour contains our boat, in which we still enjoy our evening excursions on the water. Unfortunately we do not now enjoy those brilliant skies that hailed us on our first arrival to this country. An almost perpetual rain confines us principally to the house; but when the sun bursts forth it is with a splendour and heat unknown in England. The thunder storms that visit us are grander and more terrific than I have even seen before. We watch them as they approach from the opposite side of the lake, observing the lightning play among the clouds in various parts of the heavens, and dart in jagged figures upon the piny heights of Jura, dark with the shadow of the overhanging cloud, while perhaps the sun is shining cheerily upon us. One night we enjoyed a finer storm than I had ever before beheld. The lake was lit up – the pines on Jura made visible, and all the scene illuminated for an instant, when a pitchy blackness succeeded, and the thunder came in frightful bursts over our heads amid the darkness.

2 JUNE

My verses catch fire from you as you read them

Elizabeth Barrett Browning to John Ruskin

Florence, Italy, 2 June 1855

My dear Mr Ruskin,

I believe I shall rather prove in this letter how my head turns round when I write it, than explain why I didn't write it before - and so you will go on to think me the most unsusceptible and least grateful of human beings - no small distinction in our bad obtuse world. Yet the truth is - oh, the truth is, that I am deeply grateful to you and have felt to the quick of my heart the meaning and kindness of your words, the worth of your sympathy and praise. One thing especially which you said, made me thankful that I had been allowed to live to hear it - since even to fancy that anything I had written could be the means of the least good to you, is worth all the trumpet blowing of a vulgar fame. Oh, of course, I do not exaggerate, though your generosity does. I understand the case as it is. We burn straw and it warms us. My verses catch fire from you as you read them, and so you see them in that light of your own. But it is something to be used to such an end by such a man, and I thank you, thank you, and so does my husband for the deep pleasure you have given us in the words you have written.

Champagne in the hereafter

Herman Melville to Nathaniel Hawthorne

Pittsfield, Massachusetts, June 1851

The calm, the coolness, the silent grass-growing mood in which a man *ought* always to compose, - that, I fear, can seldom be mine. My dear Sir a presentiment is on me. - I shall at last be worn out and perish, like an old nutmeg-grater, grated to pieces by the constant attrition of the wood, that is, the nutmeg. What I feel most moved to write, that is banned, - it will not pay. Yet, write the *other* way I cannot. So the product is a final hash, and all my books are botches.

Would the Gin were here! If ever, my dear Hawthorne, in the eternal times that are to come, you and I shall sit down in Paradise, in some little shady corner by ourselves; and if we shall by any means able to smuggle a basket of champagne there (I won't believe in a Termperance Heaven), and if we shall then cross our celestial legs in the celestial grass that is forever tropical, and strike our glasses and our heads together, till both musically ring in concert, - then, O my dear fellow-mortal, how shall we pleasantly discourse of all the things manifold which now so distress us, - when all the earth shall be but a reminiscence, yea, its final dissolution an antiquity. Then shall songs be composed as when wars are over; humourous, comic songs, - yes, let us look forward to such things. Let us swear that, though now we sweat, yet it is because of the dry heat which is indispensable to the nourishment of the vine which is to bear the grapes that are to give us the champagne hereafter.

O my agèd Uncle Arly!

Edward Lear to Lord Carlingford

4 June 1884

Having a notion you have a little more leisure while you are at Balmoral (as I see by the papers you are about to be) ... I shall send you a few lines just to let you know how your aged friend goes on

O my agèd Uncle Arly!
Sitting on a heap of Barley
Through the silent hours of night!
On his nose there sate a cricket;
In his hat a railway ticket –
But his shoes were far too tight!
Too! Too!
far too tight!

5 JUNE

My diamond might be coal or soot, and my theme is carbon

D H Lawrence to Edward Garnett

Spezia, Italy, 5 June 1914

You mustn't look in my novel for the old stable *ego* of the character. There is another *ego*, according to whose action the individual is unrecognisable, and passes through, as it were, allotropic states which it needs a deeper sense than any we've been used to exercise, to discover are states of the same single radically unchanged element. (Like as diamond and coal are the same pure single element of carbon. The ordinary novel would trace the history of the diamond – but I say, 'Diamond, what! This is carbon'. And my diamond might be coal or soot, and my theme is carbon). You must not say my novel is shaky – it is not perfect, because I am not expert in what I want to do. But it is the real thing, say what you like. And I shall get my reception, if not now, then before long. Again I say, don't look for the development of the novel to follow the lines of certain characters: the characters fall into the form of some other rhythmic form, as when one draws a fiddle-bow across a fine tray delicately sanded, the sand takes lines unknown.

Don't get chilly and disagreeable to me.
Au revoir,
D. H. LAWRENCE

The maddest people that the maddest times were ever plagued with

Ignatius Sancho to John Spink; Sancho, a freed Black slave, became a valet to a duke, and, at the time of writing this letter, was the owner of a grocer's store allowing him the right to vote in the British elections, the first Black British man to do so. Here he describes The Gordon Riots of 1780: several days of rioting in London against the Papists Act 1778, which was intended to reduce official discrimination against British Catholics

Charles Street, London, 6 June 1780

In the midst of the most cruel and ridiculous confusion, I am now set down to give you a very imperfect sketch of the maddest people that the maddest times were ever plagued with. - There is at this present moment at least a hundred thousand poor, miserable, ragged rabble, from twelve to sixty years of age, with blue cockades in their hats - besides half as many women and children - all parading the streets - the bridge - the park - ready for any and every mischief. Gracious God! what's the matter now? I was obliged to leave off - the shouts of the mob - the horrid clashing of swords - and the clutter of a multitude in swiftest motion - drew me to the door - when every one in the street was employed in shutting up shop. - It is now just five o'clock - the ballad-singers are exhausting their musical talents - with the downfall of Popery, S[andwic]h, and N[ort]h. Lord S[andwic]h narrowly escaped with life about an hour since; - the mob seized his chariot going to the house, broke his glasses, and, in struggling to get his lordship out, they somehow have cut his face; - the guards flew to his assistance - the light-horse scowered the road, got his chariot, escorted him from the coffeehouse, where he had fled for protection, to his carriage, and guarded him bleeding very fast home. This - this - is liberty! Genuine British liberty! - This instant about two thousand liberty boys are swearing and swaggering by with large sticks -

– Thank heaven, it rains; may it increase, so as to send these deluded wretches safe to their homes, their families and wives!

I am, dear Sir,
Yours ever by inclination,
IGN. SANCHO

We are like two secluded owls

George Eliot to Mrs Peter Taylor; Eliot (the pen name of Mary Ann Evans) describes a holiday with partner George Henry Lewes

June 1871

We have a ravishing country round us, and pure air and water; in short, all the conditions of health, if the east wind were away. I read aloud – almost all the evening – books of German science, and other gravities. So, you see, we are like two secluded owls, wise with unfashionable wisdom, and knowing nothing of pictures and French plays.

The programme of our lives

George Henry Lewes describes a holiday with George Eliot in a letter to Princess Sayn Wittgenstein-Caroline Elizabeth Iwanowska

1854

The happy hours we have spent furnish us with frequent conversation, and to have known you and the Maestro is enough to make Weimar a green spot in our lives.

We rise at eight; after breakfast read and work till between one and two, walk in the Thiergarten or pay visits till dinner, which is at three; come home to coffee, when not at the theatre or in society Miss Evans reads Goethe aloud to me & I read Shakspeare aloud to her. There you have the programme of our lives ... we stay much at home, although numerous friends attract us sometimes from our quiet.

8 JUNE

Light, beautiful letters

Rainer Maria Rilke to Lou Andreas-Salome

Paris, France, 8 June 1914

Dear Lou,

Here I am again after a long, broad and heavy time, a time that has lapsed past me like a sort of future, not lived strongly and reverently but tormented to the very end until it perished (a feat no one will succeed in imitating very easily).

--

What eventually befell so completely to my misfortune began with many, many letters, light, beautiful letters which ran trippingly off my heart; I can hardly remember ever having written such letters before. In these (as I understood more and more) a spontaneous vivacity welled up as though I had struck a new, brimming ebullience in my own being which now, unloosed in an inexhaustible spate of communication, poured itself forth over this happy gradient whilst I, writing day and night, felt its joyful streaming and at the same time the mysterious repose which seemed naturally prepared for it in the recipient. To keep this communication pure and limpid and to feel or think nothing that could be excluded by it: this suddenly, without my knowing how, became the law and measure of my doing, - and if ever a spiritually turbid person can become pure again, I was that person in those letters.

Translated from the German by R.F.C. Hull

Roses

Christina Rossetti to Caroline Gemmer

London, 1872

I will not champion stinging nettles, not to you. If we agree in liking all other flowers, our field of contention is a narrow one. Roses all-excelling shall be our common ground: of all flowers known to me I would least give up roses; and of all roses (what say you?) least give up the dog-rose of our hedges. Does any cultivated thing quite come up to its shades, its shapes, its proportions? Wild honeysuckle is lovely indeed, but not like wild roses.

Affectionately yours
Christina G. Rossetti

You are the only friend I have in the world

Charles Lamb to Samuel Taylor Coleridge

10 June 1796

Thank you for your frequent letters: you are the only correspondent, and I might add, the only friend I have in the world. I go nowhere, and have no acquaintance. Slow of speech, and reserved of manners, no one seeks or cares for my society; and I am left alone. Allen calls very occasionally, as though it were a duty rather, and seldom stays ten minutes. Then judge how thankful I am for your letters! Do not, however, burthen yourself with the correspondence. I trouble you again so soon, only in obedience to your injunctions. Complaints apart, proceed we to our task. I am called away to tea; thence must wait upon my brother; so must delay till tomorrow. Farewell!

I image to myself the little smoky room at the Salutation and Cat, where we have sat together through the winter nights, beguiling the cares of life with Poesy. When you left London I felt a dismal void in my heart. I found myself cut off, at one and the same time, from two most dear to me. 'How blest with ye the path could I have trod of quiet life!' In your conversation you had blended so many pleasant fancies that they cheated me of my grief. But in your absence the tide of melancholy rushed in again, and did its worst mischief by overwhelming my reason. I have recovered, but feel a stupor that makes me indifferent to the hopes and fears of this life. I sometimes wish to introduce a religious turn of mind; but habits are strong things, and my religious fervours are confined, alas! to some fleeting moments of occasional solitary devotion. A correspondence, opening with you, has roused me a little from my lethargy, and made me conscious of existence. Indulge me in it: I will not be very troublesome.

11 JUNE

I cannot scatter friendships like chuck-farthings

Charles Lamb to Samuel Taylor Coleridge

1797

You are all very dear and precious to me. Do what you will, Coleridge, you may hurt me and vex me by your silence, but you cannot estrange my heart from you all. I cannot scatter friendships like chuck-farthings, nor let them drop from mine hand like hour-glass sand. I have but two or three people in the world to whom I am more than indifferent, and I can't afford to whistle them off to the winds.

Now, do answer this. Friendship, and acts of friendship, should be reciprocal, and free as the air. A friend should never be reduced to beg an alms of his fellow; yet I will beg an alms: I entreat you to write, and tell me all about poor Lloyd, and all of you. God love and preserve you all!

C. Lamb.

12 JUNE

The creative urge must come from within

Langston Hughes to Charlotte Mason

June 1930

Almost all of one's life must be measured and timed as it is – meals every day at a certain hour; if I am working for a salary – to work at a certain time; to bed at a certain time ~~in order~~ to get enough sleep; letters to be answered by a certain time in order to avoid discourtesy or loss of business. So far ~~in this world~~, only my writing has been my own, to do when I wanted to do it, to finish only when I felt that it was finished, to put it aside or discard it completely if I chose. For the sake of my physical body I have washed ~~restaurant~~ thousands of hotel dishes, cooked, scrubbed decks, worked 12 to 15 hours a day on a farm, swallowed my pride for the ~~sake~~ help of philanthropy and charity – but nobody ever said to me 'You must write now, you must finish that poem tomorrow. You must begin to create on the first of the month.' Because then I could not have ~~have written, I could not have~~ created anything. I could only have put down empty words at best ... The creative urge must come from within, ~~always~~ as you know dear G., – or it is less than true ...

13 JUNE

It warmed the cockles of my heart

Lord Alfred Tennyson to Edward FitzGerald

Somersby, Lincolnshire, June 1835

Many, many times, my dear Fitz, have I both thought of you and spoken of you, and quoted your sayings and doings, as those who live with me and know me can testify and long ere this had I written to you and exprest my sincere repentance for not having answered on the instant your last kind letter – truly kind it was, and if I did not dislike warm cockles, which warm or cold are a bad fish, I would say that it warmed the cockles of my heart – but unfortunately I mislaid your letter, and your direction escaped my memory. I am not such a beast, my dear fellow, as you take me for. Grumpy at receiving a warm-hearted brief from a honest man! I may have been sometimes grumpy in the North, for I was out of health, and the climate Arctic, and Spedding had a trick of quiet banter that sometimes deranged one's equilibrium but grumpy to you – never, as I hope to be saved, and on that I take my master of keys as Brookfield used to say.

Words are very clumsy things

George Eliot to Sara Hennell

14 June 1858

Words are very clumsy things. I like less and less to handle my friends' sacred feelings with them. For even those who call themselves intimate know very little about each other – hardly ever know just how a sorrow is felt, and hurt each other by their very attempts at sympathy or consolation. We can bear no hand on our bruises. And so I feel I have no right to say that I know how the loss of your mother – 'the only person who ever leaned on you' – affects you. I only know that it must make a deeply-felt crisis in your life, and I know that the better from having felt a great deal about my own mother and father, and from having the keenest remembrance of all that experience. But for this very reason I know that I can't measure what the event is to you; and if I were near you I should only kiss you and say nothing. People talk of the feelings dying out as one gets older; but at present my experience is just the contrary. All the serious relations of life become so much more real to me – pleasure seems so slight a thing, and sorrow and duty and endurance so great. I find the least bit of real human life touch me in a way it never did when I was younger.

Dearly Beloved

Edna St Vincent Millay to her mother Cora B. Millay

Paris, France, 15 June 1921

Dearly Beloved

It is nearly six months now since I saw you. A long time. Mother, do you know, almost all people love their mothers, but I have never met anybody in my life, I think, who loved his mother as much as I love you. I don't believe there ever was anybody who did, quite so much, and quite in so many wonderful ways. I was telling somebody yesterday that the reason I am a poet is entirely because you wanted me to be and intended I should be, even from the very first. You brought me up in the tradition of poetry, and everything I did you encouraged. I can not remember once in my life when you were not interested in what I was working on, or even suggested that I should put it aside for something else. Some parents of children that are 'different' have so much to reproach themselves with. But not you, Great Spirit.

I hope you will write me as soon as you get this. If you only knew what it means to me to get letters from any of you three over there. Because no matter how interesting it all is, and how beautiful, and how happy I am, and how much work I get done, I am nevertheless away from home, - home being somewhere near where you are, mother dear.

16 JUNE

Sticking a meaning into a sentence in defiance of grammar

Leslie Stephen to his son Thoby

Hyde Park Gate, London, June 1901

My dear boy

I am trying to get a little German into Ginia*. She has a fault which I guess you may have too. Certainly I have. She rushes at her fences & insists upon sticking a meaning into a sentence in defiance of grammar. However, by insisting upon it that tenses & genders have some meaning I hope that I am getting her a little into order.

Ever your loving
LS

**Stephen's daughter, Virginia Woolf*

17 JUNE

The Elysian Fields

Lady Mary Wortley Montagu to Alexander Pope

Belgrade Village, near Constantinople, Turkey, 17 June 17--

I have already let you know, that I am still alive; but to say truth, I look upon my present circumstances to be exactly the same with those of departed spirits. The heats of Constantinople have driven me to this place, which perfectly answers the description of the Elysian fields. I am in the middle of a wood, consisting chiefly of fruit-trees, watered by a vast number of fountains, famous for the excellency of their water, and divided into many shady walks, upon short grass, that seems to me artificial, but, I am assured, is the pure work of nature – within view of the Black Sea, from whence we perpetually enjoy the refreshment of cool breezes, that make us insensible of the heat of the summer. The village is only inhabited by the richest amongst the Christians, who meet every night at a fountain, forty paces from my house, to sing and dance. The beauty and dress of the women exactly resemble the ideas of the ancient nymphs, as they are given us by the representations of the poets and painters. But what persuades me more fully of my decease, is the situation of my own mind, the profound ignorance I am in, of what passes among the living (which only comes to me by chance) and the great calmness with which I receive it.

To say truth, I am sometimes very weary of the singing, and dancing, and sunshine, and wish for the smoke and impertinencies in which you toil; though I endeavour to persuade myself, that I live in a more agreeable variety than you do; and that Monday, setting of partridges; Tuesday, reading English; Wednesday, studying in the Turkish language, (in which, by the way, I am already very learned);

Thursday, classical authors; Friday, spent in writing; Saturday, at my needle; and Sunday, admitting of visits, and hearing of music, is a better way of disposing of the week; than, Monday, at the drawing room; Tuesday, Lady Mohun's; Wednesday, at the opera; Thursday, the play; Friday, Mrs Chetwynd's, and so forth a perpetual round of hearing the same scandal, and seeing the same follies acted over and over, which here affect me no more than they do other dead people. I can now hear of displeasing things with pity, and without indignation. The reflection on the great gulph between you and me, cools all news that come hither. I can neither be sensibly touched with joy or grief, when I consider, that possibly the cause of either is removed, before the letter comes to my hands. But (as I said before) this indolence does not extend to my few friendships; I am still warmly sensible of yours and Mr Congreve's, and desire to live in your remembrance, though dead to all the world beside. I am, &c. &c.

18 JUNE

I lye dreaming of you in Moonshiny Nights

Alexander Pope to Lady Mary Wortley Montagu

1717

The poetical manner in which you paint some of the Scenes about you, makes me despise my native country and sets me on fire to fall into the Dance about your Fountain in Belgrade-village. I fancy myself, in my romantic thoughts & distant admiration of you, not unlike the man in the Alchmyist that has a passion for the Queen of the Faeries. I lye dreaming of you in Moonshiny Nights exactly in the posture of Endymion gaping for Cynthia in a Picture.

19 JUNE

The Letters of Lady Mary Wortley Montagu

Voltaire to M. le Comte d'Argental

1763

My dear angels, it is a great pity that the *Literary Gazette* allowed itself to be prejudiced in the account it gave of the Letters of Lady Mary Wortley Montagu, which are appearing in England. The Letters of Mme de Sévigné are suited to the French, those of Lady Montagu to all nations. If they are ever well translated (and that would be a difficult task) you will be delighted to find in them so much that is new and curious, embellished by knowledge, taste and good writing.

Just fancy that for more than a thousand years no traveller able to gain and give information had reached Constantinople through the countries which Lady Montagu traversed: she has seen the native land of Orpheus and Alexander: she has dined *tête-à-tête* with the widow of the Emperor Mustapha; she has translated Turkish songs and declarations of love, which are quite in the style of the Song of Songs; she has observed manners resembling those described by Homer, and has travelled with her Homer in her hand. We learn from her to rid ourselves of many of our prejudices. The Turks are neither such brutes nor so brutal as has been said.

Translated from the French by S. G. Tallentyre

20 JUNE

Madame de Sévigné: the Queen of all Letter writers

Edward FitzGerald to E B Cowell

1875

My dear Cowell,

Did you ever read Madame de Sévigné? I never did till this summer, rather repelled by her perpetual harping on her Daughter. But it is all genuine, and the same intense Feeling expressed in a hundred natural yet graceful ways: and beside all this such good Sense, good Feeling, Humour, Love of Books and Country Life, as makes her certainly the Queen of all letter writers.

21 JUNE

My dear child

Madame de Sévigné to her daughter Madame de Grignan

Paris, France, 1671

I receive your letters in the same way in which you received my ring. I am in tears while I read them. My heart seems ready to burst. Bystanders would think that you had treated me ill in your letters, or were sick, or that some accident had happened to you; whereas everything is the reverse. You love me, my dear child, you love me, and you tell me so in a manner that makes my tears flow in torrents.

You continue your journey without any disagreeable accident. To know this, is the thing I could the most desire: and yet am I in this deplorable condition! And do you then take a pleasure in thinking of me? In talking of me? And have more satisfaction in writing your sentiments to me than in telling them? In whatever way they come, they meet with a reception, the warmth of which can only be known to those who love as I do. In expressing yourself thus, you make me feel the greatest tenderness for you, that is possible to be felt: and if you think of me, be assured that I, on my side, am continually thinking of you. Mine is what the devotees call an habitual thought; it is what we ought to have for the Divine Being, were we to do our duty. Nothing is capable of diverting me from it.

I see your carriage continually driving on, never, never to come nearer to me; I fancy myself on the road, and am always in apprehensions of the carriage overturning. I am almost distracted at the violent rains we have had the last three days, and am frightened to death at the thoughts of the Rhône. I have at this instant a map before me; I know every place you sleep at. Tonight you are at Xevers, Sunday you will be at Lyons, where you will receive this letter. I have had but two letters from you; perhaps a third is on the road; they are my only comfort. I ask for no other. I am utterly incapable of seeing much company at a time; I may recover the feeling hereafter, but it is out of the question now.

Adieu, my dearest child! the only passion of my soul, the joy and anxiety of my life!

22 JUNE

Your letters always cheer our Mother

Christina Rossetti to her brother Dante Gabriel Rossetti

London, 22 June 1874

My dear Gabriel

Your letters always cheer our Mother, as a country rose cheers a Londoner, or the first Spring day overtakes all the world. With a very warm love she acknowledges the pleasure of your invitation (in which I thankfully claim my share), and weighing all circumstances on your side and on our own, thinks that Tuesday 30th (not this week, but next week (following)) will suit us all for the commencement of our visit.

23 JUNE

Our little domestic slip of mountain

William Wordsworth to Samuel Taylor Coleridge

Grasmere, The Lake District, 1799

D[orothy] is much pleased with the house and *appurtenances* the orchard especially: in imagination she has already built a seat with a summer shed on the highest platform in this our little domestic slip of mountain. The spot commands a view over the roof of our house, of the lake, the church, Helm Cragg and two thirds of the vale. We mean also to enclose the two or three yards of ground between us and the road, this for the sake of a few flowers, and because it will make it more our own. Besides, am I fanciful when I would extend the obligation of gratitude to insensate things? May not a man have a salutary pleasure in doing something gratuitously for the sake of his house, as for an individual to which he owes so much.

24 JUNE

The sweetest place on Earth

Dorothy Wordsworth to Lady Beaumont

Grasmere, The Lake District, June 1805

My dear Friend,

I write to you from the Hut, where we pass all our time except when we are walking - it has been a rainy morning, but we are here sheltered and warm, and in truth I think it is the sweetest place on Earth the little wrens often alight upon the thatch and sing their low song, but this morning *all* the Birds are rejoicing after the rain.

Before my eyes is the Church and a few houses among trees, and still beyond the hollow of Easedale which I imagine but cannot see, and the quiet mountains shutting all up. Where I sit I have no view of the Lake, but if I choose to move half a yard further along the seat, I can see it, and so on, going all round, we have a different view.

You undoe mee

Dorothy Osborne to William Temple; Osborne and Temple married in 1655, despite opposition from both families. The love letters were published posthumously

25 June 1653

For god sake doe not complaine soe that you doe not see mee, I beleeve I doe not suffer lesse in't then you, but tis not to beehelpt.

You undoe mee by but dreaming how happy wee might have bin, when I consider how farr wee are from it in reality, alasse, how can you talk of deffyeing fortune? noe body lives without it, and therfore why should you imagin you could?

26 JUNE

Guard yourself from ruminating

Fanny Burney to Mrs ----

1789

I thought with greatly added satisfaction, from what the last letter contains, of Mr's religious principles. There, indeed, you have given a basis to my hopes of your happiness, that no other consideration could have given me. To have him good is very important to me: to have you impressed with his goodness, I had almost said, is yet more so.

Only guard yourself, all you can, from ruminating, too deeply, and from indulging every rising emotion, whether of pain or pleasure. You are all made up with propensities to both; I see it with concern, yet with added tenderness: see it also yourself, and it can do no evil. We are all more in our own power than we think, till we try, or are tried. To calm your too agitated mind must be uppermost in your thoughts: - pray for strength to do it, and you will not be denied it: - but pray, I beg you: - it will not come without prayer, and prayer will impress you with the duty of exertion.

27 JUNE

A Letter always feels to me like immortality

Emily Dickinson to Thomas Wentworth Higginson

June, 1869

Dear friend

A Letter always feels to me like immortality because it is the mind alone without corporeal friend. Indebted in our talk to attitude and accent, there seems a spectral power in thought that walks alone – I would like to thank you for your great kindness but never try to lift the words which I cannot hold.

28 JUNE

The wounds all healed up clean

Ernest Hemingway to his family

American Red Cross Hospital, Milano, Italy, 1918

Dear Folks - :

The 227 wounds I got from the trench mortar didnt hurt a bit at the time, only my feet felt like I had rubber boots full of water on. Hot water. And my knee cap was acting queer. The machine gun bullet just felt like a sharp smack on my leg with an icy snow ball. However it spilled me. But I got up again and got my wounded into the dug out. I kind of collapsed at the dug out. The Italian I had with me had bled all over my coat and my pants looked like somebody had made current jelly in them and then punched holes to let the pulp out. Well the Captain who was a great pal of mine, it was his dug out, said, 'Poor Hem he'll be R.I.P. soon.' Rest In Peace, that is. You see they thought I was shot through the chest on account of my bloody coat. But I made them take my coat and shirt off. I wasn't wearing any under shirt, and the torso was intact.

...

After I came to they carried me on a stretcher three kilometers to a dressing station. The stretcher bearers had to go over lots because the road was having the 'entrails' shelled out of it. Whenever a big one would come, wheeee whoosh - Boom - they'd lay me down and get flat. My wounds were now hurting like 227 little devils were driving nails into the raw. The dressing station had been evacuated during the attack so I lay for two hours in a stable, with the roof shot off, waiting for an ambulance. When it came I ordered it down the road to get the soldiers that had been wounded first. It came back with a load and then they lifted me in.

... I sent you that cable so you wouldn't worry. I've been in the Hospital a month and 12 days and hope to be out in another month. The Italian

Surgeon did a peach of a job on my right knee joint and right foot. Took 28 stitches and assures me that I will be able to walk as well as ever. The wounds all healed up clean and there was no infection. He has my right leg in a plaster splint now so that the joint will be all right. I have some snappy souvenirs that he took out at the last operation.

Life is wonderful: I want to drink deeply – deeply

Katherine Mansfield to Lady Ottoline Morrell

June 1919

The sound of the wind is very loud in this house. The curtains fly - there are strange pointed shadows - full of meaning - and a glittering light upon the mirrors. Now it is dark - and one feels so pale - even one's hands feel pale - and now a wandering broken light is over everything. It is so exciting - so tiring, too - one is waiting for something to happen. One is not oneself at all in this weather - one is a being possessed - caught in the whirl of it - walking about very lightly - blowing about - and deeply, deeply excited ... Do you feel that, too? I feel one might say anything - do anything - wreck one's own life, wreck another's. What does it matter? Everything is flying fast. Everything is on the wing.

On Bank Holiday, mingling with the crowd I saw a magnificent sailor outside a public house. He was a cripple; his legs were crushed, but his head was beautiful - youthful and proud. On his bare chest two seagulls fighting were tatooed in red and blue. And he seemed to lift himself - above the crowd, above the tumbling wave of people and he sang:

'Heart of mine, Summer is waning.'

Oh! Heavens, I shall never forget how he looked and how he sang. I knew at the time this is one of the things one will always remember. It clutched my heart. It flies on the wind today - one of those voices, you know, crying above the talk and the laughter and the dust and the toys to sell. Life is wonderful - wonderful- bitter-sweet, an anguish and a joy - and oh! I do not want to be resigned - I want to drink deeply - deeply. Shall I ever be able to express it?

Dear Susie

Emily Dickinson to Susan Huntington Dickinson

Friday afternoon in June

I have but one thought, Susie, this afternoon of June, and that of you, and I have one prayer, only; dear Susie, that is for you.

That you and I in hand as we e'en do in heart, might ramble away as children, among the woods and fields, and forget these many fears, and these sorrowing cares, and each become a child again – I would it were so, Susie, and when I look around me and find myself alone, I sigh for you again; little sigh, and vain sigh, which will not bring you home.

I need you more and more, and the great world grows wider, and dear ones fewer and fewer, every day that you stay away – I miss my biggest heart; my own goes wandering round, and calls for Susie – Friends are too dear to sunder, oh they are far too few, and how soon they will go away where you and I cannot find them, don't let us forget these things, for their remembrance now will save us many an anguish when it is too late to love them! Susie, forgive me Darling, for every word I say – my heart is full of you, none other than you in my thoughts, yet when I seek to say to you something not for the world, words fail me; if you were here, and oh that you were, my Susie, we need not talk at all, our eyes would whisper for us, and your hand fast in mine, we would not ask for language – I try to bring you nearer, I chase the weeks away till they are quite departed, and fancy you have come, and I am on my way through the green lane to meet you, and my heart goes scampering so, that I have much ado to bring it back again, and learn it to be patient, till that dear Susie comes.

JULY

1 JULY

Give one half-hour's attention to slavery

Ignatius Sancho to Laurence Sterne

July 1766

Reverend Sir

The first part of my life was rather unlucky, as I was placed in a family who judged ignorance the best and only security for obedience. - A little reading and writing I got by unwearied application. - The latter part of my life has been - through God's blessing, truly fortunate, having spent it in the service of one of the best families in the kingdom. - My chief pleasure has been books.

In your tenth discourse* - is this very affecting passage: - 'Consider how great a part of our species - in all ages down to this - have been trod under the feet of cruel and capricious tyrants, who would neither hear their cries, nor pity their distresses. Consider slavery - what it is - how bitter a draught - and how many millions are made to drink it!' Of all my favourite authors, not one has drawn a tear in favour of my miserable black brethren - excepting yourself, and the humane author of Sir George Ellison. I think you will forgive me; - I am sure you will applaud me for beseeching you to give one half-hour's attention to slavery, as it is at this day practised in our West Indies. That subject, handled in your striking manner, would ease the yoke (perhaps) of many; - but if only of one - Gracious God! and, sure I am, you are an Epicurean in acts of charity. You, who are universally read, and as universally admired - you could not fail.

**Sterne's sermon 'Job's Account of the Shortness and Troubles of Life' (1760)*

So long bound in Chains of Misery

Laurence Sterne to Ignatius Sancho

Coxwould near York, July 1766

There is a strange coincidence, Sancho, in the little events (as well as in the great ones) of this world: for I had been writing a tender tale of the sorrows of a friendless poor negro-girl, and my eyes had scarce done smarting with it, when your Letter of recommendation in behalf of so many of her brethren and sisters, came to me –

... 'Tis no uncommon thing, my good Sancho, for one half of the world to use the other half of it like brutes, & then endeavour to make 'em so. For my own part, I never look Westward (when I am in a pensive mood at least) but I think of the burdens which our Brothers & Sisters are there carrying – & could I ease their shoulders from one once of 'em, I declare I would set out this hour upon a pilgrimage to Mecca for their sakes ...

If I can weave the tale I have wrote into the Work I'm [about]*— tis at the service of the afflicted – and a much greater matter; for in serious truth, it casts a sad Shade upon the World, that so great a part of it, are and have been so long bound in chains of darkness & in Chains of Misery; & I cannot but both respect and felicitate you, that by so much laudable diligence you have broke the one – & that by falling into the hands of so good and merciful a family, Providence has rescued You from the other.

And so, good hearted Sancho! adieu! & believe me, I will not forget [your] letter. [Yours]

L. Sterne

**he did, in Volume 9 of* Tristram Shandy *(1767)*

3 JULY

Your words are your own soul

Bram Stoker to Walt Whitman; Bram Stoker wrote this when he was 24 and Whitman 57. Stoker's novel *Dracula* was published 25 years later

Dublin, Ireland, 1872

I don't know whether it is usual for you to get letters from utter strangers who have not even the claim of literary brotherhood to write you. If it is you must be frightfully tormented with letters and I am sorry to have written this. I have, however, the claim of liking you – for your words are your own soul and even if you do not read my letter it is no less a pleasure to me to write it.

I have read your poems with my door locked late at night, and I have read them on the seashore where I could look all round me and see no more sign of human life than the ships out at sea: and here I often found myself waking up from a reverie with the book lying open before me. I love all poetry, and high generous thoughts make the tears rush to my eyes, but sometimes a word or a phrase of yours takes me away from the world around me and places me in an ideal land surrounded by realities more than any poem I ever read.

Last year I was sitting on the beach on a summer's day reading your preface to the *Leaves of Grass.* One thought struck me and I pondered over it for several hours – 'the weather-beaten vessels entering new ports,' you who wrote the words know them better than I do: and to you who sing of your own land of progress the words have a meaning that I can only imagine. But be assured of this, Walt Whitman – that a man of less than half your own age here felt his heart leap towards you across the Atlantic and his soul swelling at the words or rather the thoughts.

Bram Stoker

4 JULY

Quite lonesome, but hearty, and good spirits

Walt Whitman to Bram Stoker

1876

My dear young man,

Your letters have been most welcome to me – welcome to me as Person and as Author – I don't know which most – You did well to write me so unconventionally, so fresh, so manly, and so affectionately, too. I too hope (though it is not probable) that we shall one day meet each other. Meantime I send you my friendship and thanks.

My physique is entirely shattered – doubtless permanently, from paralysis and other ailments. But I am up and dressed, and get out every day a little. Live here quite lonesome, but hearty, and good spirits. Write to me again.

Walt Whitman

5 JULY

Intoxicate me

John Keats to Fanny Brawne

Isle of Wight, July 1819

... You must write immediately, and do all you can to console me in it – make it rich as a draught of poppies to intoxicate me – write the softest words and kiss them that I may at least touch my lips where yours have been. For myself I know not how to express my devotion to so fair a form: I want a brighter word than bright, a fairer word than fair. I almost wish we were butterflies and liv'd but three summer days – three such days with you I could fill with more delight than fifty common years could ever contain.

And how we love each other

D H Lawrence to Sallie Hopkin

Tirol, Austria, 1912

Here we are lodging awhile in a farmhouse. A mountain stream rushes by just outside. It is icy and clear.

We go out all day with our rucksacks - make fires, boil eggs, and eat the lovely fresh gruyère cheese that they make here. We are almost pure vegetarians. We go quite long ways up the valleys. The peaks of the mountains are covered with eternal snow. Water comes falling from a fearful height, and the cows, in the summer meadows, tinkle their bells. Sometimes F. undresses and lies in the sun - sometimes we bathe together - and we can be happy, nobody knows how happy.

There are millions of different bells: tiny harebells, big, black-purple mountain harebells, pale blue, hairy, strange creatures, blue and white Canterbury bells - then there's a great blue gentian, and flowers like monkey-musk. The Alpine roses are just over - and I believe we could find the edelweiss if we tried. Sometimes we drink with the mountain peasants in the Gasthaus, and dance a little. And how we love each other - God only knows.

We shall be moving on soon, walking south, by the Brenner, to Italy.

Yours,

D. H. LAWRENCE

7 JULY

Many thanks for many things

Dylan Thomas to Oscar Williams

Blaen-Cwm, near Llanstephan, Wales, July 1945

My dear Oscar

Many thanks for many things.

For your letters, long unanswered but cherished next to my heart, hair, identity disk, razorscar from a Poetry Tea, the tattooed hoofprints of Dali's mother. It is hysterical weather where I am writing, Blaen Cwm, Llangain, Carmarthenshire, Wales, in a breeding-box in a cabbage valley, in a parlour with a preserved sheepdog, where mothballs fly at night, not moths, where the Bible opens itself at Revelations; and is there money still for tea? I can hear, from far off, my Uncle Bob drinking tea and methylated spirits through 80 years of nicotine-brown fern. My father, opposite, is reading Hannibal through a magnifying glass so small he can see only one word at a time. And my wife is watching an old opera.

Next morning. Still raining, and not daffodils. A farmyard outside the window, sows and cows and the farmer's daughters, what a day of dugs. I've been reading all Lawrence's poems, some aloud to no-one in this room, and liking them more & more. Do you remember*:

O the green glimmer of apples in the orchard,
Lamps in a wash of rain!
O the wet walk of my brown hen through the stackyard!
O tears on the window pane!

Nothing now will ripen the bright green apples
Full of disappointment and of rain;
Brackish they will taste, of tears, when the yellow dapples
Of autumn tell the withered tale again.

All around the yard it is cluck! my brown hen.
Cluck! and the rain-wet wings;
Cluck! my marigold bird, and then
Cluck! for your yellow darlings.

**D H Lawrence's 'Ballad Of Another Ophelia'*

8 JULY

A merry young party

Elizabeth Gaskell to William and Mary Howitt

1838

Near the little, clean, kindly country town where I was brought up there was an old house with a moat within a park called Old Tabley, and accounted a very fine specimen of the Elizabethan style. It is beautifully kept by its owner, who lives at a new house built about a mile off, the velvet lawn up to the deep windows being mown and rolled most regularly, and the large laurels and the magnificent beeches trimmed with most excellent care.

Here on summer mornings did we often come, a merry young party, on donkey, pony or even in a cart with sacks swung across - each with our favourite book, some with sketch-books, and two baskets filled with eatables. Here we rambled, lounged and meditated: some stretched on the grass in indolent repose, half reading, half musing with a posy of musk-roses from the old-fashioned trim garden behind the house, lulled by the ripple of the waters against the grassy lawn; some in the old crazy boats, that would do nothing but float on the glassy water, singing, for one or two were of a most musical family and warbled like birds: 'Through the greenwood, through the greenwood', or 'A boat, a boat unto the ferry', or some such old catch or glee. And when the meal was spread beneath a beech tree of no ordinary size (did you ever notice the peculiar turf under beech shade?) one of us would mount up a ladder to the belfry of the old chapel and toll the bell to call the wanderers home.

Then if it rained, what merry-making in the old hall. It was galleried, with oak settles and old armour hung up, and a painted window from ceiling to floor. The strange sound our voices had in that unfrequented stone hall! The last time I was there during the fall of rain from one of those heavy clouds which add to a summer day's beauty, when every drop of rain is sun-tinged and falls merrily amongst the leaves, one or two of Shakespeare's ballads: 'Blow, blow thou winter wind', and 'Hark, hark the lark at Heaven's gate sings', and so forth were sung by the musical sisters in the gallery above, and by two other musical sisters (Mary and Ellen Needham from Lenton near Nottingham) standing in the hall below.

Your letter was as pleasant as a quiet chat

Charlotte Brontë to Elizabeth Gaskell

Haworth, Yorkshire, 9 July 1853

Thank you for your letter; it was as pleasant as a quiet chat, as welcome as spring showers, as reviving as a friend's visit; in short, it was very like a page of *Cranford.** ... A thought strikes me. Do you, who have so many friends - so large a circle of acquaintance - find it easy, when you sit down to write, to isolate yourself from all those ties, and their sweet associations, so as to be your OWN WOMAN, uninfluenced or swayed by the consciousness of how your work may affect other minds; what blame or what sympathy it may call forth? Does no luminous cloud ever come between you and the severe Truth, as you know it in your own secret and clear-seeing soul? In a word, are you never tempted to make your characters more amiable than the Life, by the inclination to assimilate your thoughts to the thoughts of those who always FEEL kindly, but sometimes fail to SEE justly? Don't answer the question; it is not intended to be answered ...

**Gaskell's* Cranford *was serialized in Dickens's* Household Words, *1851-53*

Married to a lady

Lord Alfred Tennyson to Ludovic Colquhoun; Tennyson's engagement to Emily Selwood had been previously called off in 1840

10 July 1850

My dear Colquhoun

I am free to confess that I have used you scurvily. Not that I did not ever intend to answer. You were always in my thoughts and my unfulfilled duty gave me a dyspeptic conscience. Singularly enough this very morning I was going to write when your letter was given me.

I am not going to be but am married to a lady only four years younger than myself, one who has loved me for 14 years without variableness (or any shadow of turning). She has the most beautiful nature I have met with among women. It was done very quietly at my particular request so that my own mother did not know of it till it was done.

11 JULY

Paradise Lost

Dorothy Wordsworth to Lady Beaumont

The Lake District, 1807

My dear Friend,

Oh! what reason have we not to bless the Poets, our Friends and companions in solitude or who elevate our thoughts beyond our poor weak selves and him chiefly who was your Sister's consolation that holy Bard and greatest of men. I often think of the happy evening when, by your fireside, my Brother read to us the first book of the *Paradise Lost**; and not without many hopes that we may again have the same pleasure together.

**John Milton's* Paradise Lost *(1667)*

A chaos of foam

Percy Bysshe Shelley to Thomas Love Peacock
Geneva, Switzerland, 12 July 1816

The lake appeared somewhat calmer as we left Meillerie, sailing close to the banks, whose magnificence augmented with the turn of every promontory. But we congratulated ourselves too soon; the wind gradually increased in violence, until it blew tremendously; and, as it came from the remotest extremity of the lake, produced waves of a frightful height, and covered the whole surface with a chaos of foam.

My companion, an excellent swimmer, took off his coat, I did the same, and we sat with our arms crossed, every instant expecting to be swamped. The sail was however again held, the boat obeyed the helm, and still in imminent peril from the immensity of the waves, we arrived in a few minutes at a sheltered port.

I felt in this near prospect of death a mixture of sensations, among which terror entered, though but subordinately. My feelings would have been less painful had I been alone; but I knew that my companion would have attempted to save me, and I was overcome with humiliation, when I thought that his life might have been risked to preserve mine. When we arrived at St. Gingoux, the inhabitants, who stood on the shore, unaccustomed to see a vessel as frail as ours, and fearing to venture at all on such a sea, exchanged looks of wonder and congratulation with our boatmen, who, as well as ourselves, were well pleased to set foot on shore.

Ginger-bread permanence

Gerard Manley Hopkins to Robert Bridges
Mount Street, London, 13 July 1878

I am at present writing three sermons to be preached in August; I have little else to do (of duty) and so employ myself in making up my theology, but my work will soon thicken. I am, so far as I know, permanently here, but permanence with us is ginger-bread permanence; cobweb, soapsud and frost-feather permanence.

Yours
Gerard Hopkins

14 JULY

Rhythm keeps up its perpetual beat

Virginia Woolf to John Lehman

From *A Letter to a Young Poet* (1932)

Let me try to imagine, with your letter to help me, what it feels like to be a young poet in the autumn of 1931.

On the floor of your mind, then – is it not this that makes you a poet? – rhythm keeps up its perpetual beat. Sometimes it seems to die down to nothing; it lets you eat, sleep, talk like other people. Then again it swells and rises and attempts to sweep all the contents of your mind into one dominant dance. Tonight is such an occasion. Although you are alone, and have taken one boot off and are about to undo the other, you cannot go on with the process of undressing, but must instantly write at the bidding of the dance. You snatch pen and paper; you hardly trouble to hold the one or to straighten the other. And while you write, while the first stanzas of the dance are being fastened down, I will withdraw a little and look out of the window. A woman passes, then a man; a car glides to a stop and then ... I am suddenly recalled from my observations by a cry of rage or despair. Your page is crumpled in a ball; your pen sticks upright by the nib in the carpet ... You are rasped, jarred, thoroughly out of temper. And if I am to guess the reason, it is, I should say, that the rhythm which was opening and shutting with a force that sent shocks of excitement from your head to your heels has encountered some hard and hostile object upon which it has smashed itself to pieces. Something has worked in which cannot be made into poetry; some foreign body, angular, sharp-edged, gritty, has refused to join in the dance.

Live the Questions

Rainer Maria Rilke, from *Letters to a Young Poet*
Worpswede, Germany, July 1903

I want to ask you, as clearly as I can, to bear with patience all that is unresolved in your heart, and try to love the questions themselves, as if they were rooms yet to enter or books written in a foreign language. Don't dig for answers that can't be given you yet: you live them now. For everything must be lived. Live the questions now, perhaps then, someday, you will gradually, without noticing, live into the answer.

Translated from the German by Anita Barrows and Joanna Macy

16 JULY

Rootfeelings and poemblossoms

e. e. cummings to Hildegarde Watson

Silver Lake, New Hampshire, 1947

Dear Hildegarde – well,you're a saint(not to mention anangel)sending me,for the second time,just a book whom I'd never met and who would cheer me most!

this am enjoying even more than Rilke's 'Letters To A Young Poet';& perhaps because here I recognize a variety of feelings to whom I want to cry 'you are my own!' – rootfeelings who perhaps have,over a span of some thirty years,become poemblossoms ...

17 JULY

You are the delight of my life

Jane Austen to her niece Fanny Knight

Chawton, Hampshire, 1816

My Dearest Fanny,

You are inimitable, irresistible. You are the delight of my life. Such letters, such entertaining letters, as you have lately sent! Such a description of your queer little heart! Such a lovely display of what imagination does! You are worth your weight in gold, or even in the new silver coinage. I cannot express to you what I have felt in reading your history of yourself, how full of pity and concern, and admiration and amusement I have been! You are the paragon of all that is silly and sensible, commonplace and eccentric, sad and lively, provoking and interesting. Who can keep pace with the fluctuations of your fancy, the capprizios of your taste, the contradictions of your feelings? You are so odd, and all the time so perfectly natural! So peculiar in yourself, and yet so like everybody else!

It is very, very gratifying to me to know you so intimately. You can hardly think what a pleasure it is to me to have such thorough pictures of your heart. Oh, what a loss it will be when you are married! You are too agreeable in your single state, too agreeable as a niece. I shall hate you when your delicious play of mind is all settled down into conjugal and maternal affections.

Letter to Jane Austen

Cassandra Austen to her niece Fanny Knight; Cassandra wrote this letter to Fanny after her sister Jane's death on this day in 1817

My Dearest Fanny,

Doubly dear to me now for her dear sake whom we have lost. She did love you most sincerely, and never shall I forget the proofs of love you gave her during her illness in writing those kind, amusing letters at a time when I know your feelings would have dictated so different a style. Take the only reward I can give you in the assurance that your benevolent purpose was answered; you did contribute to her enjoyment.

Even your last letter afforded pleasure. I merely cut the seal and gave it to her; she opened it and read it herself, afterwards she gave it to me to read, and then talked to me a little and not uncheerfully of its contents, but there was then a languor about her which prevented her taking the same interest in anything she had been used to do.

I have lost a treasure, such a sister, such a friend as never can have been surpassed. She was the sun of my life, the gilder of every pleasure, the soother of every sorrow; I had not a thought concealed from her, and it is as if I had lost a part of myself.

I hope I do not break your heart, my dearest Fanny, by these particulars; I mean to afford you gratification whilst I am relieving my own feelings. I could not write so to anybody else; indeed you are the only person I have written to at all, excepting your grandmamma.

19 JULY

My Last Request

Dr John Arbuthnot to Alexander Pope

July 1734

As for you, my good Friend, I think since our first acquaintance there has not been any of those little Suspicions or Jealousies that often affect the sincerest Friendships; I am sure not on my side. I must be so sincere as to own, that tho' I could not help valuing you for those Talents which the World prizes, yet they were not the Foundation of my Friendship: they were quite of another sort; nor shall I at present offend you by enumerating them: and I make it my Last Request, that you continue that noble *Disdain* and *Abhorrence* of Vice, which you seem naturally endu'd with, but still with a due regard to your own Safety; and study more to reform than chastise, tho' the one often cannot be effected without the other.

20 JULY

Fighting with Shadows

Alexander Pope to Dr Arbuthnot

July 1734

To attack Vices in the abstract, without touching Persons, may be safe fighting indeed, but it is fighting with Shadows. General propositions are obscure, misty and uncertain, compar'd with plain, full and home examples: precepts only apply to our Reason, which in most men is weak: examples are pictures, and strike the Senses, nay raise the Passions and call in those (the strongest and most general of all motives) to the aid of reformation. Every vicious man makes the case his own; and that is the only way by which such men can be affected, much less deterr'd. So that to chastise is to reform. The only sign by which I found my writings ever did any good, or had any weight, has been that they rais'd the anger of bad men. And my greatest comfort, and encouragement to proceed, has been to see, that those who have no shame, and no fear, of any thing else, have appear'd touch'd by my Satires.

21 JULY

A wrong revolutionary poetical system

Lord Byron to John Murray

1817

Dear Sir

I have read 'Lalla Rookh'*, but not with sufficient attention yet, for I ride about, and lounge, and ponder, and - two or three other things; so that my reading is very desultory, and not so attentive as it used to be. I am very glad to hear of its popularity, for [Thomas] Moore is a very noble fellow in all respects, and will enjoy it without any of the bad feeling which success - good or evil - sometimes engenders in the men of rhyme. Of the poem itself, I will tell you my opinion when I have mastered it.

With regard to poetry in general, I am convinced, the more I think of it, that he and all of us - Scott, Wordsworth, Moore, Campbell, I, - are all in the wrong, one as much as another; that we are upon a wrong revolutionary poetical system, or systems, not worth a damn in itself; and that the present and next generations will finally be of this opinion. I am the more confirmed in this by having lately gone over some of our classics, particularly Pope, whom I tried in this way, - I took Moore's poems and my own and some others, and went over them side by side with Pope's, and I was really astonished (I ought not to have been so) and mortified at the ineffable distance in point of sense, harmony, effect and even imagination, passion and invention, between the little Queen Anne's man, and us.

**by Irish poet Thomas Moore, published 1817*

I see sun-colours over all the geometry

Ralph Walden Emerson to Caroline Sturgis Tappan

Concord, Massachusetts, 22 July 1853

The universe is all chemistry, with a certain hint of a magnificent *Whence* or *Whereto* gliding or opalizing every angle of the old salt-&-acid acid-&-salt, endlessly reiterated & masqueraded through all time & space & form. The addition of that hint everywhere, saves things. Heavy & loathsome is the bounded world, bounded everywhere. An immense Boston or Hanover street with mountains of ordinary women, trains & trains of mean leathern men all immoveably bounded, no liquidity of hope or genius. But they are made chemically good, like oxen. In the absence of religion, they are polarized to decorum, which is its blockhead; - thrown mechanically into parallelism with this high *Whence* & *Whither*, which thus makes mountains of rubbish reflect the morning sun & the evening star. And we are all privy-counsellors to that Hint, which homeopathically doses the System, & can cooperate with the slow & secular escape of these oxen & semioxen from their quadruped estate, & invite them to be men, & hail them such ... Fatalism held by an intelligent soul who knows how to humour & obey the infinitesimal pulses of spontaneity, is by much the truest theory in use. All the great would call their thought fatalism, or concede that ninety nine parts are nature & one part power, though that hundredth is elastic, miraculous, and, whenever it is in energy, dissolving all the rest.

Forgive this heavy cobweb, which I did not think of spinning, & which will put you too out of all patience with my prose. But I see sun-colours over all the geometry, & am armed by thinking that our wretched interference is precluded.

The Love Letters of Edna St. Vincent Millay & her Mother

Edna St Vincent Millay to her mother Cora B. Millay

Paris, France, 23 July 1921

Dearest Mother, -

You do write the sweetest and the most wonderful letters! They are so lovely that very often I read parts of them aloud to people, just as literature. It was delicious what you told me about the turtle, - you are so gentle and kind to everything, dear - and all the things you write about birds and animals I love. Thanks for the little flower. I never saw one like it, either.

With all the love of my heart,
Vincent

PS. Do you suppose, when you & I are dead, dear, they will publish the Love Letters of Edna St Vincent Millay & her Mother?

24 JULY

The Sea of Ice

Percy Bysshe Shelley to Thomas Love Peacock

Chamouni, Switzerland, July 1816

We have returned from visiting the glacier of Montanvert, or as it is called the Sea of Ice, a scene in truth of dizzying wonder. The path that winds to it along the side of a mountain, now clothed with pines, now intersected with snowy hollows, is wide and steep.

Lines of dazzling ice occupy here and there their perpendicular rifts, and shine through the driving vapours with inexpressible brilliance: they pierce the clouds like things not belonging to this earth. The vale itself is filled with a mass of undulating ice, and has an ascent sufficiently gradual even to the remotest abysses of these horrible deserts. It is only half a league (about two miles) in breadth, and seems much less. It exhibits an appearance as if frost had suddenly bound up the waves and whirlpools of a mighty torrent. We walked some distance upon its surface. The waves are elevated about 12 or 15 feet from the surface of the mass, which is intersected by long gaps of unfathomable depth, the ice of whose sides is more beautifully azure than the sky. In these regions everything changes, and is in motion.

This vast mass of ice has one general progress, which ceases neither day nor night; it breaks and bursts for ever: some undulations sink while others rise; it is never the same. The echo of rocks, or of the ice and snow which fall from their overhanging precipices, or roll from their aerial summits, scarcely ceases for one moment. One would think that Mont Blanc, like the god of the Stoics, was a vast animal, and that the frozen blood for ever circulated through his stony veins.

25 JULY

A spring in my step and a song in my gut and poems to write

Dylan Thomas to Bonnie and John Nims

Laugharne, Wales, July 1950

My dear Bonnie and John,

Remember me? Round, red, robustly raddled, a bulging apple among poets, hard as nails made of cream cheese, gap-toothed, balding, noisome, a great collector of dust and a magnet for moths, mad for beer, frightened of priests, women, Chicago, writers, distance, time, children, geese, death, in love, frightened of love, liable to drip.

I never managed to come back, although I so much wanted to. I never answered your nice letters nor acknowledged the hollyhocks. My only damp excuse is that animal-trainer Brinnin ('Bring 'em back half alive') whipped me all over the wilds after I reluctantly left you, from British Columbia to Florida; I hardly ever knew where I was; I lost the ability to form words on paper; I ranted through my one-night stands like a ruined, sonorous mule; I spent one liquid, libidinous fortnight in New York and was wheelbarrowed on to the Queen Elizabeth by some resident firemen, a psychoanalyst's insane wife, Oscar Williams and his wife, whip-cracking Brinnin, a hosier from the Bronx, an eminent playwright (if anonymous), three unidentified men who came either from the Museum of Modern Art or from McSorley's Saloon, a lifelong friend of half an hour, a glossy woman who had made some mistake, and hairy people. Lots of hairy people, all sighing with relief. I shared a cabin with an inventor of a new kind of concrete, called, so far as I could gather, Urine – the inventor, not the concrete – and spent my days with salesmen at the bar. As a result, I have never felt physically better in my life, and go for long walks, healthy as a briar and sing in the bath (which does not exist), and have clear eyes and a new front tooth – which must have grown, for I have no memory of going to the dentist – and a spring in my step and a song in my gut and poems to write and no need to hurry to write them. I must ruin my health again: I feel so preposterously well.

26 JULY

My hands no longer stink of fish and I can write to you

Anton Chekhov to Mikhail Chekhov

1885

Misha-Terentisha!

At last I've taken off my heavy boots, my hands no longer stink of fish and I can write to you. It's six o'clock in the morning, and everyone is asleep ... The silence is extraordinary ... only the birds are chirping, as well as some creature scratching behind the wallpaper. I'm writing these lines sitting by the large, square window in my room, and as I write I glance from time to time through the window. Before my eyes unfolds an extraordinarily warm, caressing landscape: a little river, distant woods.

... Everything is marvellously comfortable and cosy. Ashtrays and matchbox stands, cigarette boxes, two washbasins and ... goodness only knows what else our kind hosts have provided. A dacha like this near Moscow would cost at least 500. You'll see when you come. I settled myself in, unpacked my suitcases and sat down to take stock, drank some vodka and a glass of wine ... and you know, it was so lovely to look out of the window at the darkened trees and the river ... I heard the song of the nightingale and could hardly believe my ears ... it was hard to forget that I wasn't still in Moscow. I slept wonderfully.

Please bring Olga's passport with you, some garlic sausage for Kiselyov (three or four sausages), bay leaves, pepper, large-format writing paper.

Please copy out June, July and August from the encyclopaedic dictionary it's easier than bringing it with you. I got up at half past three this morning. I'm now drinking tea and shall go back to bed and sleep until coffee, then after coffee I'm going off with Kiselyov to have a look at my traps. I wrote a lot yesterday and will send it off today.

The work's going well.

Your
A. Chekhov

Translated from the Russian by Rosamund Bartlett and Antony Phillips

27 JULY

A month's allowance of meat

Fanny Burney to Hester Thrale

1780

Nobody does write such sweet letters as my dear Mrs Thrale, and I would sooner give up a month's allowance of meat, than my week's allowance of an epistle.

Since I wrote last I have drunk tea with Dr Johnson. My father took me to Bolt-court, and we found him, most fortunately, with only one brass-headed cane gentleman. Since that, I have had the pleasure to meet him again at Mrs Reynolds's, when he offered to take me with him to Grub-street, to see the ruins of the house demolished there in the late riots, by a mob that, as he observed, could be no friend to the Muses!

Adieu, dearest madam, and from me accept not only, love, and not only respects, but both, and gratitude, and warmest wishes, and constancy invariable into the bargain.

F. BURNEY

Polly Sugarcake

Hester Thrale to Fanny Burney

Brighthelmstone (Brighton), July 1780

And so my letters please you, do they, my sweet Burney? I know yours are the most entertaining things that cross me in the course of the whole week; and a miserable praise too, if you could figure to yourself my most dull companions. I write now from Bowen's shop, where he has been settled about three days I think; and here comes in one man hopping, and asks for 'Russell on Sea-water' – another tripping, and begs to have the last new novel sent him home tonight; one lady tumbles the ballads about, and fingers the harpsichord which stands here at every blockhead's mercy; and another looks over the Lilliputian library, and purchases Polly Sugarcake for her longlegged missey.

Adieu, – and divide my truest kindness among all the dear Newtonians*, and keep yourself a large share. You are in no danger of invaders from the sea-coast. Susan and Sophy bathe and grow, and riot me out of my senses. I am ever, my dear girl, most faithfully yours,

H. L. T.

**the former home of Sir Isaac Newton, subsequently the Burneys' residence*

29 JULY

Sound stitched into your bones

Gerald Durrell to Lee McGeorge

July 1978

I have seen a thousand sunsets and sunrises, on land where it floods forest and mountains with honey coloured light, at sea where it rises and sets like a blood orange in a multicoloured nest of cloud, slipping in and out of the vast ocean. I have seen a thousand moons: harvest moons like gold coins, winter moons as white as ice chips, new moons like baby swans' feathers. I have seen seas as smooth as if painted, coloured like shot silk or blue as a kingfisher or transparent as glass or black and crumpled with foam, moving ponderously and murderously. I have felt winds straight from the South Pole, bleak and wailing like a lost child; winds as tender and warm as a lover's breath; winds that carried the astringent smell of salt and the death of seaweeds; winds that carried the moist rich smell of a forest floor, the smell of a million flowers. Fierce winds that churned and moved the sea like yeast, or winds that made the waters lap at the shore like a kitten. I have known silence: the cold, earthy silence at the bottom of a newly dug well; the implacable stony silence of a deep cave; the hot, drugged midday silence when everything is hypnotized and stilled into silence by the eye of the sun; the silence when great music ends. I have heard summer cicadas cry so that the sound seems stitched into your bones. I have heard tree frogs in an orchestration as complicated as Bach singing in a forest lit by a million emerald fireflies. I have heard the keas calling over grey glaciers that groaned to themselves like old people as they inched their way to the sea. I have heard the hoarse street vendor cries of the mating fur seals as they sang to their sleek golden wives, the crisp staccato admonishment of the rattlesnake, the cobweb squeak of the bat and the belling roar of the red deer knee-deep in purple heather. I have heard wolves baying at a winter's moon, red howlers making the forest vibrate with their roaring cries. I have heard the squeak, purr and grunt of a hundred multi-coloured reef fishes.

I have seen hummingbirds flashing like opals round a tree of scarlet blooms, humming like a top. I have seen flying fish, skittering like quicksilver across the blue waves, drawing silver lines on the surface with their tails. I have seen spoonbills flying home to roost like a scarlet banner across the sky. I have seen whales, black as tar, cushioned on a cornflower blue sea, creating a Versailles of fountain with their breath. I have watched butterflies emerge and sit, trembling, while the sun irons their wings smooth. I have watched tigers, like flames, mating in the long grass. I have been dive-bombed by an angry raven, black and glossy as the Devil's hoof. I have lain in water warm as milk, soft as silk, while around me played a host of dolphins. I have met a thousand animals and seen a thousand wonderful things ... but –

All this I did without you. This was my loss.
All this I want to do with you. This will be my gain.

All this I would gladly have forgone for the sake of one minute of your company, for your laugh, your voice, your eyes, hair, lips, body and above all for your sweet, ever surprising mind which is an enchanting quarry in which it is my privilege to delve.

30 JULY

Grantchester

Rupert Brooke to Erica Cotterill

The Orchard, Grantchester, near Cambridge, July 1909

I came here on Friday. It is a lovely village on the river above Cambridge. I'm in a small house, a sort of cottage, with a dear plump weather-beaten kindly old lady in control. I have a perfectly glorious time, seeing nobody I know day after day. The room I have opens straight out onto a stone verandah covered with creepers, & a little old garden full of old-fashioned flowers & crammed with roses. I work at Shakespere, read, write all day & now & then wander in the woods or by the river. I bathe every morning & by moonlight, have all my meals (chiefly fruit) brought to me out of doors, & am as happy as the day's long. I am chiefly sorry for all you people in the world. Every now & then dull bald spectacled people from Cambridge come out & take tea here. I mock them & pour the cream down their necks or roll them in the rose-beds or push them in the river, & they hate me & go away. The world smells of roses. Books? Pah!

31 JULY

The postman knocks and rings

Jane Carlyle to her husband Thomas

Cheyne Walk, Chelsea, London, 31 July 1843

Dearest, -

The postman presented me your letter tonight, in Cheyne Walk, with a bow extraordinary. He is a jewel of a postman; whenever he has put a letter from you into the box, he both knocks and rings, that not a moment may be lost in taking possession of it.

AUGUST

1 AUGUST

The red harvest moon, swollen with plenty

Willa Cather to Mariel Gere

Red Cloud, Nebraska, 1 August 1893

One of our favourite amusements out there was sitting on top of the 50 wind mill tower at night. It was great on calm evenings. We could see for miles and miles, see 'right off the edge of the world' as Ross said. The red harvest moon, swollen with plenty, rose over the lagoons and wheat fields, not very clear at first, but fleecy and cloud girt, as though timid of her own richness and fullness. But in an hour or so, when she felt the full zest of her race and the strength of her serenity, she left the vapours behind her. As soon as she was up, the little ponds all over the country began to glimmer, and the corn tassels in all those forests of corn looked white as silver. We could see the windmills and groves of cottonwoods all over the country as plainly as in day light. Moonlight has a peculiar effect on a country; it obliterates what is ugly, softens what is harsh, - and what is beautiful it raises almost to the divine and supernatural.

But the greatest thing we saw from that mill tower was the coming of a storm. The moon did not show herself at all. There was a long black bank of clouds in the west, and the lightening kept playing along it as steady as the fire of a battery. The world seemed to get ready for a storm; the cattle all huddled together in one end of the corral, the corn leaves got restless and began to toss their long blades up as if to reach for rain. In a moment the big wind struck us, [...] and we 50 feet up in the air on a four-foot platform! Roscoe howled, 'Off with your skirts, Willie or we'll never get down' you bet I peeled them off, all but a little light one. The descent was something awful, the tower shook and we shook, the wind hummed and sang and whirled all about us, if it had not been for Ross's grip on me I believe I should have fallen.

2 AUGUST

A Letter To The Dean When In England

1726

You will excuse me, I suppose,
For sending rhyme instead of prose.
Because hot weather makes me lazy,
To write in metre is more easy.

While you are trudging London town,
I'm strolling Dublin up and down;
While you converse with lords and dukes,
I have their betters here, my books:
Fix'd in an elbow-chair at ease,
I choose companions as I please.
I'd rather have one single shelf
Than all my friends, except yourself;
For, after all that can be said,
Our best acquaintance are the dead.
While you're in raptures with Faustina;
I'm charm'd at home with our Sheelina.
While you are starving there in state,
I'm cramming here with butchers' meat.
You say, when with those lords you dine,
They treat you with the best of wine,
Burgundy, Cyprus, and Tokay;
Why, so can we, as well as they.
No reason then, my dear good Dean,
But you should travel home again.
What though you mayn't in Ireland hope
To find such folk as Gay and Pope;

If you with rhymers here would share
But half the wit that you can spare,
I'd lay twelve eggs, that in twelve days,
You'd make a dozen of Popes and Gays.
Our weather's good, our sky is clear;
We've every joy, if you were here;
So lofty and so bright a sky
Was never seen by Ireland's eye!
I think it fit to let you know,
This week I shall to Quilca go;
To see M'Faden's horny brothers
First suck, and after bull their mothers;
To see, alas! my wither'd trees!
To see what all the country sees!
My stunted quicks, my famish'd beeves,
My servants such a pack of thieves;
My shatter'd firs, my blasted oaks,
My house in common to all folks,
No cabbage for a single snail,
My turnips, carrots, parsneps, fail;
My no green peas, my few green sprouts;
My mother always in the pouts;
My horses rid, or gone astray;
My fish all stolen or run away;
My mutton lean, my pullets old,
My poultry starved, the corn all sold.

A man come now from Quilca says,
'They've stolen the locks from all your keys;'
But, what must fret and vex me more,
He says, 'They stole the keys before.
They've stol'n the knives from all the forks;
And half the cows from half the sturks.'
Nay more, the fellow swears and vows,
'They've stol'n the sturks from half the cows:'
With many more accounts of woe,
Yet, though the devil be there, I'll go:
'Twixt you and me, the reason's clear,
Because I've more vexation here.

Thomas Sheridan

I am currently writing in the most awful conditions

Anton Chekhov to Nikolay Leikin

Moscow, Russia, August 1883

Dear Nikolay Alexandrovich

I am currently writing in the most awful conditions, with a great weight of non-literary activities hammering mercilessly at my conscience, a visiting relation's baby screaming in the next room, while in another room my father is reading aloud to my mother from [Leskov's] *The Sealed Angel*. Someone has got the music box going, so I have to listen to [Offenbach's] 'La Belle Héléne' ... I'd like to slope off to the dacha, but it's one o'clock in the morning ... It would be hard to imagine a worse situation for someone who wants to be a writer. My bed is occupied by the visiting relation; he keeps buttonholing me and starting to talk about medical subjects, 'My daughter probably has colic; that's why she's crying all the time.' I am unfortunate enough to be a doctor so everybody seems to think they have to talk to me about medicine. And when they get tired of discussing medicine, they start on literature.

The situation is quite impossible. I'm cursing myself for not having gone to the dacha, where I would probably have had a decent sleep and written you a story, and the main thing is, medicine and literature would have been left in peace.

Farewell. All I can think of is how and where to get my head down for a decent sleep.

Translated from the Russian by Rosamund Bartlett and Antony Phillips

4 AUGUST

So cold no fire can ever warm me

Emily Dickinson to Thomas Wentworth Higginson

August 1870

Truth is such a rare thing it is delightful to tell it.

I find ecstasy in living; the mere sense of living is joy enough.

How do most people live without any thoughts? There are many people in the world, - you must have noticed them in the street, - how do they live? How do they get strength to put on their clothes in the morning?

If I read a book and it makes my whole body so cold no fire can ever warm me, I know that is poetry. If I feel physically as if the top of my head were taken off, I know that is poetry. These are the only ways I know it. Is there any other way?

5 AUGUST

I have summoned up your image

Charlotte Brontë to Ellen Nussey

Roe-Head, Mirfield, Yorkshire, 1836

It is a stormy evening, and the wind is uttering a continual moaning sound, that makes me feel very melancholy. At such times – in such moods as these – it is my nature to seek repose in some calm tranquil idea, and I have now summoned up your image to give me rest. There you sit, upright and still in your black dress, and white scarf, and pale marble-like face – just like reality. I wish you would speak to me. If we should be separated – if it should be our lot to live at a great distance, and never to see each other again – in old age, how I should conjure up the memory of my youthful days, and what a melancholy pleasure I should feel in dwelling on the recollection of my early friend!

6 AUGUST

My hands and soul craving for self-expression

Isaac Rosenberg to Winifreda Seaton

Undated

It is horrible to think that all these hours, when my days are full of vigour and my hands and soul craving for self-expression, I am bound, chained to this fiendish mangling-machine*, without hope and almost desire of deliverance, and the days of youth go by ... I have tried to make some sort of self-adjustment to circumstances by saying, 'It is all *experience*'; but, good God! it is *all* experience, and nothing else ... I really would like to take up painting seriously; I think I might do something at that; but poetry – I despair of ever writing excellent poetry. I can't look at things in the simple, large way that great poets do. My mind is so cramped and dulled and fevered, there is no consistency of purpose, no oneness of aim; the very fibres are torn apart, and application deadened by the fiendish persistence of the coil of circumstance.

**refers to Rosenberg's apprenticeship as an engraver (1905-1911)*

I sometimes sit quite still in the boat and watch the water hens

Beatrix Potter to Noel Moore

Ambleside, The Lake District, 7 August 1896

My dear Noel,

I sometimes sit quite still in the boat and watch the water hens. They are black with red bills and make a noise just like kissing, when they are hiding in the reeds. They walk on the lily leaves, nodding their heads and peeping underneath for water snails. There are wild ducks too, but they are not so tame. One evening I went in the boat when it was nearly dark and saw a flock of lapwings asleep, standing on one leg in the water. What a funny way to go to bed! Perhaps they are afraid of foxes, the hens are.

There are some cocks and hens on the hill, who sleep right at the top of a hawthorn bush, the branches are quite covered with chickens. Those at the farm go up a stonewall into a loft. The farmer has a beautiful fat pig. He is a funny old man, he feeds the calves every morning, he rattles the spoon on the tin pail, to tell them breakfast is ready, but they won't always come, then there is a noise like a German band.

I remain yours affectionately,
Beatrix Potter

8 AUGUST

I am sitting in thy study

Mary Wordsworth to her husband William Wordsworth

August 1810

I am sitting in thy study – the rain beats against the window – the fire is flapping & the Baby in the Cradle upon the Sofa, nestling about warning me that he will presently awake, but all these quiet sounds are disturbed by a restless, noisy, chirping, dying (I am afraid) chick that is within the Fender & which the children left to *my* care therefore I have not had the heart to dismiss it –

9 AUGUST

Strawberries

Elizabeth Barrett Browning to Mary Russell Mitford

Bagni di Lucca, Italy, August 1853

We are enjoying the mountains here, riding the donkeys in the footsteps of the sheep and eating strawberries and milk by basins full. The strawberries succeed one another, generation after generation, throughout the summer, through growing on different aspects of the hills. If a tree is felled in the forests strawberries spring up just as mushrooms might, and the peasants sell them for just nothing. Our little Penini* is wild with happiness; he asks in his prayers that God would 'mate him dood and tate him on a dontey' (make him good and take him on a donkey), so resuming all aspiration for spiritual and worldly prosperity.

**The Brownings' young son, Robert, known fondly as 'Pen'*

10 AUGUST

My desire to arrive at some conception of the meaning of all things

Virginia Woolf to Gerald Brenan

Monks House, Lewes, Sussex, 10 August 1923

We came down here last week, and here we remain till October, a very happy life, on the whole, though I become rather restless with my desire to write, my desire to read, my desire to talk, and to be alone, and to explore Sussex and find a perfect house, and arrive at some conception of the meaning of all things. Why nature dangles this ancient carrot before me, I do not know. Every book is to me a glass through which I may possibly behold – I don't know what; and so with people; and so with my solitary walks on the downs, when suddenly I find I am breaking through myriads of white convolvulus, twined about the grass ...

Tonight I shall read the plays of Marlowe; tomorrow I shall walk across the meadows to Lewes and buy a chicken. Does this sketch in great blobs produce any likeness of a character? Or what do you get out of these careless, random diluted letters? I can no longer write careful letters. Moreover I am too sleepy with the heat (it is as hot today as it was in Alicante) to visualize you, your room, the brassero, the mountains, the little begging children, the pigeons, the mules, the figure of Don Giraldo, in corduroys, with a knotted tie, sitting by a plate of grapes, from which he picks a handful now and then, while he reads – Then he jumps up. Then he goes to the other room. Then he writes. Then he tears up. Then he runs out up the mountain alone making phrases? Stories? Deciding profound matters of art? Or scarcely thinking at all? – God knows. I do not pretend to know much about that young man, whom, at this moment – the church has just struck six – I see with extreme plainness. Yes, but what is he thinking?

How does it feel to be inside him? I am tormented by my own ignorance of his mind. And there is something absurd, and perhaps even insincere, in keeping up this semblance of communication in purple lines upon great white sheets.

11 AUGUST

Crows, cocks and asses

Jane Carlyle to her husband Thomas

Suffolk, 11 August 1842

Let no mortal hope to escape night-noises so long as he is above ground! Here, one might have thought that all things, except perhaps the small birds rejoicing, would have let one alone, and the fact is that, with one devilry after another, I have had hardly any sleep, for all so dead-weary as I lay down. Just as I was dropping asleep, between 11 and 12, the most infernal serenade commenced, in comparison of which the shrieking of Mazeppa is soothing melody. It was an ass, or several asses, braying as if the devil were in them, just under my open window! It ceased after a few minutes, and I actually got to sleep, when it commenced again, and I sprang up with a confused notion that all the Edinburgh watchmen were yelling round the house, and so on all night! An explosion of ass-brays every quarter of an hour! Then, about four, commenced never so many cocks, challenging each other all over the parish, with a prodigious accompaniment of rooks cawing; ever and anon enlivened by the hooing and squealing of a child, which my remembrance of East Lothian instructed me was some vermin of a creature hired to keep off the crows from the grain.

12 AUGUST

A moon-like content

Christina Rossetti to her brother William Michael Rossetti

London, August 1858

My dear William

Your letters, showing that you are enjoying yourself, cheer us like sunbeams and produce in us a moon-like content.

We have revisited the z[oological]. gardens. Lizards are in strong force, tortoises active, alligators looking up. The weasel-headed armadillo as usual evaded us. A tree-frog came to light, the exact image of a tin toy to follow a magnet in a slop-basin. The blind wombat and neighbouring porcupine broke forth into short-lived hostilities, but apparently without permanent results. The young puma begins to bite. Your glorious sea-anemones: – I well know the strawberry specimen, but do not remember the green and purple. Beware of putting them into *fresh* water, as the result is said to be fatal and nauseating.

Mamma's love: also hers and mine to Henrietta, with the useless assurance how truly I am

Your affectionate sister Christina G. Rossetti

The variations of life consist of little things

Samuel Johnson to Hester Thrale

Lichfield, Staffordshire, 13 August 1777

Dear Madam

Such tattle as filled your last sweet letter prevents one great inconvenience of absence, that of returning home a stranger and an enquirer. The variations of life consist of little things.

Important innovations are soon heard, and easily understood. Men that meet to talk of physicks or metaphysicks, or law or history, may be immediately acquainted. We look at each other in silence, only for want of petty talk upon slight occurrences. Continue therefore to write all that you would say.

His kingdom: a grain of dust

Alexander Pope to John Caryll

14 August 1713

Every hour of my life my mind is strangely distracted. This minute, perhaps, I am above the stars, with a thousand systems round about me, looking forward into the vast abyss of eternity, and losing my whole comprehension in the boundless spaces of the extended Creation ... the next moment I am below all trifles ... in the very centre of nonsense ...

Good God! What an Incongruous Animal is Man! How unsettled in his best part, his soul; and how changing and variable in his frame of Body! - the constancy of the one shook by every notion, the temperament of the other affected by every blast of wind. What an April weather in the mind! In a word, what is man altogether but one mighty inconsistency? Sickness and pain are the lot of one half of us; doubt and fear the portion of the other! What a bustle we make about passing our time, when all our space is but a point! What aims and ambitions are crowded into this little instant of our life, which, as Shakspeare finely words it, is rounded with a sleep ... Who knows what plots, what achievements a mite may perform, in his kingdom of a grain of dust, within his life of some minutes? And of how much less consideration than even this, is the life of man in the sight of that God, who is from ever, and for ever!

A kind of conversation set to flowers

Katherine Mansfield to Lady Ottoline Morrell

15 August 1917

Your glimpse of the garden, all flying green and gold, made me wonder again *who* is going to write about that flower garden. It might be so wonderful, do you know how I mean? There would be people walking in the garden - several pairs of people - their conversation - their slow pacing - their glances as they pass one another - the pauses as the flowers 'come in' as it were - as a bright dazzle, an exquisite haunting scent, a shape so formal and fine, so much a 'flower of the mind' that he who looks at it really is tempted for one bewildering moment to stoop and touch and make *sure*. The 'pairs' of people must be very different and there must be a slight touch of enchantment - some of them seeming so extraordinarily 'odd' and separate from the flowers, but others quite related and at ease. A kind of, musically speaking, conversation *set* to flowers. Do you like the idea?

A telegram poem

Louis MacNeice to Eleanor Clark

Old Ferry Lane, Kittery, Maine, August 1940

Darling,

You will be surprised to see I am still here but the air ace has not come yet because of weather. (He is supposed to be fetching me tomorrow). I left hospital 11:00 Tuesday morning & everything has been a delight since. Matthiessen & Russell Cheney, both of whom I think are very nice though old maidish in general & damned bad drivers in particular, have the dream of a little wooden house at Kittery opposite Newcastle. I sleep up in a duck's egg attic in a sumptuous double bed. There are a lot of books & very fine cooking [...]. There are two huge ginger & white cats who eat asparagus & melon & there is a luxuriant over-run garden sloping down to the sea; on the sea are some white boats all asleep.

The house seems plumb full of beds. It has enormous fireplaces & I should like to stay here in the winter. Further up the road there is a whole series of colonial houses – very attractive. Since coming here I have been amusing myself writing Ballads; I have written four already. I thought it would be almost impossible to make them seem real & other than fretwork but now am not so sure. Today I also wrote a quite different sort of poem called Jehu. I am now smoking as much as ever which makes me feel healthy though I still have a dressing.

On Tuesday I had my hair cut in Newcastle (rather short but that was nice by reaction) & bought some yellow sort of moccasin shoes made of elk which are marvellously comfortable. Yesterday I wrote you a telegram poem which I would have sent as a telegram but I thought it would have puzzled you my still being here, besides I was stingy. I will write it on the back of this. You will write to me at Roxbury, won't you, darling.

Love ever,
Louis

<u>Telegram</u>

Just left
hospital feel
beautifully real
staying by sea
with two ginger
cats golden
rod tiger
lilies to be
out is great
I eat and eat
chops lobster
ignore future
nice to think
appendix gone
for good beastly
nuisance boon
lose it lots
of love drink
my health hope
see you soon.

My first adventure as an amateur tramp

Eric Blair (pseudonym George Orwell) to Steven Runciman

Cornwall, August 1920

My dear Runciman,

I have a little spare time, and I feel I must tell you about my first adventure as an amateur tramp. Like most tramps I was driven to it.

I put my kit-bag in the cloak-room & got 12 buns for 6d: half-past-nine found me sneaking into some farmer's field - there were a few fields wedged in among rows of slummy houses. In that light I of course looked like a soldier strolling round - on my way I had been asked whether I was demobilized yet, & I finally came to anchor in the corner of a field near some allotments. I then began to remember that people frequently got fourteen days for sleeping in somebody else's field & 'having no visible means of support', particularly as every dog in the neighbourhood barked if I ever so much as moved. The corner had a large tree for shelter, & bushes for concealment, but it was unendurably cold; I had no covering, my cap was my pillow, I lay 'with my martial cloak (rolled cape) around me'. I only dozed & shivered till about 1:00, when I readjusted my puttees, & managed to sleep long enough to miss the first train, at 4:20 by about an hour, & to have to wait till 7:45 for another. My teeth were still chattering when I awoke. When I got to Looe I was forced to walk four miles in the hot sun; I am very proud of this adventure, but I would not repeat it.

Yours sincerely, E. A. Blair

Blending reality with the fading visions

Elizabeth Gaskell to Mary Howitt

18 August 1838

And now to my country customs: though a Londoner by birth, I was early motherless, and was taken when only a year old to my dear *adopted native* town, Knutsford, and some of the customs I shall mention are peculiar to the district around that little market town.

One of the customs, on any occasion of rejoicing, of strewing the ground before the houses of those who sympathize in the gladness with common red sand, and then taking a funnel filled with white sand, and sprinkling a pattern of flowers upon the red ground. This is always done for a wedding, and often accompanied by some verse of rural composition. When I was married, nearly all the houses in the town were sanded, and these were the two favourite verses:

'Long may they live,
Happy may they be,
Blest with content,
And from misfortune free.

Long may they live
Happy may they be,
And blest with a numerous
Pro-ge-ny.'

About Knutsford we have Christmas carols, such a pretty custom, calling one from dreamland to almost as mystic a state of mind; half awake and half asleep, blending reality so strangely with the fading visions; and children's voices too in the dead of the night with their old words of bygone times! ...

Many poetical beliefs are vanishing with the passing generation. A shooting star is unlucky to see. I have so far a belief in this that I always have a chill in my heart when I see one, for I have often noticed them when watching over a sick-bed and very, very anxious. The dog-rose, that pretty libertine of the hedges with the floating sprays wooing the summer air, its delicate hue and its faint perfume, is unlucky. Never form any plan while sitting near one, for it will never answer.

I was once saying to an old, blind countrywoman how much I admired the foxglove. She looked mysteriously solemn as she told me they were not like other flowers; they had 'knowledge' in them! Of course I inquired more particularly, and then she told me that the foxglove knows when a spirit passes by and always bows the head. Is not this poetical! And of the regal foxglove with its tapering crimson bells. I have respected the flower ever since.

Moreover, I know a man who has seen the Fairies and tells the story in the prettiest possible way. And if you were on Alderley Edge, the hill between Cheshire and Derbyshire, could not I point out to you the very entrance to the cave where King Arthur and his knights lie sleeping in their golden armour till the day when England's peril shall summon them to her rescue.

A wonderful naked intimacy

D H Lawrence to Mrs S.A. Hopkin

Tirol, Austria, 19 August 1912

For ourselves, Frieda and I have struggled through some bad times into a wonderful naked intimacy, all kindled with warmth, that I know at last is love. I think I ought not to blame women, as I have done, but myself, for taking my love to the wrong woman, before now. Let every man find, keep on trying till he finds, the woman who can take him and whose love he can take, then who will grumble about men or about women. But the thing must be two-sided. At any rate, and whatever happens, I do love, and I am loved. I have given and I have taken - and that is eternal. Oh, if only people could marry properly; I believe in marriage.

Re-think human life into poetry

Virginia Woolf to John Lehman

From *A Letter to a Young Poet* (1932)

Science, they say, has made poetry impossible; there is no poetry in motor cars and wireless. And we have no religion. All is tumultuous and transitional. Therefore, so people say, there can be no relation between the poet and the present age. But surely that is nonsense. These accidents are superficial; they do not go nearly deep enough to destroy the most profound and primitive of instincts, the instinct of rhythm. All you need now is to stand at the window and let your rhythmical sense open and shut, open and shut, boldly and freely, until one thing melts in another, until the taxis are dancing with the daffodils, until a whole has been made from all these separate fragments. I am talking nonsense, I know. What I mean is, summon all your courage, exert all your vigilance, invoke all the gifts that Nature has been induced to bestow. Then let your rhythmical sense wind itself in and out among men and women, omnibuses, sparrows - whatever come along the street - until it has strung them together in one harmonious whole. That perhaps is your task - to find the relation between things that seem incompatible yet have a mysterious affinity, to absorb every experience that comes your way fearlessly and saturate it completely so that your poem is a whole, not a fragment; to re-think human life into poetry and so give us tragedy again and comedy by means of characters not spun out at length in the novelist's way, but condensed and synthesized in the poet's way - that is what we look to you to do now.

21 AUGUST

I do not write for the public. You are my public

Gerard Manley Hopkins to Robert Bridges

St. Beuno's, St. Asaph, Wales, 21 August 1877

Why do I employ sprung rhythm at all? Because it is the nearest to the rhythm of prose, that is the native and natural rhythm of speech, the least forced, the most rhetorical and emphatic of all possible rhythms, combining, as it seems to me, opposite and, one would have thought, incompatible excellences, markedness of rhythm - that is rhythm's self- and naturalness of expression -

My verse is less to be read than heard, as I have told you before; it is oratorical, that is the rhythm is so! I think if you will study what I have here said you will be much more pleased with it and may I say? converted to it.

I cannot think of altering anything. Why should I? I do not write for the public. You are my public and I hope to convert you.

You say you would not for any money read my poem again*. Nevertheless I beg you will. Besides money, you know, there is love. If it is obscure do not bother yourself with the meaning but pay attention to the best and most intelligible stanzas ... If you had done this you wd. have liked it better and sent me some serviceable criticisms, but now your criticism is of no use, being only a protest memorializing me against my whole policy and proceedings.

I may add for your greater interest and edification that what refers to myself in the poem is all strictly and literally true and did all occur; nothing is added for poetical padding.

**Hopkins' poem 'The Wreck of the Deutschland', composed 1875–6 and published posthumously by Bridges in 1918 in the first edition of Hopkins' poems*

22 AUGUST

When the grape gets by, the pippin and the chestnut

Emily Dickinson to Samuel Bowles

August 1862

Dear Mr Bowles

We reckon your coming by the fruit. When the grape gets by, and the pippin and the chestnut - when the days are a little short by the clock, and a little long by the want - when the sky has new red gowns, and a purple bonnet - then we say you will come. I am glad that kind of time goes by.

It is easier to look behind at a pain, than to see it coming.

Emily

Whaddayouknowaboutthat!

Edna St Vincent Millay to Arthur Davison Ficke
New York City, 1913

My dear Mr Ficke –

Shall I give your regards to Broadway, – now that I am here within hailing of it? To any question that you might raise concerning my presence in this locality I could only answer, 'I'm here because I'm here because I'm here.'

Yesterday I got a note from Sara Teasdale, inviting me to take tea with her. Whaddayouknowaboutthat! The news of my arrival has *sprud clean* from here to East 29th Street!

How do I like New York? O, inexpressibly! Yes, the Public Library is! No, the subway isn't! O, the St. Patrick Cathedral! – Quite sweet, I assure you! And the view – charming, charming! so many roofs and things, you know; warships, and chimneys, and brewery signs – so inspiring! Yes, to the Madison Avenue Presbyterian! Dr. Cofin is *wonderful*. O, my *dear*, – tre*men*dous!

I have learned to glare with a wild hunted expression all about me at a corner, to elbow fiercely on occasion those fellow creatures whom I love as myself, and to run and grab, – literally *grab* a street-car! I have been here since Wednesday and I am become a hardened citizen of a heartless metropolis.

Adamantinely,
Vincent Millay

Reading and reading and reading

Rupert Brooke to Katharine Cox

Grantchester, near Cambridge, 1917

Rising earlyish, and bathing at noon, and a heavy lunch, make me so sleepy now (2:30) that I'm sure I'll miss the 2:55 post. Lying on this rug I'll alternately scribble a line and doze. After all, it's only just a sort of feeble attempt to cheer you. There is no wind and no sun, only a sort of warm haze, and through it the mingled country sounds of a bee, a mowing machine, a mill and a sparrow. Peace!

And the content of working all day at Webster. Reading and reading and reading. It's not noble, but it's so happy. Oh, come here!

Write to me here

Charles Dickens to Wilkie Collins

Gad's Hill Place, Kent, 25 August 1859

My Dear Wilkie

This is written on a most intensely hot night, with rain and lightning, and with shoals of little tortoises (only harder in substance) dashing in at the window, and trying in vain to smash themselves on this paper – that was one. He is now beating his eyelids to powder (I am happy to say) on the obdurate black slab of the inkstand.

I am not quite well – can't get quite well; have an instinctive feeling that nothing but sea air and sea water will set me right. I want to come to Broadstairs next Wednesday by the mid-day train and stay till Monday. As I must work every morning, will you ask the Noble Ballard [landlord of the Albion Hotel, Broadstairs] (he will contradict you, but never mind that) if he can reserve a comfortable bedroom and quiet *writeable-in* sitting-room, for those days, for his ancient friend and patron. Then you two can dine with me one day – I can dine with you another – and evenings similarly arranged. Another tortoise, two earwigs, and a spider. Will you write to me here, after seeing the gallant host of the Albion? Dine with me on the first day, and tell him we dine, or it will break his heart.

Love from all. Ever affectionately,
C. D.

I cannot paint Dirty rags & old shoes

William Blake to George Cumberland

26 August 1799

Dear Cumberland,

I ought long ago to have written to you to thank you for your kind recommendation to Dr Trusler, which, tho' it has fail'd of success, is not the less to be remember'd by me with Gratitude.

I have made him a Drawing in my best manner; he had sent it back with a Letter full of Criticisms, in which he says it accords not with his Intentions, which are to Reject all Fancy from his Work. How far he Expects to please, I cannot tell. But as I cannot paint Dirty rags & old shoes where I ought to place Naked Beauty or simple ornament, I despair of Ever pleasing one Class of Men.

A boy running races with the moon

John Clare to James Hessey
August 1823

My Dear Hessey

There is a thing or two on Spring that I am pleasd with I know the thought is new & hope it is general & true to nature tis the description of a boy running races with the moon & another hunting the landrail or landrake – I dont think you know these names but you know the bird its a little thing heard about the grass & wheat in summer & one of the most poetical images in rural nature tis like a spirit you may track it by its noise a whole day & never urge it to take wing – I will set seriously to work to make the thing as good as I can –

28 AUGUST

I should like now to promenade round your Gardens

John Keats to his sister Fanny

Winchester, Hampshire, 28 August 1819

I should like now to promenade round your Gardens - apple-tasting - pear-tasting - plum-judging - apricot-nibbling - peach-scrunching - nectarine-sucking and Melon-carving. I have also a great feeling for antiquated cherries full of sugar cracks - and a white currant tree kept for company. I admire lolling on a lawn by a water lilied pond to eat white currants and see goldfish: and go to the Fair in the Evening if I'm good. There is not hope for that - one is sure to get into some mess before evening. Have these hot days I brag of so much been well or ill for your health? Let me hear soon.

My testimony in writing

Alexander Pope to Mrs Knight

29 August 1735

Madam, -

I must keep my old custom of giving my friends now and then, once or twice a year, my testimony in writing that I love and esteem them, and that they have a place in my memory when I have been longest absent from them. I have never any thing else to say, and it is all that friendship and good will can, or ought to say: the rest is only matter of curiosity, which a newspaper can better gratify.

My head has retired and it is my heart and my pen for it

Paul Laurence Dunbar to Alice Ruth Moore, his future wife
London, 1897

Alice: My Darling,

Someday, when I can hold you in my arms and punctuate every sentence with a kiss and an embrace I may be able to tell you how happy your letter has made me. Happy and yet unhappy from the very strength of my longing to be with you, a longing not to be satisfied it seems to so distant a day.

You love me, Alice, you say; ah yes but could you know the intensity with which I worship you, you would realize that your strongest feelings are weak beside. You gave me no time to think or to resist had I willed to do so! You took my heart captive at once I yielded bravely, weak coward that I am, without a struggle. And how glad I am of my full surrender. I would rather be your captive than another woman's king. You have made life a new thing to me – a precious and sacred trust.

Will I love you tenderly and faithfully? Darling, darling, can you ask! You who are my heart, my all, my life I will love you as no man has ever loved before. Already I am living for you and working for you and through the gray days and the long nights I am longing and yearning for you; – for the sound of your voice, the touch of your hand, the magic of your presence, the thrill of your kiss.

You did wrong to kiss me? Oh sweet heart of mine, does the flower that turns its golden face up to the amorous kisses of the sun do wrong? Does the crystal wave that wrinkles at the touch of the moving wind do wrong? does the cloud that clasps the mountain close to its dewy breast do wrong? Do any of the ternal forces of nature do wrong? If so then you have done a wrong. But darling you could not have helped it. This love of ours was predestined. I had thought that

I loved you before, and I had. I loved Alice Ruth Moore the writer of 'Violets', but how I love Alice Ruth Moore, the woman, – and my queen. 'All the current of my being runs to thee.'

I am writing wildly my dear I know, but I am not stopping to think. My head has retired and it is my heart and my pen for it.

For your sake I will be true and pure. You will help me to be this for you are always in my thoughts. Last night I started out upon a rather new undertaking or rather phase of action, I took your letter with me and read it as I drove down town. 'It will give me heart,' I said. It did and I have never had before such a brilliant success. It was at a dinner of the Savage Club, artists, literateurs, scientists and actors, where every man could do some thing. I was an honoured guest and held a unique position as the representative of a whole race. I took my turn with the rest, and, – dear is this egotism? – was received with wonderful enthusiasm.

You were with me all the time! You do not leave my thoughts. Alice, Alice, how I love you! Tell me over and over again that you love me. It will hearten me for the larger task that I have set myself here. I am so afraid that you may grow to care less for me. May God forbid! But if you do, let me know at once. I love you so that I am mindful only of your happiness. This is why I shall not complain about your being in New York although I do not like it. It is a *dangerous* place. But I know, darling that you will do me no injustice, and yourself no dishonor, so I am content. Go often to Miss Brown's but do not entirely usurp my place in the heart of that queen of women. Love me, dear, and tell me so. Write to me often and believe me ever.

Your Devoted Lover, *Paul*

Baby has cut a tooth

Elizabeth Barrett Browning to Mary Russell Mitford

Bagni di Lucca, Italy, 31 August 1849

We have had a great event in our house. Baby has cut a tooth ... His little happy laugh is always ringing through the rooms. He is afraid of nobody or nothing in the world, and was in fits of ecstasy at the tossing of the horse's head, when he rode on Wilson's knee five or six miles the other day to a village in the mountains - screaming for joy, she said. He is not six months yet by a fortnight! His father loves him passionately, and the sentiment is reciprocated, I assure you.

SEPTEMBER

From a railway carriage

Robert Louis Stevenson to Frances Sitwell

17 Heriot Row, Edinburgh, 1 September 1873

We were packed very tightly all the way and I was haunted by a face that I saw looking out of a window in London and that made me very sad. I could not settle to read anything; I bought Darwin's last book in despair, for I knew I could generally read Darwin, but it was a failure. However, the book served me in good stead, for when a couple of children got in at Newcastle, I struck up a great friendship with them, on the strength of the illustrations. These two children (a girl of nine and a boy of six) had never before travelled in a railway; so that everything was a glory to them and they were never tired of watching the telegraph posts and trees and hedges go racing past us to the tail of the train; and the girl I found quite entered into the most daring personifications that I could make.

A little way on, about Alnmouth. they had their first sight of the sea; and it was wonderful how loath they were to believe that what they saw was water: indeed it was very still, and grey and solid-looking under a sky to match. It was worth the fare, yet a little farther on to see the delight of the girl when she passed into 'another country', with the black Tweed under our feet crossed by the lamps of the passenger bridge; I remembered the first time I had gone into 'another country', over the same river from the other side.

Good-bye, my dear. Ever yours
R.L.S.

2 SEPTEMBER

I want the autumn!

Rainer Maria Rilke to his wife Clara

Borgeby, Sweden, 1904

... Look! The wind is so big and wide and does not stop; it roars the whole night through and only calms down when the rain falls, and the rain grows heavier and roars too. Autumn? Why not; everything is ready, the fruit is big and the young storks can no longer be distinguished from the old. And there is a stretch of park by the high-road that is not swept and raked on Saturday evenings; weeds are there, all withered and drooping, and the half-grown chestnuts have many yellow leaves and part with them one by one; not while the gale blows, for then they gather their strength together and hold on as tight as they can, but afterwards, when it is so vastly still, then they strow themselves down, leaf by leaf, masses of big, yellow, crumpled leaves. Decaying thistles grow there with little mournful violet heads, thistles that have sprung up without thinking; there are beech-trees that are all ragged.

And in the air there is a pensive faded smell as of flowers which the sun has dried and the wind pressed, and it is the smell of autumn. And this is why I often go there now, up and down, and avoid my seat under the walnut and all my summer ways.

I want the autumn! It almost seems as if autumn were the true creator, more creative than the spring, which is too even-toned, more creative when it comes with its will-to-change and shatters the much too ready-made, self-satisfied and really almost bourgeois-complacent image of summer. This great, splendid wind piling sky upon sky – I would like to go into its country and along its highways.

Translated from the German by R.F.C. Hull

3 SEPTEMBER

A leap in the dark

Frederick Douglass to Thomas Auld; Auld was Douglass' former slave owner from whom he had run away on this day 1838
Published in *The Liberator* newspaper, September 1848

I have selected this day on which to address you, because it is the anniversary of my emancipation. Just ten years ago this beautiful September morning, yon bright sun beheld me a slave - a poor, degraded chattel - trembling at the sound of your voice, lamenting that I was a man, and wishing myself a brute. The hopes which I had treasured up for weeks of a safe and successful escape from your grasp, were powerfully confronted at this last hour by dark clouds of doubt and fear. I have no words to describe to you the deep agony of soul which I experienced on that never to be forgotten morning - (for I left by daylight). I was making a leap in the dark. The probabilities, so far as I could by reason determine them, were stoutly against the undertaking. The preliminaries and precautions I had adopted previously, all worked badly. I was like one going to war without weapons - ten chances of defeat to one of victory.

I embraced the golden opportunity, took the morning tide at the flood, and a free man, young, active and strong, is the result.

Since I left you, I have had a rich experience. I have occupied stations which I never dreamed of when a slave. Three out of the ten years since I left you, I spent as a common labourer on the wharves of New Bedford, Massachusetts. It was there I earned my first free dollar. It was mine. I could spend it as I pleased. I could buy hams or herring with it, without asking any odds of any body. That was a precious dollar to me.

We cannot set each other quite right in this matter in letters

George Eliot to Cara Bray; Eliot refers to her relationship with George Henry Lewes of which Bray disapproved

4 September 1855

No one can be better aware than yourself that it is possible for two people to hold different opinions on momentous subjects with equal sincerity, and an equally earnest conviction that their respective opinions are alone the truly moral ones. If we differ on the subject of the marriage laws, I at least can believe of you that you cleave to what you believe to be good; and I don't know of anything in the nature of your views that should prevent you from believing the same of me.

How far we differ, I think we neither of us know, for I am ignorant of your precise views; and apparently you attribute to me both feelings and opinions which are not mine. We cannot set each other quite right in this matter in letters, but one thing I can tell you in few words.

Light and easily broken ties are what I neither desire theoretically nor could live for practically ... We are leading no life of self-indulgence, except indeed that, being happy in each other, we find everything easy. We are working hard to provide for others better than we provide for ourselves, and to fulfil every responsibility that lies upon us.

I should like never to write about myself again; it is not healthy to dwell on one's own feelings and conduct, but only to try and live more faithfully and lovingly every fresh day. I think not one of the endless words and deeds of kindness and forbearance you have ever shown me has vanished from my memory.

5 SEPTEMBER

you:gorgeously attired in circusspangles

e. e. cummings to Eliena Eastman

Silver Lake, New Hampshire, 1949

Dear Eliena -

how are you? I've enjoyed many a daydream depicting your flight from NY to M's V [Martha's Vineyard]. Sometimes you had a falcon on your left wrist & a royal bengal tiger between your knees. At other moments the car was full of monkeys who have bright blue behinds;& an ostrich sits beside you,now&again dipping her head in the sandbowl which you'd kindly provided. Then(for a change)there's nobody but you:gorgeously attired in circusspangles,with a glittering crown & the most wonderful irridescent harpshaped wings in the world. But however you appeared,you were preceded & followed by an army of motorcops;lefthands at salute:caps over righteye;& a shamrock embroidered upon every heart

6 SEPTEMBER

This very noble rose

Marianne Moore to e. e. cummings

1938

Dear Mr Cummings

I marvel that one can give so much, and at your temerarious trust in our caterpillar-tractor office. After studying this very noble rose, - the turquoise under-leaf and touch of red reflected back even to the petals, I can surmise why botanical gardens and over-flowered shops do not abound in yellow roses. Yet they might, and still lack this one.

I try not to think of your loss in the fact of my having the painting. We say what a man has done, he can do again, but can he? An affect is got once. But another awaits him. At best or at worst, please know that in having the yellow rose, I study and enjoy it and am grateful.

Sincerely yours, Marianne Moore

7 SEPTEMBER

The names of 54 wildflowers

Edna St Vincent Millay to her mother Cora B. Millay

Dieppe, France, September 1921

Mother, the flowers here are almost all entirely different from those at home. Butter-and-eggs is about the only one I have seen about that I recognize, that and yarrow and what they call wild parsley, which is about the same as what we call Queen Anne's lace.

Everywhere you see a wheat field you see thousands of red poppies, single poppies, and have seen them growing, too, in a field, an immense field, of yellow mustard, a wonderful sight. And all along in front of the Tuilleries in Paris are long beds of cultivated daisies, such as both the English and the French call marguerites, but which are almost precisely the same as your own common field daisy, which does not grow wild here at all.

It is so amusing to see poppies, which we plant and thin out and weed with such diligence in little beds, growing wild all through the country; and daisies, which our farmers plough up and try their best to kill, so carefully tended and watered and fostered, along a crowded street in the very heart of Paris.

One of the men who were here told me the names of 54 wild flowers which I did not know at all, except, in the case of some, like vetches and broom, which I had come upon in poems. Such names as milk-wort, willow-herb, campion, hound's-tongue, flea-bane, ladies'-bed-straw, sweet-agrimony, rest-harrow, hard-head, bird's-foot-tre-foil, dead-nettle, silver-weed and scabius. [...] Rest-harrow gets its name from the fact that it is found for the most part around the edge of the ploughed land, where they rest their harrows. I thought at once of you when he told me that, knowing you would enjoy it.

I see the stanzas rise around me, verse upon verse, far and near

Henry David Thoreau to Lucy Brown

Concord, Massachusetts, 8 September 1841

Just now I am in the mid-sea of verses, and they actually rustle around me as the leaves would round the head of Autumnus himself should he thrust it up through some vales which I know; but, alas! many of them are but crisped and yellow leaves like his, I fear, and will deserve no better fate than to make mould for new harvests. I see the stanzas rise around me, verse upon verse, far and near, like the mountains from Agiocochook, not all having a terrestrial existence as yet, even as some of them may be clouds; but I fancy I see the gleam of some Sebago Lake and Silver Cascade, at whose well I may drink one day.

I must burn up the day's work and do it all over again

Mark Twain to Dr. John Brown

Quarry Farm, Near Elmira, New York, September 1874

DEAR FRIEND, -

I have been writing 50 pages of manuscript a day, on an average, for sometime now, on a book (a story)* and consequently have been so wrapped up in it and so dead to anything else, that I have fallen mighty short in letter-writing. But night before last I discovered that that day's chapter was a failure, in conception, moral truth to nature, and execution - enough blemish to impair the excellence of almost any chapter - and so I must burn up the day's work and do it all over again. It was plain that I had worked myself out, pumped myself dry. So I knocked off, and went to playing billiards for a change. I haven't had an idea or a fancy for two days, now - an excellent time to write to friends who have plenty of ideas and fancies of their own, and so will prefer the offerings of the heart before those of the head. Day after tomorrow I go to a neighbouring city to see a five-act-drama of mine** brought out, and suggest amendments in it, and would about as soon spend a night in the Spanish Inquisition as sit there and be tortured with all the adverse criticisms I can contrive to imagine the audience is indulging in. But whether the play be successful or not, I hope I shall never feel obliged to see it performed a second time. My interest in my work dies a sudden and violent death when the work is done.

*The Adventures of Tom Sawyer *(1876)*

**The Gilded Age *(1873)*

You are the atmosphere of beauty through which I see life

Oscar Wilde to Lord Alfred Douglas

The Haven, Worthing, 10 September 1894

My own dearest Boy,

How sweet of you to send me that charming poem. I can't tell you how it touches me, and it is full of that light lyrical grace that you always have – a quality that seems so easy, to those who don't understand how difficult it is to make the white feet of poetry dance lightly among flowers without crushing them, and to those 'who know' is so rare and so distinguished. I have been doing nothing here but bathing and playwriting. My play is really very funny: I am quite delighted with it*. But it is not shaped yet. It lies in Sibylline leaves about the room, and Arthur has twice made a chaos of it by 'tidying up'. The result, however, was rather dramatic. I am inclined to think that Chaos is a stronger evidence for an Intelligent Creator than Kosmos is: the view might be expanded.

Yesterday (Sunday) Alphonso, Stephen and I sailed to Littlehampton in the morning, bathing on the way. We took five hours in an awful gale to come back! did not reach the pier till eleven o'clock at night, pitch dark all the way, and a fearful sea. I was drenched, but was Viking-like and daring. It was, however, quite a dangerous adventure. All the fishermen were waiting for us. I flew to the hotel for hot brandy and water, on landing with my companions, and found a letter for you from dear Henry, which I send you: they had forgotten to forward it. As it was past ten o'clock on a Sunday night the proprietor could not sell us any brandy or spirits of any kind! So he had to give it to us. The result was not displeasing, but what laws! A hotel proprietor is not allowed to sell 'necessary harmless' alcohol to three shipwrecked mariners, wet to the skin, because it is Sunday!

Both Alphonso and Stephen are now anarchists, I need hardly say.

Dear, dear boy, you are more to me than any one of them has any idea; you are the atmosphere of beauty through which I see life; you are the incarnation of all lovely things.

When we are out of tune, all colour goes from things for me, but we are never really out of tune. I think of you day and night.

Write to me soon, you honey-haired boy! I am always devotedly yours

Oscar

*The Importance of Being Earnest *(1895)*

Where's that happiness business?

Rupert Brooke to Frances Cornford

London, September 1912

I shan't write much now. I'm in an infinitely tired, muddy, flabby state. I got into London at eight this morning, and I'm reduced by the miseries of the journey to pulp. Several times this morning I've almost taken the train to the North Pole - but now it's lunch, and for the rest of the day I'm going to attach myself firmly to several friends, and refuse to be left alone.

Oh Lord, this England place you all talk so much about, turns out to be grey with rain and drizzle. I've been so thirsting for England (not that I've really got much feeling for place - but England = places + atmosphere + people I know). Do you know the feeling when one's looked forward to a thing very much a long time, and pictured it vividly, and then, when it comes (a party it used to be perhaps) you're a little tired possibly, and you've thought about it too much - and it doesn't come off. Everything's *there*, just as it ought to be, only - the emotions don't come. There's the ices, and the games, and the lights, and the decoration, and the laughter, and the supper-table, only - where's that happiness business? It's really a state of tiredness. It generally passes in a minute. I've now got it. I expected England and my friends to be - so wonderfully fresh and beautiful and invigorating ... and now I'm here, and there's only the Strand, and the National Liberal, and X. and Y. and Z. - trotting their round ...

Words can never tell how perfectly dear you are to me

Robert Browning to Elizabeth Barrett Browning; written on their wedding day, which took place in secret at St Marylebone Parish Church, on this day in 1846

1pm Saturday.

You will only expect a few words - what will those be? When the heart is full it may run over, but the real fulness stays within.

You asked me yesterday 'if I should repent?' Yes - my own Ba, - I could wish all the past were to do over again, that in it I might somewhat more, - never so little more, conform in the outward homage to the inward feeling: what I have professed ... (for I have performed nothing -) seems to fall short of what my first love required even - and when I think of this moment's love ... I could repent, as I say.

Words can never tell you, however, - form them, transform them anyway, - how perfectly dear you are to me - perfectly dear to my heart and soul.

I look back, and in every one point, every word and gesture, every letter, every silence - you have been entirely perfect to me - I would not change one word, one look.

My hope and aim are to preserve this love, not to fall from it - for which I trust to God who procured it for me, and doubtlessly can preserve it.

Enough now, my dearest, dearest, own Ba! You have given me the highest, completest proof of love that ever one human being gave another. I am all gratitude - and all pride, (under the proper feeling which ascribes pride to the right source -) all pride that my life has been so crowned by you.

God bless you prays your very own, RB

13 SEPTEMBER

It is but in a very narrow circle that friendship walks in this world

Alexander Pope to Martha Blount

September 1733

The greatest pain I know, is to say things so very short of one's meaning, when the heart is full.

I feel the going out of life fast enough, to have little appetite left to make compliments, at best useless, and for the most part unfelt speeches. It is but in a very narrow circle that friendship walks in this world, and I care not to tread out of it more than I needs must; knowing well, it is but to two or three (if quite so many) that any man's welfare, or memory, can be of consequence: the rest I believe, I may forget, and be pretty certain they are already even, if not before-hand with me.

Life, after the first warm heats are over, is all downhill: and one almost wishes the journey's end, provided we were sure but to lie down easy whenever the Night should over-take us.

My hall clock

Charles Dickens to Mr John Bennett

Gad's Hill Place, Kent, 14 September 1863

My dear Sir,

Since my hall clock was sent to your establishment to be cleaned it has gone (as indeed it always has) perfectly well, but has struck the hours with great reluctance, and after enduring internal agonies of a most distressing nature, it has now ceased striking altogether. Though a happy release for the clock, this is not convenient to the household. If you can send down any confidential person with whom the clock can confer, I think it may have something on its works that it would be glad to make a clean breast of.

Faithfully yours.

15 SEPTEMBER

The dead man touch'd me from the past

From Lord Alfred Tennyson's poem *In Memoriam* (1850) which was a response to the death of Tennyson's friend Arthur Hallam who had died on this day 1833, aged 22. In these verses, Tennyson describes his feelings on reading Hallam's letters

A hunger seized my heart; I read
    Of that glad year which once had been,
    In those fall'n leaves which kept their green,
The noble letters of the dead:

And strangely on the silence broke
    The silent-speaking words, and strange
    Was love's dumb cry defying change
To test his worth; and strangely spoke

The faith, the vigour, bold to dwell
    On doubts that drive the coward back,
    And keen thro' wordy snares to track
Suggestion to her inmost cell.

So word by word, and line by line,
    The dead man touch'd me from the past,
    And all at once it seem'd at last
The living soul was flash'd on mine.

Lord Alfred Tennyson

The beauty of this house

Katherine Mansfield to John Middleton Murry

Very late Friday night, September 1916

I must write and tell you ...

That it only dawned on me this evening that perhaps you will not be here again for a long time ... that you won't see the dahlias of this year again reflected in your mirror ... and that the lemon verbena in a jar on my table will be all withered and dry. As I thought that, sitting, smoking in the dusky room, Peter Wilkins [a black kitten] came in with a fallen-all-too-fallen leaf in his mouth, and I remembered that the Michaelmas daisies were out and, lo! it was autumn.

Is it just my fancy - the beauty of this house to-night? This round lamp on the round table, the rich flowers, the tick of the clock dropping into the quiet - and the dark outside and the apples swelling and a swimming sense of deep water. May brought me this evening some of this year's apples ... 'Good to eat.' They are small and coloured like pale strawberries. I wish that you were with me. It is not because you are absent that I feel so free of distraction, so poised and so still. I feel that I am free even of sun and wind, like a tree whose every leaf has 'turned'.

An ugly little house

Katherine Mansfield to Lady Ottoline Morrell

September 1916

M. is away in London. He left last Tuesday morning and since then I have had no news from him. I am very anxious.

Being here alone in rather an ugly little house with no news of what has happened is damnable. I sit up at night with all the doors and windows locked and wait for daylight with a hammer on the table by my side to bear me company. What the hammer would do in an hour of need I really don't know, but I feel that to come upon a woman armed with a hammer might be damping to the spirits of the most Hardened Fiend ... The frightening thing about this little house is its smugness – an eternal, a kind of Jesus-Christ-yesterday-to-day-and-for-ever quality of smugness which is most sinister.

18 SEPTEMBER

Words are the quoits, the bows, the stave that furnish the gymnasium of the mind

George Eliot to Maria Lewis
September 1841

When a sort of haziness comes over the mind, making one feel weary of articulated or written signs of ideas, does not the notion of a less laborious mode of communication, of a perception approaching more nearly to intuition, seem attractive? Nathless, I love words: they are the quoits, the bows, the staves that furnish the gymnasium of the mind. Without them, in our present condition, our intellectual strength would have no implements. I have been rather humbled in thinking that if I were thrown on an uncivilized island, and had to form a literature for its inhabitants from my own mental stock, how very fragmentary would be the information with which I could furnish them! It would be a good mode of testing one's knowledge to set one's self the task of writing sketches of all subjects that have entered into one's studies entirely from the chronicles of memory.

19 SEPTEMBER

Stars of flame dance and sparkle and go out

Samuel Taylor Coleridge to his wife Sara

Hamburg, Germany, 19 September 1798

The Ocean is a noble thing by night; a beautiful white cloud of foam at momentary intervals roars and rushes by the side of the vessel, and stars of flame dance and sparkle and go out in it, and every now and then light detachments of foam dart away from the vessel's side with their galaxies of stars and scour out of sight like a Tartar troop over a wilderness. What these stars are I cannot say; the sailors say they are fish spawn, which is phosphorescent.

20 SEPTEMBER

The great 'fairy tale of my life'

Hans Christian Andersen to Signe Laessöe

Locle in the Juras, Switzerland, September 1833

This day fourteen years ago I left Odense and began the great 'fairy tale of my life'; now fourteen years afterwards I am sitting in the Jura Mountains, with a family of friends who have invited me. They don't understand a word of Danish, and the little children shout at me, because they think I am deaf, when I don't understand their foreign baby talk. A fire is blazing in the stove, it is snowing outside, the clouds are gathered over the forest; but I know that lower down the mountain I shall find summer and ripe grapes. I shall soon again drink in the warm air beyond the Alps. How much of beautiful nature have I not seen, since I left Paris! From the Jura Mountains I had the first view over the Alps. Our road lay close to the deep abyss, where the clouds were drifting below; but suddenly we came to an opening through the mountains, and far below all was of a lovely, deep green, a land such as you only see in your dreams. It was Geneva, its lake as clear as the azure heavens. There runs the Rhone, so blue that the water almost seemed coloured. The mountains stood high over the horizon like waves of violet glass tipped with creamy foam.

The faculty of imagination lifted me when I was sinking

Charlotte Brontë to William S. Williams

Haworth, Yorkshire, 21 September 1849

I shall bend as my powers tend. The two human beings who understood me, and whom I understood, are gone*: I have some that love me yet, and whom I love, without expecting, or having a right to expect, that they shall perfectly understand me. I am satisfied; but I must have my own way in the matter of writing. The loss of what we possess nearest and dearest to us in this world, produces an effect upon the character we search out what we have yet left that can support, and, when found, we cling to it with a hold of new-strung tenacity. The faculty of imagination lifted me when I was sinking, three months ago; its active exercise has kept my head above water since; its results cheer me now, for I feel they have enabled me to give pleasure to others. I am thankful to God, who gave me the faculty; and it is for me a part of my religion to defend this gift, and to profit by its possession.

**her sisters Emily and Anne who had died within five months of each other (Emily, in December 1848 and Anne, in May 1849)*

My letters! all dead paper, ... mute and white!

From *Sonnets from the Portuguese* (28)

My letters! all dead paper, ... mute and white! -
And yet they seem alive and quivering
Against my tremulous hands which loose the string
And let them drop down on my knee to-night.
This said, ... he wished to have me in his sight
Once, as a friend: this fixed a day in spring
To come and touch my hand ... a simple thing,
Yet I wept for it! - this, ... the paper's light ...
Said, Dear, I love thee; and I sank and quailed
As if God's future thundered on my past.
This said, I am thine - and so its ink has paled
With lying at my heart that beat too fast.
And this ... O Love, thy words have ill availed,
If, what this said, I dared repeat at last!

Elizabeth Barrett Browning

23 SEPTEMBER

Issuing from some deep, unbewildered place in the poet

Rainer Maria Rilke to the Baroness Gudrun Uexkuell

Capri, Italy, 1907

I have a pleasant daily work at my back, a translation of the 44 wonderful *Sonnets from the Portuguese* of Elizabeth Barrett Browning, for the tackling of which I have to thank my hostess. One day it will grow into a little book, and I am looking forward particularly to placing it in your hands! These English love-sonnets have such perfection and accuracy of expression: crystals of feeling, so clear, so right, shiningly mysterious and issuing from some deep, unbewildered place in the poet. And it was somehow possible for me to allow the German rendering to take shape at a similar depth, so that I am pleased with the success of the translation.

Translated from the German by R.F.C. Hull

Mrs Coleridge was delivered of a SON

Samuel Taylor Coleridge to Thomas Poole

24 September 1796

On Tuesday morning I was surprised by a letter from Mr Maurice, our medical attendant, informing me that Mrs Coleridge was delivered on Monday, September 19, 1796, half past two in the morning, of a SON, and that both she and the child were uncommonly well. I was quite annihilated with the suddenness of the information, and retired to my own room to address myself to my Maker, but I could only offer up to Him the silence of stupefied feelings. I hastened home. When I first saw the child, I did not feel that thrill and overflowing of affection which I expected. I looked on it with a melancholy gaze; my mind was intensely contemplative and my heart only sad. But when two hours after I saw it at the bosom of its mother, on her arm, and her eye tearful and watching its little features, then I was thrilled and melted, and gave it the KISS of a *father* ...

My men will have eaten the Michaelmas Goose

Edward FitzGerald to E B Cowell

Woodbridge, Suffolk, 1867

My dear Cowell,

My Ship is still afloat: but I have scarce used her during the last cold weather. I may, however, run to Lowestoft and back; but by the end of next week I suppose she (the Ship) will be laid up in the Mud; my Men will have eaten the Michaelmas Goose which I always regale them with on shutting up shop; and I may come home to my Fire here to read *The Woman in White* and play at Patience - which (I mean the Game at Cards so called) I now do by myself for an hour or two every night. Perhaps old Montaigne may drop in to chat with and comfort me: but Sophocles, Don Quixote and Boccaccio - I think I must leave them with their Halo of Sea and Sunshine about them.

Letter of Consolation

Montaigne to his wife; from his dedicatory epistle to La Boetie's translation of Plutarch's *Letter of Consolation to his Wife*

September 1570*

I send you the Consolatory Letter written by Plutarch to his Wife, translated by him into French; regretting much that fortune has made it so suitable a present for you, and that, having had but one child, and that a daughter, long looked for, after four years of your married life, it was your lot to lose her in the second year of her age. But I leave to Plutarch the duty of comforting you, and acquainting you with your duty herein, begging you to put your faith in him for my sake; for he will reveal to you my own ideas, and will express the matter far better than I should myself.

- Your good husband,

Michel de Montaigne

**this letter was dated about two weeks after the death of their first child, at about two months of age. Montaigne's 'second year' may be an earlier printer's error (Ref: Frame, 1958)*

Translated from the French by Charles Cotton

27 SEPTEMBER

I can set a measure to the magnitude of our loss

Plutarch to his wife on the loss of their two-year-old daughter

My dear wife, in your emotion keep me as well as yourself within bounds. For I know and can set a measure to the magnitude of our loss, taken by itself; but if I find any extravagance of distress in you, this will be more grievous to me than what has happened. Yet neither was I born 'from oak or rock'*; you know this yourself, you who have reared so many children in partnership with me, all of them brought up at home under our own care. And I know what great satisfaction lay in this that after four sons the longed-for daughter was born to you, and that she made it possible for me to call her by your name. Our affection for children so young has, furthermore, a poignancy all its own: the delight it gives is quite pure and free from all anger or reproach.

... as she was herself the most delightful thing in the world to embrace, to see, to hear, so too must the thought of her live with us and be our companion, bringing with it joy in greater measure, nay in many times greater measure, than it brings sorrow and we must not sit idle and shut ourselves in, paying for those pleasures with sorrows many times as great.

**Homer,* Iliad. *XXII.126;* Odyssey. *XIX.163*

Translated from the Greek by Phillip H. De Lacy and Benedict Einarson

That feeling went through my whole body like sweetest nectar

William Carlos Williams to his wife Florence

On Board SS. Pennland, Wednesday, 7:45am, 28 September 1927

Dearest Flossie: This is mid-ocean. The wind has shifted again to the north where there is a small freighter on the horizon steaming in the same direction as ourselves. It is a gray threatening sort of day but not too cold. The sea is fairly quiet.

This simple life on the ocean, without close companions, without work to do and without temptation or irritation of any sort about me - unless there be a temptation to read too much - has put me in a thoughtful mood - full of love for you.

I was really an unhappy, disappointed child - in general - during my early years. And yet underneath it all there was an enormous faith and solidity. Inside me I was like iron and with a love for the world and a determination to do good in the world that was like the ocean itself.

But if, one way and another, I was a disappointed and unhappy - lit by wild flashes - boy, though this is true I am a most happy man. And the greatest thing which has caused that has been yourself. For some uncanny reason you saw through me and you saw me good. I in my turn recognized in a flash of intuition, that you were the queen of the world for me at that moment. I tell you now that that feeling went through my whole body like sweetest nectar and that I knew it would last forever. And I mean just exactly forever. There was the eternal in that and I knew it at once.

What 'love' is I don't know if it is not the response of our deepest natures to one another. I went direct to you through my own personal hell of doubt and hesitation and I have never changed the millionth part of one inch since that first decision.

All my life I have grown from that moment when I asked you to marry me, always into a clearer and more satisfying realization of what really took place at that time. I love you and you love me and so only at the end will I know what love is –

It is wise that we have adventured once again, this time on a separation. You are the one to have made this 'necessary evil' of separation possible. I am sure it is good. I feel it all over me in many ways not yet fully come to light: in power to work, in clarity of conception of some of my emotional difficulties, in firmness within myself and in decision and fuller realization concerning my love for you.

I believe that with love – (how I hate the word, mistrust it I mean) with love we can dare to understand each other.

There, I'm written out on that topic. I wanted so much to say it, but it is so hard to say well. The damned words keep jumping and slipping, until before long we've said just the opposite of what was intended. But a strong emotional bias keeps the words straight – pretty well. And that's what they mean when they say that in spite of faults the truth shines through.

Love,
BILL

A cup of tea with milk in it

Edna St Vincent Millay to her mother Cora B. Millay
Letchworth, Hertfordshire, September 1921

Dearest Mother,

Here I am in a little English town, visiting the daughter of an English rector in her home. It is not a rectory, because the rector is dead now, and they are living in a house; but it is much more like a rectory than the houses in which I usually visit, you may be sure. We have just had tea. I was out for a walk with Judy, my friend, who was with me at Pourville, and her sister, and suddenly they put their noses to the wind and began streaking it for home, - tea-time! The tea was poured when we got to the table, and there was milk in it, for everybody, without a question asked. I drank it, of course, and do you know, rather liked it. I remember you used to take it that way, mother, when I was a little child, very hot, and with milk in it, and I used to come to you with a hard, round, 'common' cracker, and beg to soak it in your cup, after which I would butter it and eat it. Oh, the butter melted so quickly, and slid all around, usually dripping on me before I could prevent it, I remember, and nothing was ever so good! The next time I see you, you shall have a cup of tea with milk in, and I shall soak my common cracker in it, and butter it, and eat it, and we shall be very gay.

Damn this pen

Leslie Stephen to his wife Julia
Padstow, Cornwall, September 1885

My own,

Confound this pen, it is worse than the last & the paper is shiny – damn them both. That being settled I may say that we have had a very successful walk. Whilst I remember it I gave 4s to the guard. I had no more to spare. I cannot yet find out about my route; but if you do not see me at Bodmin Road, I shall probably have settled to go by Launceton & the Southwestern reaching Waterloo at 10:00. How the devil is anybody to write with a pen like this? Well, we had a very good walk. We started at 9:30. I remembered New Quay so well that I felt a shiver in all my bones as I used to do when I saw you cowering under the bushes in the garden. The place has a dismal sensation for me & even for miles I remembered it. So, beloved, we walked to Bodrutha Steps which is a very fine cliff 400 feet high. We felt it a duty to go down by a steep path to the bottom & back which added considerably to the labour. Then we walked on & your chocolates came in very useful for no village or public appeared & C.B. (Clarke) was obviously empty. I walked slowly to spare him & is really an excellent companion.

...

This is a quaint little place rather like Polperro & a harbour wh looks as fine as Falmouth at high tide, but they say it is all sand when the tide is out. We have a clean old-fashioned inn with a jolly landlady & have had a dinner of beefsteak, apple pie, Cornish cream & cheese, I feel very comfortable after it & C.B. is well that he is writing ten letters. I said nothing s[houl]d induce me to write to any but you. Kiss all my pets.

Your loving LS
Damn this pen

OCTOBER

Delicious autumn!

George Eliot to Maria Lewis

1 October 1841

Is not this a true autumn day? Just the still melancholy that I love – that makes life and nature harmonize. The birds are consulting about their migrations, the trees are putting on the hectic or the pallid hues of decay, and begin to strew the ground, that one's very footsteps may not disturb the repose of earth and air, while they give us a scent that is a perfect anodyne to the restless spirit. Delicious autumn! My very soul is wedded to it, and if I were a bird I would fly about the earth seeking the successive autumns.

Papa thinks that I have sold my soul – for genius

Elizabeth Barrett Browning to her sisters

Roanne, France, 2 October 1846

No one judge of this act, except some one who knows thoroughly the man I have married. He rises on me hour by hour. If ever a being of a higher order lived among us with a glory round his head, in these latter days, he is such a being.

Papa thinks that I have sold my soul – for genius ... mere genius. Which I might have done when I was younger, if I had had the opportunity ... but am in no danger of doing now. For my sake, for the love of me, from an infatuation which from first to last has astonished me, he has consented to occupy for a moment a questionable position.

But those who question most, will do him justice fullest – and we must wait a little with resignation. In the meanwhile, what he is, and what he is to me, I would fain teach you. – Have faith in me to believe it. He puts out all his great faculties to give me pleasure and comfort ... charms me into thinking of him when he sees my thoughts wandering ... forces me to smile in spite of all of them – if you had seen him that day at Orleans.

He laid me down on the bed and sate by me for hours, pouring out floods of tenderness and goodness, and promising to win back for me, with God's help, the affection of such of you as were angry. And he loves me more and more. Today we have been together a fortnight, and he said to me with a deep, serious tenderness ... 'I kissed your feet, my Ba, before I married you – but now I would kiss the ground under your feet, I love you with a so much greater love.' And this is true, I see and feel. I feel to have the power of making him happy ... I feel to have it in my hands. It is strange that anyone so brilliant should love me, but true and strange it is and it is impossible for me to doubt it any more.

The far-off world seems nearer than the present

Lord Alfred Tennyson to Emily Sellwood before they were married

October 1839

All life is a school, a preparation, a purpose: nor can we pass current in a higher college, if we do not undergo the tedium of education in this one.

Annihilate within yourself these two dreams of Space and Time. To me often the far-off world seems nearer than the present, for in the present is always something unreal and indistinct, but the other seems a good solid planet, rolling round its green hills and paradises to the harmony of more steadfast laws. There steam up from about me mists of weakness, or sin, or despondency, and roll between me and the far planet, but it is there still.

Dim mystic sympathies with tree and hill reaching far back into childhood. A known landskip is to me an old friend, that continually talks to me of my own youth and half-forgotten things, and indeed does more for me than many an old friend that I know. An old park is my delight, and I could tumble about it for ever.

Sculpture is particularly good for the mind: there is a height and divine stillness about it which preaches peace to our stormy passions. Methinks that, in looking upon a great statue like the Theseus (maim'd and defaced as it is), one becomes as it were God-like, to feel things in the Idea.

4 OCTOBER

That purple edge outside most people's vision

Edna St Vincent Millay to Arthur Davison Ficke

Rome, Italy, October 1921

Arthur, my dearest,

Do you remember that poem in *Second April* which says, 'Life is a quest & love a quarrel, Here is a place for me to lie!'? – That is what I want of you – out of the sight & sound of other people, to lie close to you & let the world rush by. To watch with you suns rising & moons rising in that purple edge outside most people's vision – to hear high music that only birds can hear – oh, my dearest, dearest, would it not be wonderful, just once to be together again for a little while?

Arthur, I am glad that you love me. Your letters have hurt me & healed me. Such sweetness, to be loved like that. But to be loved like that by you, – how shaking & terrible besides.

5 OCTOBER

Such soar, but never set

Emily Dickinson to Sue Huntington Dickinson; Sue's youngest child Thomas Gilbert died on 5 October 1883, aged eight

Dear Sue –

The vision of immortal life has been fulfilled. How simply at last the fathom comes! The passenger and not the sea surprises us. Gilbert rejoiced in secrets. His life was panting with them. With what a menace of light he cried, 'Don't tell, Aunt Emily.' My ascended playmate must instruct me now. Show us, prattling preceptor, but the way to thee! He knew no niggard moment. His life was full of boon. The playthings of the Dervish were not so wild as his. No crescent was this creature – he travelled from the full. Such soar, but never set. I see him in the star and meet his sweet velocity in everything that flies.
His life was like a bugle
That winds itself away:
His elegy an echo.
His requiem ecstasy.
Dawn and meridian in one, wherefore should he wait, wronged only of night, which he left for us? Pass to thy rendezvous of light pangless except for us who slowly ford the mystery which thou hast leapt across!

Your letter is almost like folding you to my heart

Percy Bysshe Shelley to his wife Mary Wollstonecraft Shelley

London, 6 October 1817

Dearest and best of living beings, how much do your letters console me when I am away from you! Your letter today gave me the greatest delight; so soothing; so powerful, and quiet are your expressions, that it is almost like folding you to my heart. Tomorrow, therefore, beloved, I shall not come, but the day after certainly, if you decide on that.

Kiss all the little ones; poor little William – is he so cold? – and Alba and Clara.

I can scarcely write today, but shall be better tomorrow. Adieu, my dearest love; twenty kisses to your sweet lips.

P. B. S.

7 OCTOBER

The stillness seemed to be not of this world

Dorothy Wordsworth to Reverend William Johnson

1818

On the summit of the Pike, there was not a breath of air to stir even the papers containing our refreshment, as they lay spread out upon a rock. The stillness seemed to be not of this world: – we paused, and kept silence to listen; and no sound could be heard: we were far above the reach of the Cataracts of Scafell; and not an insect was there to hum in the air.

We sat down to our repast, and gladly would we have tempered our beverage (for there was no spring or well near us) with such a supply of delicious water as we might have procured, had we been on the rival summit of Great Gavel; for on its highest point is a small triangular receptacle in the native rock, which, the shepherds say, is never dry. There we might have slaked our thirst plenteously with a pure and celestial liquid, for the cup or basin, it appears, has no other feeder than the dews of heaven, the showers, the vapors, the hoar frost and the spotless snow.

I know not how long we might have remained on the summit of the Pike, without a thought of moving, had not our Guide warned us that we must not linger; for a storm was coming. We looked in vain to espy the signs of it. Mountains, vales and sea were touched with the clear light of the sun. 'It is there,' said he, pointing to the sea beyond Whitehaven, and there we perceived a light vapour unnoticeable but by a shepherd accustomed to watch all mountain bodings. We gazed around again, and yet again, unwilling to lose the remembrance of what lay before us in that lofty solitude; and then prepared to depart.

I ought to have mentioned that round the top of Scafell Pike not a blade of grass is to be seen. Cushions or tufts of moss, parched and brown, appear between the huge blocks and stones lie in heaps on all sides to a great distance, like skeletons or bones of the earth not needed at the creation, and there left to be covered with never-dying lichens, which the clouds and dews nourish; and adorn with colours of vivid and exquisite beauty. Flowers, the most brilliant feathers and even gems, scarcely surpass in colouring some of those masses of stone, which no human eye beholds, except the shepherd or traveller be led thither by curiosity: and how seldom must this happen! For the other eminence is the one visited by the adventurous stranger; and the shepherd has no inducement to ascend the Pike in quest of his sheep; no food being there to tempt them.

We certainly were singularly favored in the weather; for when we were seated on the summit, our conductor, turning his eyes thoughtfully round, said, 'I do not know that in my whole life, I was ever, at any season of the year, so high upon the mountains on so calm a day.' (It was the 7th of October.) Afterwards we had a spectacle of the grandeur of earth and heaven commingled; yet without terror. We knew that the storm would pass away; - for so our prophetic Guide had assured us.

8 OCTOBER

This, Madam, is the history of one of my toes

Samuel Johnson to Hester Thrale

London, 8 October 1779

Dear Madam

I begin to be frighted at your omission to write; do not torment me any longer, but let me know where you are, how you got thither, how you live there, and every thing else that one friend loves to know of another.

I will show you the way.

On Sunday the gout left my ankles, and I went very commodiously to Church. On Monday night I felt my feet uneasy. On Tuesday I was quite lame. That night I took an opiate, having first taken physick and fasted. Towards morning on Wednesday the pain remitted. – Bozzy came to me, and much talk we had. I fasted another day; and on Wednesday night could walk tolerably. On Thursday, finding myself mending, I ventured on my dinner, which I think has a little interrupted my convalescence. Today I have again taken physick, and eaten only some stewed apples. I hope to starve it away. It is now no worse than it was at Brighthelmstone.

This, Madam, is the history of one of my toes; the history of my head would perhaps be much shorter.

Surely I shall have a letter tomorrow.

I am, &c.,

Sam Johnson

9 OCTOBER

Wet paint poisoning one's soul

Jane Carlyle to her husband Thomas

Chelsea, London, October 1852

I write, dear, since you bid me write again; but upon my honour it were better to leave me silent; all the thoughts of my heart just now are curses on Mr ---- I have not a word of comfort to give; I am wearied and sad and cross; feel as if death had been dissolved into a liquid, and I had drunk of it till I was full! Good gracious! That wet paint should have the power of poisoning one's soul as well as one's body! But it is not the wet paint simply; it is the provocation of having an abominable process spun out so interminably, and the prospect of your finding your house hardly habitable after such long absence and weary travel. Never in all my life has my temper been so tried. So anxious I have been to get on, and the workmen only sent here, seemingly, when they have nowhere else to go, and Mr ---- dwindled away into a myth!

I have never printed a single line in my life

Lady Mary Wortley Montagu to her daughter the Countess of Bute
Brescia, Italy, 10 October 1752

This letter will be very dull or very peevish (perhaps both). I am at present much out of humour, being on the edge of a quarrel with my friend and patron, the Cardinal Querini.

Yesterday here arrived one of his chief chaplains, with a long compliment, which concluded with desiring I would send him my works; having dedicated one of his cases to English books, he intended my labours should appear in the most conspicuous place. I was struck dumb for some time with this astonishing request; when I recovered my vexatious surprize (foreseeing the consequence), I made answer, I was highly sensible of the honour designed me, but, upon my word, I had never printed a single line in my life. I was answered in a cold tone, that his Eminence could send for them to England, but they would be a long time coming, and with some hazard; and that he had flattered himself I would not refuse him such a favour, and I need not be ashamed of seeing my name in a collection where he admitted none but the most eminent authors. It was to no purpose to endeavour to convince him. He would not stay dinner, though earnestly invited; and went away with the air of one that thought he had reason to be offended. I know his master will have the same sentiments, and I shall pass in his opinion for a monster of ingratitude, while it is the blackest of vices in my opinion, and of which I am utterly incapable – I really could cry for vexation.

Sure nobody ever had such various provocations to print as myself. I have seen things I have wrote, so mangled and falsified, I have scarce known them. I have seen poems I never read, published with my name at length; and others, that were truly and singly wrote by me, printed under the names of others. I have made myself easy under all these mortifications, by the reflection I did not deserve them, having never aimed at the vanity of popular applause; but I own my philosophy is not proof against losing a friend, and it may be making an enemy of one to whom I am obliged.

11 OCTOBER

Squirrel-houses, rabbit hutches and bird-cages

William Cowper to Mrs King

Weston Lodge, Buckinghamshire, 11 October 1788

There was a time when I amused myself in a way somewhat similar to yours; allowing, I mean, for the difference between masculine and feminine operations. The scissors and the needle are your chief implements; mine were the chisel and the saw. In those days you might have been in some danger of too plentiful a return for your favours. Tables, such as they were, and joint-stools such as never were, might have travelled to Pertenhall in most convenient abundance. But I have long since discontinued this practice, and many others which I found it necessary to adopt, that I might escape the worst of all evils, both in itself and in its consequences - an idle life.

Many arts I have exercised with this view for which nature never designed me; though among them were some in which I arrived at considerable proficiency by mere dint of the most heroic perseverance. There is not a squire in all this country who can boast of having made better squirrel-houses, hutches for rabbits, or bird-cages, than myself; and in the article of cabbage-nets I had no superior.

12 OCTOBER

I began with lettuces and cauliflowers

William Cowper to Mrs King

Weston Lodge, Buckinghamshire, October 1788

Gardening was, of all employments, that in which I succeeded best, though in this I did not suddenly attain perfection. I began with lettuces and cauliflowers; from them I proceeded to cucumbers; next to melons. I then purchased an orange tree, to which, in due time, I added two or three myrtles. These served me day and night with employment during a whole severe winter. To defend from the frost, in a situation that exposed them to its severity, cost me much ingenuity and much attendance. I contrived to give them a fire heat; and have waded night after night through the snow with the bellows under my arm, just before going to bed, to give the latest possible puff to the embers, lest the frost should seize them before morning. Very minute beginnings have sometimes important consequences. From nursing two or three little evergreens I became ambitious of a greenhouse, and accordingly built one; which, verse excepted, afforded me amusement for a longer time than any expedient of all the many to which I have fled for refuge from the misery of having nothing to do.

13 OCTOBER

I have had many thoughts

George Eliot to Sara Hennell

13 October 1847

I heartily wish you had been with me to see all the beauties which have gladdened my soul and made me feel that this earth is as good a heaven as I ought to dream of.

Fancy a very high precipice, the strata upheaved perpendicularly in rainbow-like streaks of the brightest maize, violet, pink, blue, red, brown and brilliant white, worn by the weather into fantastic fretwork, the deep blue sky above and the glorious sea below. It seems an enchanted land, where the earth is of more delicate, refined materials than this dingy planet of ours is wrought out of. You might fancy the strata formed of the compressed pollen of flowers, or powder from bright insects. You can think of nothing but Calypsos, or Prosperos and Ariels, and such-like beings.

I find one very great spiritual good attendant on a quiet, meditative journey among fresh scenes. I seem to have removed to a distance from myself when I am away from the petty circumstances that make up my ordinary environment. I can take myself up by the ears and inspect myself, like any other queer monster on a small scale. I have had many thoughts, especially on a subject that I should like to work out – 'The superiority of the consolations of philosophy to those of (so-called) religion.' Do you stare?

The sea, the firmament, the forest are the work of pure soul

Ralph Waldo Emerson to Sarah Ann Clarke

Concord, Massachusetts, October 1840

Nature - what is it but the circumference of which I am the centre, the outside of my inside, object whereof I am subject? Nature is the body which the spirit animates, -

It is by the soul that the world exists and planets revolve and as the soul enters into me I share & become the power will or science, call it what you please, by which the largest & all effects are wrought equally with the petty ones of my present experience.

This external unity & kindred of production and producer is the account of that feeling of self recognition we always find in the landscape. The sea, the firmament, the forest are the work of pure soul; in them therefore we can so easily pray & aspire; whilst we are so easily checked in the presence of man & his works, or Impure Soul. In these beautiful days which are now passing, go into the forest & the leaves hang silent & sympathetic, unobtrusive & related, like the thoughts which they so hospitably enshrine. Could they tell their sense, they would become the thoughts we have; could our thoughts take form they would hang as sunny leaves. And yet it is not by direct study of these enchantments that their sense is to be extorted, but by manlier & total methods, by doing & being. Conscience is the key to botany by more life & not by microscopes must I learn the essence of a tree.

Your affectionate servant,
R W Emerson

We can fake as much as we like

P G Wodehouse to William Townend

New York, October 1951

I think the letters scheme is terrific.

The great thing, as I see it, is not to feel ourselves confined to the actual letters. I mean, nobody knows what was actually in the letters, so we can fake as much as we like. That is to say, if in a quickly written letter from – say – Hollywood, I just mention that Winston Churchill is there and I have met him, in the book I can think up some amusing anecdote, describing how his trousers split up the back at the big party or something. See what I'm driving at?

You see, all the letters I have written to you were written very quickly. I just poured out the stuff as if we were talking to each other. But for the book we need more carefully written stuff.

(There's an example for you in that paragraph. I used 'written' three times and 'stuff' twice. The letters, as they appear in the book, must be much more polished. Naturally not artificial, but avoiding the same verb twice in a sentence.)

Also, these letters give me a wonderful opportunity of shoving thoughts on life to a much greater extent than I do in my actual letters.

The way to work this thing, as I see it, is for you to complete the book and then hand it over to me, and I will go through it and add stuff and make it all more vivid. I have always wanted to write my autobiography but felt too self-conscious. This will be a way of doing the thing obliquely ...

Well, laddie, I was seventy yesterday. I tried my hardest to think solemn thoughts like Somerset Maugham in *A Writer's Notebook*, but couldn't dig up any. I felt just the same as usual. (Now there's a case of what I mean when I say that we must fake a bit in the book. It ought to be possible, with thought, to turn out a complete letter dated Oct 15, 1951 which will be an amusing essay on 'How It Feels To Be 70'.

In fact, that is how the book ought to end. That should be the last letter in it. But an essay like that takes careful thinking out, and I can't possibly compose it in a letter which I want to get off to you this afternoon! See what I mean?)

Float along an infinite ocean cradled in the flower of the Lotus

Samuel Taylor Coleridge to John Thelwall; Coleridge probably composed *Kubla Khan* around the time of writing this letter

16 October 1797

I can *at times* feel strongly the beauties you describe, in themselves and for themselves; but more frequently *all things* appear *little*, all the knowledge that can be acquired child's play; the universe itself! what but an immense heap of *little* things? I can contemplate nothing but *parts*, and parts are all *little*! My mind feels as if it ached to behold and know something *great*, something *one* and *indivisible*. And it is only in the faith of that that rocks or waterfalls, mountains or caverns, give me the sense of sublimity or majesty! But in this faith *all things* counterfeit infinity.

'Struck with the deepest calm of joy,' I stand
Silent, with swimming sense; and gazing round
On the wide landscape, gaze till all doth seem
Less gross than bodily, a living Thing
Which acts upon the mind and with such hues
As clothe th' Almighty Spirit, where He makes
Spirits perceive His presence! ...

It is but seldom that I raise and spiritualize my intellect to this height; and at other times I adopt the Brahmin creed, and say, 'It is better to sit than to stand, it is better to lie than to sit, it is better to sleep than to wake, but Death is the best of all!' I should much wish, like the Indian Vishnu, to float about along an infinite ocean cradled in the flower of the Lotus, and wake once in a million years for a few minutes just to know that I was going to sleep a million years more.

17 OCTOBER

The strong serious smell of sprigs of heather

Rainer Maria Rilke to his wife Clara

Paris, France, 1907

Never have I been so affected and well-nigh smitten by heather as I was the other day, when I found these three sprigs in your letter. Since then they have been lying in my Buck der Bilder and permeating it with their strong serious smell, which is really only the scent of autumn earth.

But how wonderful it is, this scent. Never, it seems to me, does the earth allow itself to be inhaled so much in one single scent, the mellow earth; in a scent that is no whit smaller than the scent of the sea, bitter where it borders on the sense of taste, and more than honey-sweet where you think it must strike on more solemn tones. Harbouring depths in itself, darkness and sepulture, and yet again the wind; tar and turpentine and Ceylon tea. Grave and needy like the smell of a mendicant friar, yet resinous and heartening like precious incense. And to look at: like embroidery - marvellous; like three cypresses woven into a Persian carpet with violet silk: a violet so puissant and dewy as to be the colour-complement of the sun. You ought to see it.

One of the sprigs is now lying, by chance, on the dark-blue velvet of an old writing-casket. It is like a firework: no, just like a Persian carpet. Are they all, all these millions of little branches, of such wonderful workmanship? Look at the colouring of the green, in which there is a splash of gold, and the sandalwood-brown of the stem and the break with its new, fresh, barely-green interior. - Ah, for days I've been marvelling at the magnificence of these three fragments and am thoroughly ashamed that I was not happy when I had the chance to wander about in all the abundance of it.

So badly does one live, because one always comes incomplete into the present, inept and scatter-brained. When I think back there is no period of my life without such, and even greater, reproaches. Only the ten days after Ruth's birth, I think, have I lived without loss; finding Reality as indescribable, even in its smallest part, as it probably always is. – But I suppose it is the stale city-summer that makes me so susceptible to the glory of little bits of heather springing from the splendours of the northern year.

Translated from the German by R.F.C. Hull

I am now upon my own footing

From Phillis Wheatley to Colonel David Worcester; recounts a trip to England, Wheatley's emancipation and the prospect of the publication of her book of poetry, the first to be published by an African-American

Boston, 18 October 1773

Sir

I was reciev'd in England with such kindness Complaisance, and so many marks of esteem and real Friendship, as astonishes me on the reflection.

- Was introduced to Lord Dartmouth and had near half an hour's conversation with his Lordship.

Then to Lady Cavendish, and Lady Carteret Webb, - Mrs Palmer a Poetess, an accomplishd Lady, - Dr Thos. Gibbons, Rhetoric Proffessor, to Israel Mauduit Esqr., Benjamin Franklin Esqr. F.R.S., Grenville Sharp Esqr. who attended me to the Tower & Show'd the Lions, Panthers, Tigers, &c. the Horse Armoury, small Armoury, the Crowns, Sceptres, Diadems, the Font for christening the Royal Family. Saw Westminster Abbey, British Museum Coxe's Museum, Saddler's wells, Greenwich Hospital, Park and Chapel, The Royal Observatory at Greenwich, &c. &c. too many things & Places to trouble you with in a Letter.

- The Earl of Dartmouth made me a Compliment of five Guineas, and desir'd me to get the whole of Mr Pope's Works, as the best he could recommend to my perusal, this I did, also got *Hudibrass* [sic], *Don Quixot* [sic] , & *Gay's Fables* [sic] - was presented with a Folio Edition of Milton's *Paradise Lost*, printed on a Silver Type, so call'd from its elegance, (I suppose).

- Since my return to America my Master, has at the desire of my friends in England given me my freedom. The Instrument is drawn, so as to secure me and my property from the hands of the Executers. adminstrators, &c. of my master, & secure whatsoever should be given me as my Own.

I expect my Books which are publishd in London in Capt. Hall, who will be here I believe in eight or ten days. I beg the favour that you would honour the enclos'd Proposals, & use your interest with Gentlemen & Ladies of your acquaintance to subscribe also, for the more subscribers there are, the more it will be for my advantage as I am to have half the sale of the Books. This I am the more solicitous for, as I am now upon my own footing and whatever I get by this is entirely mine, & it is the Chief I have to depend upon.

My dutiful respects attend your Lady and Children and I am ever respectfully your oblig'd Hume sert.

Phillis Wheatley

I found my mistress very sick on my return
But she is some what better, we wish we could depend on it.

19 OCTOBER

A Letter from Phillis Wheatley

Robert Hayden's epistolary poem (1978) imagines Phillis Wheatley's visit to London

London, 1773

Dear Obour

Our crossing was without
event. I could not help, at times,
reflecting on that first – my Destined –
voyage long ago (I yet
have some remembrance of its Horrors)
and marvelling at God's Ways.
Last evening, her Ladyship presented me
to her illustrious Friends.
I scarce could tell them anything
of Africa, though much of Boston
and my hope of Heaven. I read
my latest Elegies to them.
'O Sable Muse!' the Countess cried,
embracing me, when I had done.
I held back tears, as is my wont,
and there were tears in Dear
Nathaniel's eyes.
At supper – I dined apart
like captive Royalty –
the Countess and her Guests promised
signatures affirming me
True Poetess, albeit once a slave.
Indeed, they were most kind, and spoke,
moreover, of presenting me
at Court (I thought of Pocahontas) –

an Honour, to be sure, but one,
I should, no doubt, as Patriot decline.
    My health is much improved;
I feel I may, if God so Wills,
entirely recover here.
Idyllic England! Alas, there is
no Eden without its Serpent. Under
the chiming Complaisance I hear him Hiss;
I see his flickering tongue
when foppish would-be Wits
murmur of the Yankee Pedlar
and his Cannibal Mockingbird.
    Sister, forgive th'intrusion of
my Sombreness – Nocturnal Mood
I would not share with any save
your trusted Self. Let me disperse,
in closing, such unseemly Gloom
by mention of an Incident
you may, as I, consider Droll:
Today, a little Chimney Sweep,
his face and hands with soot quite Black,
staring hard at me, politely asked:
'Does you, M'lady, sweep chimneys too?'
I was amused, but dear Nathaniel
(ever Solicitous) was not.

I pray the Blessings of our Lord and Saviour Jesus Christ be yours Abundantly. In His Name,

Phillis

Arthur says such letters as mine never ought to be kept

Charlotte Brontë to Ellen Nussey

Haworth, Yorkshire, 20 October 1854

Arthur* has just been glancing over this note – he thinks I have written too freely ... Men don't seem to understand making letters a vehicle of communication – they always seem to think us incautious. I'm sure I don't think I have said anything rash – however, you must burn it when read. Arthur says such letters as mine never ought to be kept – they are dangerous as lucifer matches – so be sure to follow a recommendation he has just given 'fire them' – or 'there will be no more' such is his resolve. I can't help laughing – this seems to me so funny. Arthur however says he is quite 'serious' and looks it, I assure you – he is bending over the desk with his eyes full of concern.

**Arthur Bell Nichols, Charlotte Brontë's husband, whom she had married four months earlier*

Love of Individuals

Alexander Pope to Jonathan Swift

October 1725

I really enter as fully as you desire, into your Principle, of Love of Individuals: And I think the way to have a Publick Spirit, is first to have a Private one: For who the devil can believe any man can care for a hundred thousand people, who never cared for One? No ill humoured man can ever be a Patriot, and more than a Friend.

22 OCTOBER

Your friend

Gerard Manley Hopkins to Robert Bridges

St. Joseph's, Bedford Leigh, near Manchester, 22 October 1879

If I were not your friend I should wish to be the friend of the man that wrote your poems. They shew the eye for pure beauty and they shew, my dearest, besides, the character which is much more rare and precious. Did time allow I should find a pleasure in dwelling on the instances, but I cannot now. Since I must not flatter or exaggerate I do not claim that you have such a volume of imagery as Tennyson, Swinburne or Morris, though the feeling for beauty you have seems to me pure and exquisite; but in point of character, of sincerity or earnestness, of manliness, of tenderness, of humour, melancholy, human feeling, you have what they have not and seem scarcely to think worth having.

23 OCTOBER

The poetry runs as hard as sap from a frozen maple tree

Herman Melville to Richard Henry Dana

New York, 1850

My Dear Dana -

About the 'whaling voyage'*- I am half way in the work, & am very glad that your suggestion so jumps with mine. It will be a strange sort of a book, tho', I fear; blubber is blubber you know: tho' you may get oil out of it, the poetry runs as hard as sap from a frozen maple tree; - & to cook the thing up, one must needs throw in a little fancy, which from the nature of the thing, must be ungainly as the gambols of the whales themselves. Yet I mean to give the truth of the thing, spite of this.

Sincerely Yours
H Melville

**Melville's novel* Moby Dick *(1851)*

24 OCTOBER

In my writingbox was all my worldly wealth

Jane Austen to her sister Cassandra

Bull and George, Dartford, Kent, 24 October 1798

My Dear Cassandra

I should have begun my letter soon after our arrival, but for a little adventure which prevented me. After we had been here a quarter of an hour it was discovered that my writing and dressing boxes had been by accident put into a chaise which was just packing off as we came in, and were driven away toward Gravesend in their way to the West Indies. No part of my property could have been such a prize before, for in my writingbox was all my worldly wealth, 7l, and my dear Harry's deputation. Mr Nottley immediately despatched a man and horse after the chaise, and in half an hour's time I had the pleasure of being as rich as ever; they were got about two or three miles off.

25 OCTOBER

The shock of moral earthquakes wakens a vivid sense of life

Charlotte Brontë to Margaret Wooler

Haworth, Yorkshire, 1848

I have now out-lived youth; and, though I dare not say that I have outlived all its illusions - that the romance is quite gone from life - the veil fallen from truth, and that I see both in naked reality - yet, certainly, many things are not what they were ten years ago: and, amongst the rest, the pomp and circumstance of war have quite lost in my eyes their fictitious glitter. I have still no doubt that the shock of moral earthquakes wakens a vivid sense of life, both in nations and individuals; that the fear of dangers on a broad national scale, diverts men's minds momentarily from brooding over small private perils, and for the time gives them something like largeness of views; but, as little doubt have I, that convulsive revolutions put back the world in all that is good, check civilisation, bring the dregs of society to its surface; in short, it appears to me that insurrections and battles are the acute diseases of nations, and that their tendency is to exhaust, by their violence, the vital energies of the countries where they occur.

Tired head that won't rest

Louisa May Alcott to her aunt

October 1887

DEAR AUNTIE –

As you and I belong to the 'Shut-in Society', we may now and then cheer each other by a line. Your note and verse are very good to me today, as I sit trying to feel all right in spite of the stiffness that won't walk, the rebel stomach that won't work, and the tired head that won't rest.

My verse lately has been from the little poem found under a good soldier's pillow in the hospital.

I am no longer eager, bold, and strong,
    All that is past;
I am ready not to do
    At last– at last.
My half-day's work is done,
    And this is all my part.
I give a patient God
    My patient heart.

The learning not to do is so hard after being the hub to the family wheel so long. But it is good for the energetic ones to find that the world can get on without them, and to learn to be still, to give up, and wait cheerfully.

As we have 'fell into poetry', as Silas Wegg* says, I add a bit of my own; for since you are Marmee now, I feel that you won't laugh at my poor attempts any more than she did, even when I burst forth at the ripe age of eight.

Love to all the dear people, and light to the kind eyes that have made sunshine for others so many years.

Always your
Lu

**a character in Dickens's* Our Mutual Friend

27 OCTOBER

The great epistolick art

Samuel Johnson to Hester Thrale

Lichfield, Staffordshire, 27 October 1777

Dear Madam

You talk of writing and writing, as if you had all the writing to yourself. If our correspondence were printed, I am sure posterity, for posterity is always the author's favourite, would say that I am a good writer too . - *Anch'io sono pittore.** To sit down so often with nothing to say: to say something so often, almost without consciousness of saying, and without any remembrance of having said, is a power of which I will not violate my modesty by boasting, but I do not believe that every body has it. Some, when they write to their friends, are all affection; some are wise and sententious; some strain their powers for efforts of gaiety: some write news, and some write secrets; but to make a letter without affection, without wisdom, without gaiety, without news, and without a secret, is, doubtless, the great epistolick art.

In a man's letters, you know, Madam, his soul lies naked, his letters are only the mirror of his breast; whatever passes within him is shown undisguised in its natural process; nothing is inverted, nothing distorted; you see systems in their elements; you discover actions in their motives.

Of this great truth, sounded by the knowing to the ignorant, and so echoed by the ignorant to the knowing, what evidence have you now before you! Is not my soul laid open in these veracious pages? Do not you see me reduced to my first principles? This is the pleasure of corresponding with a friend, where doubt and distrust have no place, and every thing is said as it is thought. The original idea is laid down in its simple purity, and all the supervenient conceptions are spread over it *stratum super stratum*, as they happen to be formed.

These are the letters by which souls are united, and by which minds naturally in unison move each other as they are moved themselves. I know, dearest Lady, that in the perusal of this, such is the consanguinity of our intellects, you will be touched as I am touched. I have indeed concealed nothing from you, nor do I expect ever to repent of having thus opened my heart.

I am, &c.,
Sam Johnson

**And I also, I am a painter*

28 OCTOBER

Penny post maddened

Lord Alfred Tennyson to William Cox Bennett

October 1864

My dear Sir

Look at this pile which on my return from abroad I find heaped on my table. I ought to have thanked you before for your generous lines - but look at the pile - some three feet high - and let that apologize for my silence - and believe me, though penny post maddened,

Yours ever
A. Tennyson

My last words in these last lines

Sir Walter Raleigh to his wife; written on the eve of his scheduled execution for treason. In fact, he was reprieved, remaining imprisoned for many years. He was pardoned in 1617 but beheaded the following year, on this day 1618.

1603

You shall now receive (my deare wife) my last words in these last lines. My love I send you that you may keep it when I am dead, and my councell that you may remember it when I am no more. I would not by my will present you with sorrowes (dear Besse) let them go to the grave with me and be buried in the dust. And seeing that it is not God's will that I should see you any more in this life, beare it patiently, and with a heart like thy selfe.

I send you all the thankes which my heart can conceive, or my words can rehearse for your many travailes, and care taken for me, which though they have not taken effect as you wished, yet my debt to you is not the lesse: but pay it I never shall in this world.

I cannot write much, God he knows how hardly I steale this time while others sleep, and it is also time that I should separate my thoughts from the world.

I can say no more, time and death call me away.

Written with the dying hand of sometimes thy Husband, but now alasse overthrowne.

Yours that was, but now not my own.
Walter Rawleigh

You will never grow old to me, or die, or be lost in any way

Edna St Vincent Millay to Arthur Davison Ficke

New York City, October 1920

Arthur, -

I love you, too, my dear, and shall always, just as I did the first moment I saw you. You are a part of Loveliness to me. - Sometimes at night, when you were in France, I would read over the sonnets you had sent me - just as you have been doing now with mine - & long for you in an anguish of sweet memory, & send all my spirit out to you in passion. - It seemed incredible you were not in the room with me, you were so much nearer than anything else, nearer than the dress I was wearing. - It doesn't matter at all that we never see each other, & that we write so seldom. We shall never escape from each other.

It is very dear to me to know that you love me, Arthur, - just as I love you, quietly, quietly, yet with all your strength, & with a strength greater than your own that drives you towards me like a wind. It is a thing that exists, simply, like a sapphire, like anything roundly beautiful; there is nothing to be done about it, & nothing one would wish to do.

- There are moments, of course, when I am with you, that it is different. One's body, too, is so lonely. And then, too, it is as if I knew of a swamp of violets, & wanted to take you there, & share them with you, because you are my friend. - But all that is the least of it, my dear. - And you must never think that I don't understand. -

You will never grow old to me, or die, or be lost in any way.
- Vincent

Greek wines or March beer

Lady Mary Wortley Montagu to Abbot ----

Dover, 31 October 1718

I arrived this morning at Dover, after being tossed a whole night in the packet-boat.

I cannot help looking with partial eyes on my native land. That partiality was certainly given us by nature, to prevent rambling, the effect of an ambitious thirst after knowledge, which we are not formed to enjoy. All we get by it, is a fruitless desire of mixing the different pleasures and conveniencies which are given to the different parts of the world, and cannot meet in any one of them. After having read all that is to be found in the languages I am mistress of, and having decayed my sight by midnight studies, I envy the easy peace of mind of a ruddy milk-maid, who, undisturbed by doubt, hears the sermon, with humility, every Sunday, not having confounded the sentiments of natural duty in her head by the vain inquiries of the schools, who may be more learned, yet, after all, must remain as ignorant.

And, after having seen part of Asia and Africa, and almost made the tour of Europe, I think the honest English squire more happy, who verily believes the Greek wines less delicious than March beer; that the African fruits have not so fine a flavour as golden pippins; that the Beca figuas of Italy are not so well tasted as a rump of beef; and that, in short, there is no perfect enjoyment of this life out of Old England. I pray God I may think so for the rest of my life; and, since I must be contented with our scanty allowance of daylight, that I may forget the enlivening sun of Constantinople.

NOVEMBER

1 NOVEMBER

A Letter from Home

Published 1964

She sends me news of blue jays, frost,
Of stars and now the harvest moon
That rides above the stricken hills.
Lightly, she speaks of cold, of pain,
And lists what is already lost.
Here where my life seems hard and slow,
I read of glowing melons piled
Beside the door, and baskets filled
With fennel, rosemary and dill,
While all she could not gather in
Or hid in leaves, grow black and falls.
Here where my life seems hard and strange,
I read her wild excitement when
Stars climb, frost comes, and blue jays sing.
The broken year will make no change
Upon her wise and whirling heart; -
She knows how people always plan
To live their lives, and never do.
She will not tell me if she cries.

I touch the crosses by her name;
I fold the pages as I rise,
And tip the envelope, from which
Drift scraps of borage, woodbine, rue.

Mary Oliver

A letter: from you was like a messenger from the land of shadows

Lord Alfred Tennyson to Richard Monckton Milnes

Somersby, Lincolnshire, 1833

My dear Milnes

A letter from you was like a messenger from the land of shadows - it is so long since I have looked upon and conversed with you, that I will not deny but that you had withdrawn a little into the twilight - yet you do me wrong in supposing that I have forgotten you. I shall not easily forget you, for you have that about you which one remembers with pleasure.

I am rejoiced to hear that you intend to present us with your Grecian impressions. Your gay and airy mind must have caught as many colours from the landskip you moved through, as a flying soap bubble - a comparison truly somewhat irreverent - yet I meant it not as such, - though I care not if you take it in an evil sense, for is it not owed to you, for your three-years silence to me whom you professed to love and to care for, and, in the second place, for your profane expression, 'cleaning one's mind of Greek thoughts and Greek feelings to make way for something better': it is a sad thing to have a dirty mind full of Greek thoughts and feelings - what an Augean [stable] it must have been before the Greek thoughts got there.

To have done with this idle banter. I hope that in your book you have given us much glowing description and little mysticism. I know that you can describe richly and vividly - give orders to Moxon and he will take care that the volume is conveyed to me. Believe me, dear Richard,

ever thine
A.T.

I took my letter; I broke its seal

From Chapter 22, 'The Letter', of Charlotte Brontë's novel *Villette* (1853) which is narrated by the character Lucy Snowe

Taking a key whereof I knew the repository, I mounted three staircases in succession, reached a dark, narrow, silent landing, opened a worm-eaten door and dived into the deep, black, cold garret. Here none would follow me – none interrupt – not Madame herself. I shut the garret-door; I placed my light on a doddered and mouldy chest of drawers; I put on a shawl, for the air was ice-cold; I took my letter; trembling with sweet impatience, I broke its seal.

'Will it be long – will it be short?' thought I, passing my hand across my eyes to dissipate the silvery dimness of a suave, south-wind shower.

It was long.

'Will it be cool? – will it be kind?'

It was kind.

To my checked, bridled, disciplined expectation, it seemed very kind: to my longing and famished thought it seemed, perhaps, kinder than it was.

So little had I hoped, so much had I feared; there was a fulness of delight in this taste of fruition – such, perhaps, as many a human being passes through life without ever knowing. The poor English teacher in the frosty garret, reading by a dim candle guttering in the wintry air, a letter simply good-natured – nothing more; though that good-nature then seemed to me godlike – was happier than most queens in palaces.

Of course, happiness of such shallow origin could be but brief; yet, while it lasted it was genuine and exquisite: a bubble – but a sweet bubble – of real honey-dew. Dr John had written to me at length; he had written to me with pleasure; he had written with benignant mood, dwelling with sunny satisfaction on scenes that had passed before his eyes and mine, - on places we had visited together - on conversations we had held - on all the little subject-matter, in short, of the last few halcyon weeks. But the cordial core of the delight was, a conviction the blithe, genial language generously imparted, that it had been poured out not merely to content *me* - but to gratify *himself*. A gratification he might never more desire, never more seek - an hypothesis in every point of view approaching the certain; but *that* concerned the future. This present moment had no pain, no blot, no want; full, pure, perfect, it deeply blessed me. A passing seraph seemed to have rested beside me, leaned towards my heart, and reposed on its throb a softening, cooling, healing, hallowing wing. Dr John, you pained me afterwards: forgiven be every ill - freely forgiven - for the sake of that one dear remembered good!

I don't take the cigarette out of my mouth when I write Deceased over their letters

Wilfred Owen to Siegfried Sassoon; Owen wrote this letter a month before his death: killed in action, on this day in 1918

1918

It is a strange truth: that your 'Counter-Attack'* frightened me much more than the real one: though the boy by my side, shot through the head, lay on top of me, soaking my shoulder, for half an hour.

Catalogue? Photograph? Can you photograph the crimson-hot iron as it cools from the smelting? That is what Jones's blood looked like, and felt like. My senses are charred.

I shall feel again as soon as I dare, but now I must not. I don't take the cigarette out of my mouth when I write Deceased over their letters.

**poem by Siegfried Sassoon*

I whisper good-night in your ears

John Keats to George And Georgiana Keats; from a long journal-letter written over three months to Keats's brother and sister-in-law who had emigrated to America

1819

... The candles are burnt down and I am using the wax taper - which has a long snuff on it - the fire is at its last click - I am sitting with my back to it with one foot rather askew upon the rug and the other with the heel a little elevated from the carpet - I am writing this on the *Maid's Tragedy*, which I have read since tea with great pleasure - Besides this volume of Beaumont and Fletcher, there are on the table two volumes of Chaucer and a new work of Tom Moore's, called *Tom Cribb's Memorial to Congress* - nothing in it. These are trifles - but I require nothing so much of you but that you will give one a like description of yourselves, however it may be when you are writing to me. Could I see the same thing done of any great Man long since dead it would be a great delight: as to know in what position Shakspeare sat when he began 'To be or not to be' - such things become interesting from distance of time or place. I hope you are both now in that sweet sleep which no two beings deserve more than you do - I must fancy so - and please myself in the fancy of speaking a prayer and a blessing over you and your lives - God bless you - I whisper goodnight in your ears, and you will dream of me.

6 NOVEMBER

I feel suppled and anointed now

Virginia Woolf to Vita Sackville-West

Tavistock Square, London, 1928

Dearest Creature

It was a very very nice letter you wrote by the light of the stars at midnight. Always write then, for your heart requires moonlight to deliquesce it. And mine is fried in gaslight, as it is only nine o'clock and I must go to bed at eleven. And so I shant say anything: not a word of the balm to my anguish – for I am always anguished – that you were to me. How I watched you! How I felt – now what was it like! Well, somewhere I have seen a little ball kept bubbling up and down on the spray of a fountain: the fountain is you; the ball me. It is a sensation I get only from you. It is physically stimulating, restful at the same time I feel suppled and anointed now – and then, here, in Tavistock Square, hour after hour passes, in rasping chatter. Oh I've seen so many people: talked so much, and woken up shot through the heart in the night by a sense of doom and frustration – cant escape: and why, and why?

But what I was about to say was, I have found my spectacles. Leonard says will you dose Pinka for worms. I cant decide what to say to your mother. Oh and if you're coming on Wednesday, let me know in good time.

Ajoskyboskybayso

Edward Lear to Chichester Fortescue

London, November 1859

All through next week I shall be here,
To work as best I may,
On my last picture, which is near-
er finished every day.

But after the thirteenth; – (that's Sunday)
I must – if able – start
(Or on the Tuesday if not Monday,)
For England's Northern part.

So then I hope to hear your ways
are bent on English moves
For that I trust once more to gaze
Upon the friend I loves.

But if you are not coming now
Just write a line to say so –
And I shall still consider how
Ajoskyboskybayso.

No more my pen; no more my ink:
No more my rhyme is clear.
So I shall leave off here I think. –
Yours ever,

Edward Lear

The first letter I ever wrote

Lord Byron, aged 10, to his aunt

Newstead Abbey, Nottinghamshire, 8 November 1798

Dear Madam, -

My Mamma being unable to write herself desires I will let you know that the potatoes are now ready and you are welcome to them whenever you please.

She begs you will ask Mrs Parkyns if she would wish the poney to go round by Nottingham or to go home the nearest way as it is now quite well but too small to carry me.

I have sent a young Rabbit which I beg Miss Frances will accept off and which I promised to send before. My Mamma desires her best compliments to you all in which I join.

I am, Dear Aunt, yours sincerely,
Byron

I hope you will excuse all blunders as it is the first letter I ever wrote.

9 NOVEMBER

To nourish sleek optimism

George Eliot to the Brays

1852

I am in clover - an elegant house, glorious fires, and a comfortable carriage - in short just in the circumstances to nourish sleek optimism.

I have a beautiful view from my room window - masses of wood, distant hills, the Firth, and four splendid buildings dotted far apart. When I look out in the morning it is as if I had waked up in Utopia or Icaria or one of Owen's parallelograms. The weather is perfect - all the more delightful to me for its northern sharpness which is just what I wanted to brace me.

10 NOVEMBER

Such a mockturtle gabble of wrecked convivial hydrographers

Dylan Thomas to Madame Caetani

c. 1953

What can I say? Why do I bind myself always into these imbecile grief-knots, blindfold my eyes with lies, wind my brass music around me, sew myself in a sack, weight it with guilt and pig-iron, then pitch me squealing to sea, so that time and time again I must wrestle out and unravel in a panic, like a seaslugged windy Houdini, and ooze and eel up wheezily, babbling and blowing black bubbles, from all the claws and bars and breasts of the mantrapping seabed?

Deep dark down there, where I chuck the sad sack of myself, in the slimy squid-rows of the sea there's such a weed-drift and clamour of old plankton drinkers, such a mockturtle gabble of wrecked convivial hydrographers tangled with polyps and blind prawns, such a riffraff of seabums in the spongy dives, so many jellyfish soakers jolly & joking in the smoke-blue basements, so many salty sea-damaged daughters stuffing their wounds with fishes, so many lightning mid-night makers in the luminous noon of the abysmal sea, and such fond despair there, always there, that time and time again I cry to myself as I kick clear of the cling of my stuntman's sacking. Oh, one time the last time will come and I'll never struggle I'll sway down here forever handcuffed and blindfold, sliding my woundaround music, my sack trailed in the slime, with all the rest of the self-destroyed escapologists in their cages, drowned in the sorrows they drown and in my piercing own, alone and one with the coarse and cosy damned seahorsey dead, weeping my tons.

The man who every day dreams of home

Cecil Frost, of the Canadian Machine Gun Corps, to his parents; letter writing was the main form of communication between soldiers and their families during the First World War. By Autumn 1916, the postal system was handling around 10 million letters from home to the Front per week

Belgium, November 1918

You will never realize what it felt like to know that the war was over. We didn't know till 10:30am of the 11th that armistice started at eleven o'clock. Suddenly the news flashed through. The advance continued right up to the hour of eleven. Every man had a grin from ear to ear on his face. Nobody yelled or showed uncontainable enthusiasm – everybody just grinned and I think the cause was, that the men couldn't find words to express themselves. I think of the man who every day has his life in danger and who dreams of home more than heaven itself – suddenly finds that the danger is past and that his return is practically assured – that he has won after personally risking his life – no wonder they couldn't say much – they simply grinned.

12 NOVEMBER

This is my letter to the World

This is my letter to the World
That never wrote to Me -
The simple News that Nature told -
With tender Majesty

Her Message is committed
To Hands I cannot see -
For love of Her- Sweet - countrymen -
Judge tenderly - of Me

Emily Dickinson

A friendship interwoven with the texture of life

Samuel Johnson to Hester Thrale

London, 13 November 1783

Dear Madam

Since you have written to me with the attention and tenderness of ancient time, your letters give me a great part of the pleasure which a life of solitude admits. You will never bestow any share of your good will on one who deserves better. Those that have loved longest love best. A sudden blaze of kindness may by a single blast of coldness be extinguished, but that fondness which length of time has connected with many circumstances and occasions, though it may for a while be suppressed by disgust or resentment, with or without a cause, is hourly revived by accidental recollection. To those that have lived long together, every thing heard and every thing seen recals some pleasure communicated, or some benefit conferred, some petty quarrel, or some slight endearment. Esteem of great powers, or amiable qualities newly discovered, may embroider a day or a week, but a friendship of twenty years is interwoven with the texture of life. A friend may be often found and lost, but an *old friend* never can be found, and Nature has provided that he cannot easily be lost.

Madam,
Your most humble servant,
Sam Johnson

I am a poet – if they will give me time

Edgar Allan Poe to John Neal

Baltimore, 1829

I am young - not yet 20 - *am* a poet - if deep worship of all beauty can make me *one* - and wish to be so in the common meaning of word. I would give the world to embody one half the ideas afloat in my imagination. (By the way, do you remember, or did you ever read the exclamation of Shelley about Shakspeare, 'What a number of ideas must have been afloat befor such an author could arise!')

I appeal to you as a man that loves the same beauty which I adore - the beauty of the natural blue sky and the sunshiny earth - there can be no tie more strong than that of brother for brother - it is so much that they love one another as that they both love the same parent - their affections are always running in the same direction - the same channel and cannot help mingling. I am and have been from my childhood, an idler. It cannot therefore be said that,

'I left a calling for this idle trade
'A duty broke - a father disobeyed -

for I have no father - nor mother.'

I am about to publish a volume of 'Poems' - the greater part written before I was 15. Speaking about 'Heaven', the Editor of the *Yankee* says, 'He might write a beautiful, if not a magnificent poem,' (the very first words of encouragement I ever remember to have heard). I am very certain that, as yet I have not written *either* - but that I can, I will take my oath - if they will give me time.

A perishing coalblack day, wet, dripping wet, foggy, folded, drear

Katherine Mansfield to John Middleton Murry

15 November 1919

I have just come downstairs and lighted my fire. Do you smell the blue gum wood and the pommes de pin? It's a perishing coalblack day, wet, dripping wet, foggy, folded, drear. The fire is too lovely: it looks a stag's head with two horns of flame. I managed to get the review off yesterday, but not without a struggle. I wanted to be sincere: I felt I had a duty to perform. Oh dear, oh dear! What's it all come to, I wonder?

16 NOVEMBER

Over-grown with sand-plants, thorns, and wild roses

Hans Christian Andersen to the Grand-Duke of Weimar

Copenhagen, Denmark, 1859

The scenery of Jutland has been a great revelation to me. The storms of the North Sea whip up the great sand-dunes, the whirling sand cuts the face, the sea dashes and rolls like a seething cataract against the coast, and loosens the clay of the precipices. But the most striking sight of all was 'Skagen', – this desert, with a small town but no streets, – for the houses lie miles apart from each other, according as the whirling sandhills permit: pieces of 'wrack' bound with rope indicate where the street ought to be. The little town stretches for half a mile along the Cattegat, and from thence there is just as long a road over the plains to old Skagen, where the gates and doors are decorated with the figure-heads of ships. It looks as if 'Neptune', 'Hope', and other exalted deities lived here; for their figures, taken from stranded ships, are to be seen at every entrance.

The most remarkable feature, however, is the large Gothic church buried in the sand. First the sand covered the churchyard, then the walls; but the services were still continued, until one Sunday a sand-bank settled in front of the door. Then the clergyman turned to his congregation: 'God,' said he, 'has now closed this house; we must build Him a new one elsewhere'; and another now stands in a new portion of the town.

Just as in the fairy tale of the enchanted forest the castle is surrounded by an impenetrable thicket, so is the church here over-grown with sand-plants, thorns, and wild roses, which spread like a stockade over the mighty plains. Like a buried Pompeii, the church now lies with its gravestones and monuments till a westerly storm comes and sets the sands in motion; and this will happen, for the dunes are always moving eastwards and new ones rising up. It is like coming into the birds' kingdom here, especially outside the town. For a quarter of a mile from the light-house a tongue of land, strewn with rolling stones stretches out into the sea, and ends in a point just wide enough for a man to stand on and let the North Sea play over his left boot and the Cattegat over his right. It is very plainly seen how the two seas meet here; but the North Sea always holds the mastery.

17 NOVEMBER

I wonder what became of my letter?

E Nesbit to Mavis, Kathleen and Cecily, young readers of E Nesbit's fiction
1909

My Dears,

I *did* write to you, in answer to your other letters. I wonder what became of *my* letter? perhaps it perished in one of those conflagrations caused by bad boys who drop lighted fuses into pillar boxes. Or perhaps it was delivered at your house and was put in a drawer and then slipped over the back edge into the house the drawer lives in, and when the house-maid found it at spring cleaning time she thought it was an old letter and put it in the dustpan. But I suppose we shall never know. Its fate will remain forever a mystery ...

I am very pleased to have your letters, and to know that you like my books. You are quite right to like Kingsley and Dickens and George Macdonald better than you like me, my dear Cecily. There is one other person whose you ought to like better than mine - and that is Mrs Ewing. Oh - and Hans Andersen is another. If I had a magic carpet I would lend it to Kathleen for a month. Then you could all come and see me on it, and that would be jolly for all of us. I wish Mavis could have magic adventures like my children: the best I can do for her is to call the next child I write about Mavis*.

Your loving friend,
E. Nesbit

**Nesbit later dedicated* The Wonderful Garden *(1911) to the three children and named the heroines in* Wet Magic *(1913) Mavis and Kathleen*

18 NOVEMBER

Something to do with the way you have met the problem of time

Gertrude Stein to Samuel M. Steward

Bilignin par Belley, Ain, France, 1936

My dear Sam,

The book* came and I have just finished it and I like it I like it a lot, you have really created a piece of something, by the way how old are you, I have just finished it and I am not sure that I am not going to read it again. It quite definitely did something to me. There are things I might say but it is not that, I have to read it again to know what it is, the first 25 pages did not do it and from then on it did, something came into xistence and remained there, I have to read it again to know more just what, it has something to do with the way you have met the problem of time, as I say I will read it again and then I will write again, you have succeeded in reaching a unity without connecting, I often think that the American contribution is making anything dead, nobody else in writing xcept Americans ever made a thing xist without life be without life and you do that but you do do something else it is a certain level that is there, well anyway I will read it again and write to you again, and with that level you do make it and it is all that, it will be nice meeting some time and don't worry you can eat just what you need and nothing else and so we are looking forward to your coming, that was a funny story about Time, that is not part of the weekly newspaper is it, because if it is, I do not know them but it is strange that they would do that, things are very mixed up in Paris just now but here in the country everything is relatively peaceful xcept the weather, there is snow where there should no snow and consequently there are other things that are not, I will read the book again and write again and I can tell you that I like it and that it did something to me

Always
Gertrude Stein

**Steward's novel* Angels on the Bough *(1936)*

Have we quarrelled? I am sure we have not

Samuel Johnson to Fanny Burney
19 November 1783

Madam, - You have now been at home this long time, and yet I have neither seen nor heard from you. Have we quarrelled? I have met with a volume of the *Philosophical Transactions*, which I imagine to belong to Dr Burney. Miss Charlotte will please to examine. Pray send me a direction where Mrs Chapone lives; and pray, some time, let me have the honour of telling you how much I am, madam, your most humble servant,
Sam Johnson

Fanny Burney to Dr. Samuel Johnson

Dear Sir, - May I not say dear? For quarrelled I am sure we have not. The bad weather alone has kept me from waiting upon you; but now you have condescended to give me a summons, no lion shall stand in the way of my making your tea this afternoon, unless I receive a prohibition from yourself, and then I must submit; for what, as you said of a certain great lady, signifies the barking of a lap-dog, if once the lion puts out his paw? The book was very right. Mrs Chapone lives at either No. 7 or 8 in Dean Street, Soho. I beg you, sir, to forgive a delay for which I can only 'tax the elements with unkindness', and to receive, with your usual goodness and indulgence, your ever most obliged and most faithful humble servant,
F. BURNEY

20 NOVEMBER

Negative Capability

John Keats to his brothers George and Thomas Keats
Hampstead, London, 1817

... Several things dove-tailed in my mind, and at once it struck me what quality went to form a Man of Achievement, especially in Literature, and which Shakspeare possessed so enormously – I mean Negative Capability, that is, when a man is capable of being in uncertainties, mysteries, doubts, without any irritable reaching after fact and reason.

John

I read and reread your letters

Pliny the Younger to his wife Calpurnia
c.100 CE

Caius Plinius to his dear Calpurnia, good health. You write that you are feeling my absence very much and that your only consolation when you don't have me is to hold my books and frequently even place them in my imprint beside you. I am happy to know that you miss me and happy too that you can ease the pain with this sort of medication. I for my part read and reread your letters and return to them again and again as if they had just arrived. But this only fans the flames of my longing for you: if there is such pleasure in reading what you write, think what joy it is to talk with you! Do write as often as you can, even though it will torture me as much as delight me.

Farewell.

Translated from the Latin by Michael Trapp

22 NOVEMBER

Dear tender one

George Eliot to John Cross; Eliot's partner of 25 years, George Henry Lewes, had died in 1878. Eliot married John Cross the year after she wrote him this letter

The Heights, Witley, Surrey, 1879

Best and loving one - the sun it shines so cold, so cold, when there are no eyes to look love on me. I cannot bear to sadden one moment when we are together, but *wenn Du bist nicht da** I have often a bad time. It is a solemn time, dearest. And why should I complain if it is a painful time? What I call my pain is almost a joy seen in the wide array of the world's cruel suffering.

Through everything else, dear tender one, there is the blessing of trusting in thy goodness. Thou dost not know anything of verbs in Hiphil and Hophal or the history of metaphysics or the position of Kepler in science, but thou knowest best things of another sort, such as belong to the manly heart - secrets of lovingness and rectitude.

**when you are not there*

23 NOVEMBER

Paths of fancy

Mary Robinson to John Taylor, proprietor of *The Sun* newspaper

1794

I was really happy to receive your letter. Your silence gave me no small degree of uneasiness, and I began to think some demon had broken the links of that chain which I trust has united us in friendship forever. Life is such a scene of trouble and disappointment that the sensible mind can ill endure the loss of any consolation that renders it supportable. How, then, can it be possible that we should resign, without a severe pang, the first of all human blessings, the friend we love? Never give me reason again, I conjure you, to suppose you have wholly forgot me.

Now I will impart to you a secret, which must not be revealed. I think that before the 10th of December next I shall quit England forever. Yet, my dear Juan, I shall feel a very severe struggle in quitting those paths of fancy I have been childish enough to admire false prospects. They have led me into the vain expectation that fame would attend my labours, and my country be my pride. How have I been treated? I need only refer you to the critiques of last month, and you will acquit me of unreasonable instability. When I leave England – adieu to the muse forever – I will never publish another line while I exist, and even those manuscripts now finished I WILL DESTROY.

Perhaps this will be no loss to the world, yet I may regret the many fruitless hours I have employed to furnish occasions for malevolence and persecution.

24 NOVEMBER

7 Men in black

Fanny Burney to Esther Burney; describes a mastectomy before availability of general anaesthetic

1812

When all was ready ... I rang for my Maid & Nurses. But before I could speak to them, my room, without previous message, was entered by seven Men in black. M. Dubois ordered a bed stead into the middle of the room ... I stood suspended, for a moment, whether I should not abruptly escape – I looked at the door, the windows – I felt desperate – but it was only for a moment, my reason then took the command ... I mounted, therefore, unbidden, the bed stead & M. Dubois spread a cambric handkerchief upon my face but when, Bright through the cambric, I saw the glitter of polished Steel – I closed my Eyes Yet – when the dreadful steel was plunged into the breast – cutting through veins – arteries – flesh – nerves – I needed no injunctions not to restrain my cries.

I began a scream that lasted unintermittingly during the whole time of the incision – & I almost marvel that it rings not in my Ears still! so excruciating was the agony. When the wound was made, & the instrument was withdrawn, the pain seemed undiminished, for the air that suddenly rushed into those delicate parts felt like a mass of minute but sharp & forked poniards, that were tearing the edges of the wound ... again I felt the instrument – describing a curve – cutting against the grain. The instrument this second time withdrawn, I concluded the operation over – Oh no! presently the terrible cutting was renewed – & worse than ever, to separate the bottom, the foundation of this dreadful gland from the parts to which it adhered – Again all description would be baffled – yet again all was not over ... Oh Heaven! – I then felt the Knife rackling against the breast – scraping it!

Twice, I believe, I fainted; at least, I have two total chasms in my memory of this transaction, that impede my tying together what passed.

God bless my dearest Esther – I fear this is all written confusedly, but I cannot read it – & I can write it no more.

A magnificent glimmering moonlight night

Robert Louis Stevenson to Frances Sitwell

17 Heriot Row, Edinburgh, 1873

My dear, it is a magnificent glimmering moonlight night, with a wild, great west wind abroad, flapping above one like an immense banner and every now and again swooping furiously against my windows. The wind is too strong perhaps, and the trees are certainly too leafless for much of that wide rustle that we both remember; there is only a sharp angry sibilant hiss, like breath drawn with the strength of the elements, through shut teeth, that one hears between the gusts only. I am in excellent humour with myself for I have worked hard and not altogether fruitlessly; and I wished before I turned in just to tell you that things were so. My dear friend, I feel so happy all over when I think that you remember me kindly.

Life is doubled for me. I have been up tonight lecturing to a friend on life and duties and what a man could do; a coal off the altar had been laid on my lips, and I talked quite above my average and I hope I spread, what you would wish to see spread, into one person's heart; and with a new light upon it.

I shall tell you a story. Last Friday, I went down to Portobello, in the heavy rain, with an uneasy wind blowing *par rafales* off the sea (or *en rafales* should it be? or what?). As I got down near the beach a poor woman, oldish and seemingly lately, at least, respectable, followed me and made signs. She was drenched to the skin, and looked wretched below wretchedness. You know I did not like to look back at her; it seemed as if she might misunderstand and be terribly hurt and slighted; so I stood at the end of the street – there was no one else within sight in the wet – and lifted up my hand very high with some money in it. I heard her steps draw heavily near behind me and, when she was near enough to see, I let the money fall in the mud and went off at my best walk without ever turning round. There is nothing in the story; and yet you will understand how much there is, if one chose to set it forth. You see, she was so ugly; and you know there is something terribly, miserably pathetic in a certain smile, a certain sodden aspect of invitation on such faces. It is so terrible, that it is in a way sacred; it means the outside of degradation and (what is worst of all in life) false position. I hope you understand me rightly.

The prince started chopping at the wall with an axe

Anton Chekhov to his nephew Mikhail

Melikhovo, Russia, November 1896

On 26 November at six o'clock in the evening a fire broke out at home. It started in the passage round Mother's stove. From lunchtime until evening there had been a terrible smell of smoke and we all complained of the fumes, then by evening we could see tongues of flame in the gap between the stove and the wall. At first it was difficult to see what had actually caught fire, whether it was inside the stove or in the wall. The prince happened to be visiting us at the time, and he started chopping at the wall with an axe. But the wall would not give way, we couldn't manage to introduce any water into the gap and the flames kept climbing higher and higher, meaning there must have been a draught somewhere. Meanwhile, it was obvious that it wasn't just soot burning, but wood. We ring the bell. Smoke. Everybody crowds round. The dogs are howling. The peasants drag the fire engine into the yard. Commotion in the passage. Commotion in the attic. The fire hose splutters. The prince hacks away with his axe. A woman comes with an icon.

Result: one wrecked stove, one wrecked wall, wallpaper torn to shreds on the wall between Mother's room and the stove, one wrecked door, floors covered in dirt, everywhere stinking of soot and nowhere for Mother to sleep.

Best respects.
A. Chekhov
The stove had been extremely stupidly constructed.

Translated from the Russian by Rosamund Bartlett and Antony Phillips

Dead and buried and gone

Patrick Brontë to the Reverend John Buckworth

Haworth, Yorkshire, 27 November 1821

My dear wife was taken dangerously ill on the 29th of January last; and in a little more than seven months afterwards she died. During every week and almost every day of this long tedious interval I expected her final removal. For the first three months I was left nearly quite alone, unless you suppose my six little children and the nurse and servants to have been company.

I was at H[aworth], a stranger in a strange land. It was under these circumstances, after every earthly prop was removed, that I was called on to bear the weight of the greatest load of sorrows that ever pressed upon me. One day, I remember it well; it was a gloomy day, a day of clouds and darkness, three of my little children were taken ill of a scarlet fever; and, the day after, the remaining three were in the same condition. Just at that time death seemed to have laid his hand on my dear wife in a manner which threatened her speedy dissolution. She was cold and silent and seemed hardly to notice what was passing around her. This awful season however was not of long duration. My little children had a favourable turn, and at length got well; and the force of my wife's disease somewhat abated. A few weeks afterwards her sister, Miss Branwell, arrived, and afforded great comfort to my mind, which has been the case ever since, by sharing my labours and sorrows, and behaving as an affectionate mother to my children. At the earliest opportunity I called in different medical gentlemen to visit the beloved sufferer; but all their skill was in vain. Death pursued her unrelentingly. Her constitution was enfeebled, and her frame wasted daily; and after above seven months of more agonizing pain than I ever saw anyone endure she fell asleep in Jesus, and her soul took its flight to the mansions of glory. During many years she had walked with God, but the great enemy, envying her life of holiness, often disturbed her mind in the last conflict. Still, in general she had peace and joy in believing, and died, if not triumphantly, at least calmly and with a holy yet humble confidence that Christ was her Saviour and heaven her eternal home.

Do you ask how I felt under all these circumstances? I would answer to this, that tender sorrow was my daily portion; that oppressive grief sometimes lay heavy on me and that there were seasons when an affectionate, agonizing something sickened my whole frame, and which is I think of such a nature as cannot be described, and must be felt in order to be understood. And when my dear wife was dead and buried and gone, and when I missed her at every corner, and when her memory was hourly revived by the innocent yet distressing prattle of my children, I do assure, my dear sir, from what I felt, I was happy at the recollection that to sorrow, not as those without hope, was no sin; that our Lord himself had wept over his departed friend, and that he had promised us grace and strength sufficient for such a day.

They seem all stuck about my heart

Edward FitzGerald to John Allen

London, November 1832

My dear Allen,

I have been reading Shakespeare's Sonnets: and I believe I am unprejudiced when I say, I had but half an idea of him, Demigod as he seemed before, till I read them carefully –

I have truly been lapped in these Sonnets for some time: they seem all stuck about my heart, like the ballads that used to be on the walls of London. I have put a great many into my Paradise, giving each a fair white sheet for himself: there being nothing worthy to be in the same page. I could talk for an hour about them: but it is not fit in a letter ...

I think I shall come out right

Louisa May Alcott to her father on her twenty-fourth birthday
Boston, 29 November 1856

DEAREST FATHER, -

Your little parcel was very welcome to me as I sat alone in my room, with snow falling fast outside, and a few tears in (for birthdays are dismal times to me); and the fine letter, the pretty gift, and, most of all, the loving thought so kindly taken for your old absent daughter, made the cold, dark day as warm and bright as summer to me.

And now, with the birthday pin upon my bosom, many thanks on my lips, and a whole heart full of love for its giver, I will tell you a little about my doings, stupid as they will seem after your own grand proceedings. How I wish I could be with you, enjoying what I have always longed for, - fine people, fine amusements, and fine books. But as I can't, I am glad you are; for I love to see your name first among the lecturers, to hear it kindly spoken of in papers and inquired about by good people here, - to say nothing of the delight and pride I take in seeing you at last filling the place you are so fitted for, and which you have waited for so long and patiently.

I am very well and very happy. Things go smoothly, and I think I shall come out right, and prove that though an *Alcott* I *can* support myself. I like the independent feeling; and though not an easy life, it is a free one, and I enjoy it. I can't do much with my hands; so I will make a battering-ram of my head and make a way through this rough-and-tumble world.

Goodbye, and a happy birthday from your ever loving
Louisa

An out-of-the-heart letter

Jane Carlyle to her sister-in-law Jean Aitken

5 Cheyne Row, London, 1849

My dear Jane, -

Your letter was one of the letters that one feels a desire to answer the instant one is done reading it - an out-of-the-heart letter that one's own heart (if one happen to have one) jumps to meet. But writing with Mr C. waiting for his tea was, as you will easily admit, a moral impossibility; and after tea there were certain accursed flannel shirts (oh, the alterations that have been made on them!) to 'piece'; and yesterday, when I made sure of writing you a long letter, I had a headache. Today I write; but with no leisure, though I have no 'small clothes' to make, nor any disturbance in that line (better for me if I had); still I get into as great bustles occasionally as if I were the mother of a fine boisterous family.

So you see, dear, it is not the right moment for writing you the letter that is lying in my heart for you. But I could not, under any circumstances, refrain longer from telling you that your letter was very, very welcome; that the tears ran down my face over it - though Mr C. was sitting opposite, and would have scolded me for 'sentimentality' if he had seen me crying over kind words merely; and that I have read it three times, and carried it in my pocket ever since I got it, though my rule is to burn all letters. Oh, yes; there is no change in me, so far as affection goes, depend upon that. But there are other changes, which give me the look of a very cold and hard woman generally.

Please burn this letter - I mean don't hand it to the rest; there is a circulation of letters in families that frightens me from writing often; it is so difficult to write a circular to one.

DECEMBER

1 DECEMBER

The superior quality of your plum pudding

Christina Rossetti to Amelia Barnard Heimann

London, 1862

My dear Mrs Heimann

Recollecting the superior quality of your Plum Pudding, I am desired by Mamma to write and request the great favour of your recipe for our immediate benefit. Last year our pudding was concocted by Aunt Eliza's Sarah; but this was supposed to have occasioned some disappointment to our Elizabeth: who this year is to be indulged with the work according to some good receipt.

Our heartiest best wishes, true Christmas wishes, to you and all yours.

Your often obliged
Affectionate friend
Christina G. Rossetti

2 DECEMBER

Burning the letters

Lord Alfred Tennyson to W E Gladstone, Prime Minister; this postscript completed a letter discussing details of the peerage which Tennyson had recently accepted

2 December 1883

P.S. I heard of an old lady the other day to whom all the great men of her time had written. When Froude's *[Life of] Carlyle* came out, she rushed up to her room, and to an old chest there wherein she kept their letters, and flung them into the fire. 'They were written to me,' she said, 'not to the public!' and she set her chimney on fire, and her children and grandchildren ran in – 'The chimney's on fire!' 'Never mind!' she said, and went on burning. I should like to raise an altar to that old lady, and burn incense upon it.

3 DECEMBER

Our Letters are our selves and in them absent friends meet

John Donne to George Gerrard

c. 1630

I should not only send you an account by my servant, but bring you an account often myself, (for our Letters are ourselves and in them absent friends meet) how I do, but that two things make me forbear that writing: first, because it is not for my gravity, to write of feathers, and straws, and in good faith, I am no more, considered in my body, or fortune. And then because whensoever I tell you how I do, by a Letter, before that Letter comes to you, I shall be otherwise, then when it left me. At this time, I humbly thank God, I am only not worse; for I should as soon look for Roses at this time of the year, as look for increase of strength.

These old fools last night laughed till they cried

Mark Twain (the pen name of Samuel Clemens) to his wife

December 1893

LIVY DARLING, -

Last night at John Mackay's the dinner consisted of soup, raw oysters, corned beef and cabbage, and something like a custard. I ate without fear or stint, and yet have escaped all suggestion of indigestion. The men present were old gray Pacific-coasters whom I knew when I and they were young and not gray. The talk was of the days when we went gypsying a long time ago - thirty years. Indeed it was a talk of the dead. Mainly that. And of how they looked, and the harum-scarum things they did and said. For there were no cares in that life, no aches and pains, and not time enough in the day (and three-fourths of the night) to work off one's surplus vigor and energy. Of the mid-night highway robbery joke played upon me with revolvers at my head on the windswept and desolate Gold Hill Divide, no witness is left but me, the victim. All the friendly robbers are gone. These old fools last night laughed till they cried over the particulars of that old forgotten crime.

John Mackay has no family here but a pet monkey - a most affectionate and winning little devil. But he makes trouble for the servants, for he is full of curiosity and likes to take everything out of the drawers and examine it minutely; and he puts nothing back. The examinations of yesterday count for nothing today - he makes a new examination every day. But he injures nothing.

Dear heart, this is from one who loves you - which is Saml.

We lost a part of ourselves

Alexander Pope to Jonathan Swift; following the death of playwright and poet John Gay

5 December 1732

Good God! How often are we to die before we go quite off this stage? In every friend we lost a part of ourselves, and the best part. God keep those we have left! few are worth praying for, and one's self the least of all.

I shall never see you now I believe; one of your principal calls to England is at an end. Indeed he was the most amiable by far, his qualities were the gentlest, but I love you as well and as firmly.

The thred of Life

George Herbert to his mother
Trinity College, Cambridge, 6 December 1620

Madam,

As the Earth is but a point in respect of the heavens, so are earthly Troubles compar'd to heavenly Joyes; therefore, if either Age or Sickness lead you to those Joyes? consider what advantage you have over *Youth* and *Health*, who are now so near those true Comforts.

I have alwaies observ'd the thred of Life to be like other threds or skiens of silk, full of snarles and incumbrances: Happy is he, whose bottom is wound up and laid ready for work in the New *Jerusalem*. – For my self, *dear Mother*, I alwaies fear'd sickness more then death, because sickness hath made me unable to perform those Offices for which I came into the world, and must yet be kept in it; but you are freed from that fear, who have already abundantly discharg'd that part, having both ordered your Family, and so brought up your Children that they have attain'd to the years of Discretion, and competent Maintenance. – So that now if they do not well the fault cannot be charg'd on you; whose Example and Care of them will justifie you both to the world and your own Conscience: insomuch, that whether you turn your thoughts on the life past, or on the Joyes that are to come, you have strong preservatives against all disquiet. –

7 DECEMBER

With a new listening in my heart

Rainer Maria Rilke to his wife Clara

Capri, Italy, December 1906

I could read your (fifth) letter over and over again. Each time with a new listening in my heart.

I thank you for passing on to me those words which must have been work and exertion enough for you even to accept, arrange and, where you thought it good, reject ... So this, too, belongs to the many, many things in which you are implicated. It came and needed you, needed all your strength, your memories of words, facts, sadnesses, of all the ruthless, almost desperate exaggerations by means of which I sometimes try to plumb the depths of sincerity, only causing pain both to myself and you. You saw all this rising up before you, with all the menace, hardness and momentary hopelessness that come with it, and you had to find the resolve to set yourself above it, superbly clear-headed.

This is how it is with me: I am passionately determined not to miss any of the voices that may come. I will hear each one of them, I will take out my heart and hold it in the midst of these condemning and chiding words so that it shall not be touched by them on one side only and from a distance. But at the same time I will not give up my perilous and often irresponsible standpoint and exchange it for a more comprehensible and renunciatory one before the last, uttermost and final voice has spoken to me; for only on this spot am I accessible and open to them all, only on this spot can I be reached by the fate, the encouragement, the powers that want to reach me; only from here can I one day obey as absolutely as I now resist.

Translated from the German by R.F.C. Hull

Nobody can have the soul of me

D H Lawrence to Rachel Annand Taylor

Lynn Croft Eastwood, Nottingham, December 1910

I have been at home now ten days. My mother is very near the end. Today I have been to Leicester. I did not get home till half past nine. Then I ran upstairs. Oh she was very bad. The pains had been again.

'Oh my dear,' I said, 'is it the pains?'

'Not pain now—oh the weariness,' she moaned, so that I could hardly hear her. I wish she could die tonight.

My sister and I do all the nursing. My sister is only 22. I sit upstairs hours and hours till I wonder if ever it were true that I was at London. I seem to have died since, & that is an old life, dreamy.

I will tell you. My mother was a clever, ironical, delicately moulded woman of good, old burgher descent. She married below her. My father was dark, ruddy, with a fine laugh. He is a coal miner. He was one of the sanguine temperament, warm & hearty, but unstable: he lacked principle, as my mother would have said. He deceived her & lied to her. She despised him - he drank.

Their marriage life has been one carnal, bloody fight. I was born hating my father: as early as ever I can remember. I shivered with horror when he touched me. He was very bad before I was born.

This has been a kind of bond between me and my mother. We have loved each other, almost with a husband & wife love, as well as filial & maternal. We knew each other by instinct. She said to my aunt - about me:

'But it has been different with him. He has seemed to be part of me.' And that is the real case. We have been like one, so sensitive to each other that we never needed words. It has been rather terrible & has made me, in some respects, abnormal.

I think this peculiar fusion of soul (don't think me highfalutin) never comes twice in a lifetime – it doesn't seem natural. When it comes it seems to distribute one's consciousness far abroad from oneself, & one understands! I think no one has got 'Understanding' except through love. Now my mother is nearly dead, and I don't quite know how I am.

I have been to Leicester today, I have met a girl who has always been warm for me – like a sunny happy day – and I've gone & asked her to marry me: in the train, quite unpremeditated, between Rothley & Quorn – she lives at Quorn. When I think of her I feel happy with a sort of warm radiation – she is big & dark and handsome. There were five other people in the carriage. Then when I think of my mother: – if you've ever put your hand round the bowl of a champagne glass and squeezed it & wondered how near it is to crushing-in & the wine all going through your fingers – that's how my heart feels – like the champagne glass. There is no hostility between the warm happiness & the crush of misery: but one is concentrated in my chest, & one is diffuse – a suffusion, vague.

Muriel is the girl I have broken with. She loves me to madness, & demands the soul of me. I have been cruel to her, & wronged her, but I did not know.

Nobody can have the soul of me. My mother has had it, & nobody can have it again. Nobody can come into my very self again, and breathe me like an atmosphere.

I would as soon kill a pig as write a letter

Lord Alfred Tennyson to Dr and Mrs Robert James Mann

December 1858

Dear Doctor and Mrs. Mann

You know that any day I would as soon kill a pig as write a letter –

Yet I feel that to friends over the sea a word is due – if it be only to say how well we remember you and how often we wish you back again.

I don't I know deserve to be answered, but shall be grateful if answered, at your convenience: you know *you* have not to cast about, *you* have something to tell – we living in the old place and looking on the old views and running in the old ruts, little or nothing but what you know already.

Yours ever
A. Tennyson

Procrastination became irresistible to me

William Wordsworth to Sir George Beaumont
Grasmere, The Lake District, 1803

Owing to a set of painful and uneasy sensations which [I have] more or less at all times about my chest, from a disease which chiefly affects my nerves and digestive organs, and which makes my aversion from writing little less than madness, I deferred writing to you.

This feeling was indeed so strong in me, as to make me look upon the act of writing to you, not as a work of a moment, but as a business with something little less than awful in it, a task, a duty, a thing not to be done but in my best, my purest, and my happiest moments.

Many of these I had, but then I had not my pen and ink, my paper before me, my conveniences, my appliances and means to boot all which, the moment that I thought of them, seemed to disturb and impair the sanctity of my pleasure. I contented my self with thinking over my complacent feelings, and breathing forth solitary gratulations and thanksgivings, which I did in many a sweet and many a wild place.

In this shape, procrastination became irresistible to me; at last I said I will write at home, from my own fireside, [w]hen I shall be at ease and in comfort. I have now been more than [a] fortnight at home, but the uneasiness in my chest has made [me] beat off the time when the pen was to be taken up. I do not know from what cause it is, but during the last three [y]ears I have never had a pen in my hand for five minutes, [b]efore my whole frame becomes one bundle of uneasiness, [a] perspiration starts out all over me, and my chest is [o]ppressed in a manner which I can not describe. This is a sad weakness, for I am sure, though, it is chiefly owing to the state of my body, that by exertion of the mind [I] might be able to control it. So however it is, and I mention it, because I am sure when you are made acquainted with the circumstances, though the extent to which it exists nobody can well conceive, you will look leniently upon my silence, and rather pity than blame me.

11 DECEMBER

My fountain pen is not very well today

E Nesbit to Joan Palmer

December 1913

My dear Reviewer

I have just read your article on *Five Children and It* in the *Clarion*. Thank you! It is the best review I have ever had. It gives an idea of the events of the story, and expresses charmingly your opinion of it.

I am glad you like the children – I am rather fond of them myself. They are second cousins once removed of the Bastables whom you may have met.

Have you read the other two books of the adventures of Anthea, Robert and the rest?

The reason why those children are like real children is that I was a child once myself, and by some fortunate magic I remember exactly how I used to feel and think about things.

I am sorry this letter is so badly written, but my fountain pen is not very well today. It is suffering from cramp in the iridium, a very painful disorder, but not, fortunately, dangerous.

If you go on as you have begun you ought to be a successful author. You have a grasp of essentials. Do you ever write poetry? It is the best possible training for writing prose. It teaches you the value of words and cadences.

I send you my love – Your friend, E. Nesbit

12 DECEMBER

You are not phlegmatic and impenetrable

Charlotte Brontë to Margaret Wooler

Haworth, Yorkshire, 12 December 1853

I wonder how you are spending these long winter evenings. Alone, probably, like me. The thought often crosses me, as I sit by myself, how pleasant it would be if you lived within a walking distance, and I could go to you sometimes, or have you to come and spend a day and night with me. Yes; I did enjoy that week at Hornsea, and I look forward to spring as the period when you will fulfil your promise of coming to visit me. I fear you must be very solitary at Hornsea. How hard to some people of the world it would seem to live your life! how utterly impossible to live it with a serene spirit and an unsoured disposition! It seems wonderful to me, because you are not, like Mrs ----, phlegmatic and impenetrable, but received from nature feelings of the very finest edge. Such feelings, when they are locked up, sometimes damage the mind and temper. They don't with you. It must be partly principle, partly self-discipline, which keeps you as you are.

I have some things to say about acacias and sea-weeds and serpents

Marianne Moore to Bryher (Annie Winifred Ellerman); Moore and Bryher exchanged over 500 letters

13 December 1920

Dear Bryher:

I shall like any name you select for me; I am in my family, a weasel, a coach-dog, a water-rat, a basilisk and an alligator and could be an armadillo, a bull-frog or anything that seems suitable to you. [...]

I like what you say about me and marvel that you can say anything at all for it is true that I have not expressed so far, any of the things that I particularly wish to say. You could not see any education that I have had, with a microscope so I do not know that I am justified in blaming education with my ice-bound state. I should attempt observations in prose I think – nothing absolute. To put my remarks in verse form, is like trying to dance the minuet in a bathing-suit but for the time-being I have some things to say about acacias and sea-weeds and serpents in plane-trees that will have to appear in fragments.

Since I have no sweet flower to send you, I enclose my heart

Emily Dickinson to Mary Bowles

December 1858

Dear Mrs Bowles

Since I have no sweet flower to send you, I enclose my heart; a little one, sunburnt, half broken sometimes, yet close as the spaniel, to it's friends. Your flowers came from Heaven, to which if I should ever go, I will pluck you palms.

My words are far away when I attempt to thank you, so take the silver tear instead, from my full eye. You have often remembered me.

I have little dominion – are there not wiser than I, who with curious treasure, could requite your gift. Angels fill the hand that loaded

Emily's!

The human heart is the fairy-lamp of poetry

Hans Christian Andersen to the Grand-Duke of Weimar

Copenhagen, Denmark, December 1850

Christmas is approaching – the childish, happy Christmas fête. In every house they are decorating the trees; in the grand-ducal castle at Weimar also the Christmas tree stands. Joy reigns supreme with young and old on this most beautiful fairy night of the year, which is also for the grown-up people a veritable children's night.

Thanks for your friendship in the old year: may the new one prove a bright and happy one for us all.

For me the human heart is the fairy-lamp of poetry, which I firmly grasp, and I stand like Aladdin with this lamp in the glowing cavern of science; neither will the powers of nature be able to make me their servant. No, I will call forth the spirits, which at my bidding must build me a new castle of poetry.

A bright Christmas and a happy New Year to you all is the wish of

H. C. Andersen

I shall tell you a story about four little rabbits

Beatrix Potter to Noel Moore; the first telling of *The Tale of Peter Rabbit* from one of Potter's illustrated letters to a young friend. Published on this day in 1901

Eastwood Dunkeld, Scotland, 1893

My dear Noel

I don't know what to write to you, so I shall tell you a story about four little rabbits whose names were Flopsy, Mopsy, Cottontail and Peter. They lived with their mother in a sand bank under the root of a big fir tree.

'Now my dears,' said old Mrs Bunny, 'you may go into the field or down the lane, but don't go into Mr McGregor's garden.'

Flopsy, Mopsy & Cottontail, who were good little rabbits went down the lane to gather blackberries, but Peter, who was very naughty, ran straight away to Mr McGregor's garden and squeezed underneath the gate.

First he ate some lettuce and some broad beans, then some radishes, and then feeling rather sick, he went to look for some parsley, but round the end of a cucumber frame whom should he meet but Mr McGregor!

Mr McGregor was planting out young cabbages but he jumped up and ran after Peter waving a rake and calling out 'stop thief'.

Peter was most dreadfully frightened & rushed all over the garden for he had forgotten the way back to the gate. He lost one of his shoes among the cabbages and the other shoe amongst the potatoes. After losing them he ran on four legs & went faster, so that I think he would have got away altogether, if he had not unfortunately run into a gooseberry net and got caught fast by the large buttons on his jacket. It was a blue jacket with brass buttons, quite new.

Mr McGregor came up with a basket which he intended to pop on the top of Peter, but Peter wriggled out just in time, leaving his jacket behind, and this time he found the gate, slipped underneath and ran home safely.

Mr McGregor hung up the little jacket & shoes for a scarecrow, to frighten the blackbirds.

Peter was ill during the evening, in consequence of overeating himself. His mother put him to bed and gave him a dose of camomile tea, but Flopsy, Mopsy and Cottontail had bread and milk and blackberries for supper.

I am coming to London next Thursday, so I hope I shall see you soon, and the new baby.

I remain, dear Noel, yours affectionately
Beatrix Potter

Directions for coughing or sneezing before the King and Queen

Fanny Burney to her sister Hetty
Windsor, 17 December 1785

My dearest Hetty, -

I am sorry I could not more immediately write; but I really have not had a moment since your last. Now I know what you next want is, to hear accounts of kings, queens and such royal personages. O ho! Do you so? Well. Shall I tell you a few matters of fact? Or, had you rather a few matters of etiquette? Oh, matters of etiquette, you cry! For matters of fact are short and stupid, and anybody can tell, and everybody is tired with them. Very well, take your own choice.

You would never believe - you, who, distant from courts and courtiers, know nothing of their ways - the many things to be studied, for appearing with a proper propriety before crowned heads. Heads without crowns are quite other sort of rotundas. Now, then, to the etiquette. I inquired into every particular, that no error might be committed. And as there is no saying what may happen in this mortal life, I shall give you those instructions I have received myself, that, should you find yourself in the royal presence, you may know how to comport yourself.

Directions for coughing, sneezing or moving, before the King and Queen.
In the first place you must not cough. If you find a cough tickling in your throat, you must arrest it from making any sound; if you find yourself choking with the forbearance, you must choke - but not cough. In the second place, you must not sneeze. If you have a vehement cold, you must take no notice of it; if your nose membranes

feel a great irritation, you must hold your breath; if a sneeze still insists upon making its way, you must oppose it, by keeping your teeth grinding together; if the violence of the repulse breaks some blood-vessel, you must break the blood-vessel - but not sneeze. In the third place, you must not, upon any account, stir either hand or foot. If, by chance, a black pin runs into your head, you must not take it out. If the pain is very great, you must be sure to bear it without wincing; if it brings the tears into your eyes, you must not wipe them off; if they give you a tingling by running down your cheeks, you must look as if nothing was the matter. If the blood should gush from your head by means of the black pin, you must let it gush; if you are uneasy to think of making such a blurred appearance, you must be uneasy, but you must say nothing about it. If, however, the agony is very great, you may, privately, bite the inside of your cheek, or of your lips, for a little relief; taking care, meanwhile, to do it so cautiously as to make no apparent dent outwardly. And, with that precaution, if you even gnaw a piece out, it will not be minded; only be sure either to swallow it, or commit it to a corner of the inside of your mouth till they are gone - for you must not spit.

I have many other directions, but no more paper; I will endeavor, however, to have them ready for you in time. Perhaps, meanwhile, you will be glad to know if I have myself had opportunity to put in practice these receipts? How can I answer in this little space?

Most affectionately yours, F. B.

The most astonishing, the most surprising, the most marvellous

Madame de Sévigné to her cousin Monsieur de Coulanges

Paris, France, December 1670

I am going to tell you a thing the most astonishing, the most surprising, the most marvellous, the most miraculous, the most magnificent, the most confounding, the most unheard of, the most singular, the most extraordinary, the most incredible, the most unforeseen, the greatest, the least, the rarest, the most common, the most public, the most private till today, the most brilliant, the most enviable; in short, a thing of which there is but one example in past ages, and that not an exact one either; a thing that we cannot believe in Paris; how then will it gain credit at Lyons?

I cannot bring myself to tell it you: guess what it is. I give you three times to do it in. What, not a word to throw at a dog? Well then, I find I must tell you. Monsieur de Lauzun is to be married next Sunday at the Louvre, to, pray guess to whom! I give you four times to do it in, I give you six, I give you a hundred ... He is to be married next Sunday, at the Louvre, with the King's leave, to Mademoiselle, Mademoiselle de, Mademoiselle ... guess, pray guess her name: he is to be married to Mademoiselle, the great Mademoiselle; Mademoiselle, daughter of the late Monsieur; Mademoiselle, grand-daughter of Henri IV; Mademoiselle d'Eu, Mademoiselle de Donibes, Mademoiselle de Montpensier, Mademoiselle d'Orleans, Mademoiselle, the King's first cousin. Mademoiselle, destined to the throne, Mademoiselle, the only match in France that was worthy of Monsieur. What glorious matter for talk!

Falling from the clouds

Madame de Sévigné to her cousin Monsieur de Coulanges

Paris, France, 19 December 1670

What is called falling from the clouds, happened last night at the Tuileries; but I must go farther back. You have already shared in the joy, the transport, the ecstasies, of the Princess and her happy lover. It was just as I told you, the affair was made public on Monday. Tuesday was passed in talking, astonishment, and compliments.

The contract was then drawn up ... Thursday morning, which was yesterday, Mademoiselle was in expectation of the King's signing the contract, as he had said he would do; but, about seven o'clock in the evening, the Queen, Monsieur, and several old dotards who were about him, had so persuaded His Majesty that his reputation would suffer in this affair, that, sending for Mademoiselle and Monsieur de Lauzun, he announced to them, before the Prince, that he forbade them absolutely to think any further of this marriage. Monsieur de Lauzun received the prohibition with all the respect, submission, firmness and, at the same time, despair, that could be expected in so great a reverse of fortune. As for Mademoiselle, she gave a loose to her feelings, and burst into tears, cries, lamentations and the most violent expressions of grief; she keeps her bed all day long, and takes nothing within her lips but a little broth. What a fine dream is here! What a glorious subject for a tragedy, or romance, but especially talking and reasoning eternally! This is what we do day and night, morning and evening, without end, and without intermission; we hope you do the same.

20 DECEMBER

A vortex of debts, dishpans, and despondency

Louisa May Alcott to her sister Anna

I feel very moral today, having done a big wash alone, baked, swept the house, picked the hops, got dinner and written a chapter in *Moods*. May gets exhausted with work, though she walks six miles without a murmur.

It is dreadfully dull, and I work so that I may not 'brood'. Nothing stirring but the wind; nothing to see but dust; no one comes but rose-bugs; so I grub and scold at the 'A'. because it takes a poor fellow's tales and keeps 'em years without paying for 'em. If I think of my woes I fall into a vortex of debts, dishpans and despondency awful to see. So I say, 'every path has its puddle'–, and try to play gayly with the tadpoles in *my* puddle, while I wait for the Lord to give me a lift, or some gallant Raleigh to spread his velvet cloak and fetch me over dry shod.

You ask what I am writing. Well, two books half done, nine stories simmering and stacks of fairy stories moulding on the shelf. I can't do much, as I have no time to get into a real good vortex. It unfits me for work, worries Ma to see me look pale, eat nothing and ply by night. These extinguishers keep genius from burning as I could wish, and I give up ever hoping to do anything unless luck turns for your

Lu

A little rocky Island with a legended past

W B Yeats to Katharine Tyan; includes an early draft of Yeats's poem 'The Lake Isle of Innisfree'

London, 21 December 1888

My dear Miss Tynan

Here are two verses I made the other day: there is a beautiful Island of Innisfree in Lough Gill, Sligo. A little rocky Island with a legended past. In my story I make one of the characters whenever he is in trouble long to go away and live alone on that Island - an old daydream of my own. Thinking over his feelings I made these verses about them -

I will arise and go now and go to the island of Innisfree
And live in a dwelling of wattles, of woven wattles and woodwork made.
Nine bean-rows will I have there, a yellow hive for the honey-bee
And this old care shall fade.

There from the dawn above me peace will come down dropping slow,
Dropping from the veils of the morning to where the household cricket sings;
And noontide there be all a glimmer, and midnight be a purple glow,
And evening full of the linnets' wings.

I write this letter today hoping it will be in time for Xmas and close it with many good wishes. Yours always

WB YEATS

No more than a minute was left me to live

Fyodor Dostoevsky to his brother

The Peter and Paul Fortress, St. Petersburg, Russia, 22 December 1849

Brother, my precious friend! All is settled! I am sentenced to four years' hard labour in the fortress (I believe, of Orenburg), and after that to serve as a private. Today, the 22nd of December we were taken to the Semionov Drill Ground. There the sentence of death was read to all of us, we were told to kiss the Cross, our swords were broken over our heads and our last toilet was made (white shirts). Then three were tied to the pillar for execution. I was the sixth. Three at a time were called out; consequently, I was in the second batch and no more than a minute was left me to live.

I remembered you, brother, and all yours; during the last minute you, you alone, were in my mind, only then I realized how I love you, dear brother mine! Finally the retreat was sounded, and those tied to the pillar were led back, and it was announced to us that His Imperial Majesty granted us our lives. Then followed the present sentences.

Brother! I have not become downhearted or low-spirited. Life is everywhere life, life in ourselves, not in what is outside us. There will be people near me, and to be a man among people and remain a man for ever, not to be downhearted nor to fall in whatever misfortunes may befall me – this is life; this is the task of life. I have realized this. This idea has entered into my flesh and into my blood.

Yes, it's true! The head which was creating, living with the highest life of art, which had realized and grown used to the highest needs of the spirit, that head has already been cut off from my shoulders. There remain the memory and the images created but not yet incarnated by me. They will lacerate me, it is true! But there remains in me my heart and the same flesh and blood which can also love, and suffer, and desire, and remember, and this, after all is life. *On voit le soleil!* Now,

Don’t grieve for me!

...

When I look back at the past and think how much time has been wasted in vain, how much time was lost in delusions, in errors, in idleness, in ignorance of how to live, how I did not value time, how often I sinned against my heart and spirit – my heart bleeds. Life is a gift, life is happiness, each minute might have been an age of happiness. *Si jeunesse savait!* Now, changing my life, I am being reborn into a new form. Brother! I swear to you that I shall not lose hope and shall preserve my spirit and heart in purity. I shall be reborn to a better thing. That is my whole hope, my whole comfort!

23 DECEMBER

The grooves of life

Leslie Stephen to Charles Eliot Norton

London, December 1900

My dear Norton,

I shall never be as strong as I was not long go; but I have still a little work left in me. I found it necessary to do something if only by way of distraction. The outside world has been so dismal that thoughts of it have often broken my sleep and my isolation by deafness leaves me to brood over all manner of dismal reflections. I try to exorcise them & with tolerable success by a bit of scribbling. My children are all well. Thoby enjoying Cambridge immeasurably & Vanessa her studio and Virginia as literary as her papa. It is cheering to see them all interested & hopeful & so long as that lasts, I should be a coward to give in to the blue devils. As one gets old, the grooves of life seem to have become polished & one slips down them with wondrous rapidity. I feel as if I were about entering the rapids and getting ready for a plunge over Niagara.

Our ball was very thin, but by no means unpleasant

Jane Austen to her sister Cassandra
Steventon, Oxfordshire, 24 December 1798

My dear Cassandra

I returned from Manydown this morning, and found my mother certainly in no respect worse than when I left her. She does not like the cold weather, but that we cannot help. I spent my time very quietly and very pleasantly with Catherine. Miss Blackford is agreeable enough. I do not want people to be very agreeable, as it saves me the trouble of liking them a great deal. I found only Catherine and her when I got to Manydown on Thursday. We dined together and went together to Worting to seek the protection of Mrs Clarke, with whom were Lady Mildmay, her eldest son, and a Mr and Mrs Hoare.

Our ball was very thin, but by no means unpleasant. There were 31 people, and only 11 ladies out of the number, and but five single women in the room. Of the gentlemen present you may have some idea from the list of my partners – Mr Wood, G. Lefroy, Rice, a Mr Butcher (belonging to the Temples, a sailor and not of the eleventh Light Dragoons), Mr Temple (not the horrid one of all), Mr William Orde (cousin to the Kingsclere man), Mr John Harwood, and Mr Calland, who appeared as usual with his hat in his hand, and stood every now and then behind Catherine and me to be talked to and abused for not dancing. We teased him, however, into it at last. I was very glad to see him again after so long a separation, and he was altogether rather the genius and flirt of the evening. He inquired after you. There were 20 dances, and I danced them all, and without any fatigue ... My black cap was openly admired by Mrs Lefroy, and secretly I imagine by everybody else in the room ...

Tuesday. I was to have dined at Deane today, but the weather is so cold that I am not sorry to be kept at home by the appearance of snow. We are to have company to dinner on Friday: the three Digweeds and James. We shall be a nice silent party, I suppose.

You deserve a longer letter than this, but it is my unhappy fate seldom to treat people so well as they deserve ... God bless you!

Yours affectionately, Jane Austen

Wednesday. - The snow came to nothing yesterday, so I *did* go to Deane, and returned home at nine o'clock at night in the little carriage, and without being very cold.

My little book: my 'first-born'

Louisa May Alcott to her mother; Alcott gave a copy of her first book *Flower Fables* (1854) to her mother, accompanied by this note

Boston, Christmas Day 1854

Dear Mother

– Into your Christmas stocking I have put my 'first-born', knowing that you will accept it with all its faults (for grandmothers are always kind), and look upon it merely as an earnest of what I may yet do; for, with so much to cheer me on, I hope to pass in time from fairies and fables to men and realities.

Whatever beauty or poetry is to be found in my little book is owing to your interest in and encouragement of all my efforts from the first to the last; and if ever I do anything to be proud of, my greatest happiness will be that I can thank you for that, as I may do for all the good there is in me; and I shall be content to write if it gives you pleasure.

To dear mother, with many kind wishes for a happy New Year and merry Christmas.

I am ever your loving daughter
Louy

Never to beat and bruise one's wings

George Eliot to Clifford Allbutt

December 1868

Never to beat and bruise one's wings against the inevitable but to throw the whole force of one's soul towards the achievement of some possible better, is the brief heading that need never be changed, however often the chapter of more special rules may have to be re-written.

27 DECEMBER

I have a thirst for Happiness, that never will be quenched again

Katherine Mansfield to the Hon. Dorothy Brett

1919

We had a superb Xmas - stockings - a tree, decorations, crackers, pudding, drink - most potent and plentiful - parcels pouring in and out. Murry seemed to wear a paper hat (a large red and yellow butterfly) from Xmas Eve until after Boxing Day - We gradually, under the influence of wine and Chinese mottoes, gave a party - Charades - Kot, Gertler, Campbell, etc. Oh, I did love it so - loved everybody. They were all fluttering and twinkling like candles in the darkest, most mysterious Tree of all - I wanted to say to everybody - Let us stay forever just as we are. Don't let us ever wake up and find it is all over.

It made me realize all over again how thrilling and enchanting life can be, and that we are not old - the blood still flows in our veins. We still laugh. The red chairs became a pirate ship. Koteliansky wore a muff on his head and Campbell a doormat tied under the chin - can't this happen more often? Ought not Life to be divided into work and play - real play? We ought not to have to sit in corners when our work is over. I feel that I have a thirst for Happiness, that never will be quenched again.

- Hurrah for Life! But this isn't a letter. It is a hail -

I touched the keys in unison with his Imagination

James Boswell to William Johnson Temple; Boswell describes an encounter with Voltaire

Château de Ferney, France, 28 December 1764

I returned yesterday to this enchanted castle. The Magician appeared a very little before dinner. But in the evening he came into the drawing room in great spirits. I placed myself by him.

I touched the keys in unison with his Imagination. I wish you had heard the Music. He was all Brilliance. He gave me continued flashes of Wit. I got him to speak English which he does in a degree that made me, now and then, start up and cry, 'Upon my soul this is astonishing.'

When he talked our language He was animated with the Soul of a Briton. He had bold flights. He had humour. He had an extravagance; he had a forcible oddity of stile that the most comical of our *Dramatis Personae* could not have exceeded. He swore bloodily as was the fashion when he was in England. He hum'd a Ballad; he repeated nonsence.

At last we came upon Religion. Then did he rage. The Company went to Supper. M. de Voltaire and I remained in the drawing room with a great Bible before us; and if ever two mortal men disputed with vehemence we did. Yes, upon that occasion He was one Individual and I another. For a certain portion of time there was a fair opposition between Voltaire and Boswell. The daring bursts of his Ridicule confounded my understanding. He stood like an Orator of ancient Rome. Tully was never more agitated than he was. He went far. His aged frame trembled beneath him. He cried, 'O I am very sick; my head turns round.'

...

Before I left Britain, I was idle, dissipated, ridiculous and regardless of Reputation. Often was I unworthy to be the freind of Mr Temple. Now I am a very different Man. I have got a character which I am proud of. Speak thou who hast known me from my earliest years, couldst thou have imagined eight years ago that thy Companion in the Studies of Antiquity who was debased by an unhappy education in the smoak of Edinburgh, couldst thou have imagined him to turn out the Man that he now is?

29 DECEMBER

A powerful remedy

Voltaire to a friend in bereavement

England, 1728

I know no more powerful remedy for the sorrows of the heart than deep and serious application of the mind to other objects.

This application changes the gloomy tenor of the spirits – sometimes even makes us insensible to bodily ills. Anyone who devotes himself to music or to reading a good book, which appeals at once to the mind and to the imagination, finds speedy relief from the sufferings of an illness: he also finds that, little by little, the pangs of the heart lose their sharpness.

He is obliged to think of something quite other than that which he is trying to forget. The strongest chains are, in the long run, those of custom. It depends, I believe, on ourselves to break the links which bind us to our sorrows and to strengthen those which attach us to happier things.

Not, indeed, that we are absolute masters of our thoughts: that implies much: but neither are we absolute slaves: and, once again, I believe that the Supreme Being has given us a little of His *liberty*, as He has given us a little of His *power of thought*.

Let us make use, then, of such weapons as we have. We undoubtedly add, by reading and thinking, to our *power of thought*: why should we, then, not also add to what is called our *liberty*? There is not one of our senses or our powers which has not been helped by effort. Why should liberty be the only one of man's attributes which he cannot increase?

Suppose, for instance, we see round us trees hung with a delicious but poisoned fruit, which a raging hunger incites us to pick: if we feel ourselves too weak to abstain, let us go (and going depends on ourselves) to places where there are no such fruits.

These are counsels which, like so many others, are no doubt easier to give than to follow: but we are in the presence of a disease wherein the patient must minister to himself.

Translated from the French by S. G. Tallentyre

You pierce my soul

From the penultimate chapter of Jane Austen's novel *Persuasion* which was first published in December 1817: a letter from Captain Wentworth to Anne Elliot

I can listen no longer in silence. I must speak to you by such means as are within my reach. You pierce my soul. I am half agony, half hope. Tell me not that I am too late, that such precious feelings are gone for ever. I offer myself to you again with a heart even more your own than when you almost broke it, eight years and a half ago. Dare not say that man forgets sooner than woman, that his love has an earlier death. I have loved none but you. Unjust I may have been, weak and resentful I have been, but never inconstant. You alone have brought me to Bath. For you alone, I think and plan. Have you not seen this? Can you fail to have understood my wishes? I had not waited even these ten days, could I have read your feelings, as I think you must have penetrated mine. I can hardly write. I am every instant hearing something which overpowers me. You sink your voice, but I can distinguish the tones of that voice when they would be lost on others. Too good, too excellent creature! You do us justice, indeed. You do believe that there is true attachment and constancy among men. Believe it to be most fervent, most undeviating, in

F. W.

I must go, uncertain of my fate; but I shall return hither, or follow your party, as soon as possible. A word, a look, will be enough to decide whether I enter your father's house this evening or never.

A happy New Year

Rainer Maria Rilke to his wife Clara

Capri, Italy, 1907

The midnight of the New Year is struck, strangely significant, stroke slowly following stroke, each one smooth, widespread, foldless, as though being laid away in store.

I had gone back to my little house again and stood on the roof and wanted to see in all this a good end and find a good beginning in myself. And now let us have faith in the long new year which is given us, new, untouched, full of things that have never been, full of work never before done, full of tasks, demands and encouragement, and let us try to receive it without letting fall the gifts it has to bestow on those who ask the necessary things, the grave and great things ... A happy New Year ...

Translated from the German by R.F.C. Hull

Author Biographies

Louisa May Alcott (1832-1888). American writer best known for her novel *Little Women* and its sequels. After she died, in accordance with her wishes, many of her letters were destroyed. Of those that survive, most were addressed to family members.

Hans Christian Andersen (1805-1875). Danish writer known for his literary fairy tales including *The Emperor's New Clothes, The Little Mermaid* and *The Snow Queen*.

Maya Angelou (1928-2014). Influential Black American author and poet. She wrote *Letter to My Daughter* (2009), a book of essays dedicated to 'the daughter she never had'.

Dr John Arbuthnot (1667-1735). Physician and writer, friend to writer Alexander Pope. Pope was to immortalise him in his satirical poem *Epistle to Dr. Arbuthnot*. Pope wrote to Arbuthnot that it was 'the best Memorial that I can leave, both of my Friendship to you, & of my own Character'.

Jane Austen (1775-1817). Author of *Pride and Prejudice*, a novel structured around letters. Austen also wrote one epistolary novella, unpublished in her lifetime, *Lady Susan*. Much of Austen's correspondence was burned by her sister Cassandra, probably to protect her legacy and her family and friends' privacy. Only 160 of what would likely have been thousands of letters survive.

Cassandra Austen (1773-1845). Only sister of Jane Austen. When they were apart they would correspond frequently. Cassandra, an amateur watercolourist, produced the only two surviving lifetime likenesses of Jane.

Elizabeth Barrett Browning (1806-1861). Popular and well-regarded English poet. Robert Browning initiated a correspondence with Barrett that was to lead to them falling in love, Barrett Browning's love poetry (including *Sonnets of the Portuguese*) and their elopement. They moved to Florence, Italy.

JM Barrie (1860-1937). Novelist and playwright. Author of *Peter Pan; or, The Boy Who Wouldn't Grow Up*, featuring Peter Pan, Wendy and Captain Hook, the latter pursued by a crocodile who had swallowed a ticking clock.

Elizabeth Bishop (1911-1979). American poet.

William Blake (1757-1827). Poet, painter and engraver from London who claimed to have visions. Ninety-five of his letters survive.

James Boswell (1740-1795). Best known for his renowned biography of Samuel Johnson, *Life of Samuel Johnson* (1791). During his Grand Tour of Europe, aged 24, Boswell spent three days with his hero, famed French writer and philosopher Voltaire.

Anne Brontë (1820-1849). Youngest of the Brontë sisters. Author of *The Tenant of Wildfell Hall*, a groundbreaking account of domestic abuse. Lived most of her life at Haworth in Yorkshire. Anne died away from home in Scarborough, Yorkshire, aged 29. Unlike their sister Charlotte, very few of Anne and Emily's letters survive.

Charlotte Brontë (1816-1855). English novelist (notably of *Jane Eyre*) and poet, from Haworth close to the Yorkshire moorlands that inspired her and her sisters' writing. Charlotte's husband, as recounted in a letter by Charlotte, advised that her correspondence to best friend Ellen Nussey be burnt when read: 'be sure to follow a recommendation he has just given "fire them"'. Ellen disregarded the advice. As well as hundreds of surviving letters, Brontë made use of the epistolary form as a literary device in novels *The Professor* and *Villette*.

Patrick Brontë (1777-1861). Father of six children, including writers Charlotte, Emily and Anne. Born in Ireland, he became an Anglican priest and settled in Haworth, Yorkshire. His wife Maria neé Branwell died in 1821 when the children were aged between 19 months and seven years old.

Rupert Brooke (1887-1915). English poet. One of his best-known poems *The Old Vicarage, Grantchester*, written in Berlin, reflects back to his time living in the village of Grantchester near Cambridge.

Robert Browning (1812-1889). Poet and husband of fellow poet Elizabeth Barrett Browning. They met five months after Browning sent his first letter to her in January 1845. The almost daily letters continued until their marriage in September 1846.

Robert Burns (1759-1796). Scottish poet, widely regarded as the Bard of Scotland, he left a large legacy of poetry, songs and letters. He would often include poems or drafts of poems in his letters to friends.

Lord Byron (1788-1824). Poet and celebrity, Byron was a prolific letter-writer to his many friends and acquaintances, especially when scandals surrounding him impelled him to move abroad, spending several years living in Italy and Greece. Thousands of his letters survive.

Jane Carlyle (1801-1866). Wife of historian Thomas Carlyle and prolific letter writer. Thomas described reading her correspondence following her death: 'such an electric shower of all-illuminating brilliancy, penetration, recognition, wise discernment, just enthusiasm, humour, grace, patience, courage, love, [...] as I know not where to parallel!' (*Reminiscences*, July 1866).

Willa Cather (1873-1947). Born on her grandmother's farm in Virginia, USA, Cather documented life at the turn of the 20th century on the Great Plains of the Mid-West in her novels *O Pioneers!* and *My Ántonia*.

Anton Chekhov (1860-1904). Russian doctor and writer. His plays include *The Cherry Orchard* and *Three Sisters*. He was also an acclaimed short story writer.

John Clare (1793-1864). English 'peasant poet' from Northamptonshire who worked as a farm labourer. He had several spells in asylums, struggling with mental illness. He often included poems in his letters which contain many idiosyncrasies of spelling and punctuation.

Samuel Taylor Coleridge (1772-1834). English poet (*The Rime of the Ancient Mariner*, *Kubla Khan*) and close friend of William Wordsworth. He married Sara Fricker in 1795 with whom he had four children. He suffered frequent bouts of illness, and became addicted to laudanum (a form of opium) which was used as a treatment.

Wilkie Collins (1824-1889). English novelist (*The Woman in White*, *The*

Moonstone) and playwright. Close friend of Charles Dickens.

William Cowper (1731–1800). English poet, one of the most popular of his day. *The Task*, a 5000-line poem in six books was inspired by a friend who suggested he write about a sofa. He lived with mental illness for many years, finding solace in countryside pursuits and gardening at home in Olney, Buckinghamshire. Jane Austen quotes from his works in four of her novels.

ee cummings (1894–1962). americanpoet; his poetic style was to use idiosyncratic syntax and lower-case spellings as do his:letters

Madame d'Arblay (Fanny Burney) (1752–1840). Novelist, diarist and prolific letter writer. *Evelina*, an epistolary novel, first published anonymously, was her most successful and unfolds in the course of 84 letters written by the heroine and seven other characters. Burney's extraordinary life is captured in her journal-letters, letters and diaries, including her time at the royal court as 'Keeper of the Robes' to Queen Charlotte, wife of George III.

Charles Dickens (1812–1870). Hugely popular English novelist. Author of 15 novels including *Oliver Twist* and *David Copperfield*, he also ran a weekly journal and performed public readings of his work. He was a prolific letter writer and was said to receive around 60 to 80 letters a day.

Emily Dickinson (1830–1886). Little known as a poet in her lifetime, thousands of her poems were discovered and published after her death. She lived all her life in Amherst, Massachusetts in growing seclusion so that sending and receiving letters became an increasingly important form of communication. Many of her letters have been classified as 'letter-poems'.

John Donne (1572–1631). English metaphysical poet and Dean of St Paul's Cathedral in London.

Fyodor Dostoevsky (1821–1881). Russian novelist, including of *Crime and Punishment*. After being imprisoned for anti-government activities in 1849 (for reading and distributing banned books), he was sentenced to death by firing squad but reprieved moments before the planned execution.

Frederick Douglass (1818–1895). African American abolitionist, orator, publisher and author of *Narrative of the Life of Frederick Douglass, an American Slave, Written by Himself*. Writing letters became a tool for his abolitionist work, including letters that were published in the abolitionist newspaper *The Liberator*.

Paul Laurence Dunbar (1872–1906). African American poet and novelist, son of two formally enslaved people. He had many books published and achieved international success. He married poet Alice Ruth Moore.

Alice Ruth Moore Dunbar-Nelson (1875–1935). Born in New Orleans, USA, the daughter of a formerly enslaved African American seamstress and a white merchant marine. She published her first book of poetry at the age of 20. Married to poet Paul Laurence Dunbar.

Gerald Durrell (1925–1995). Writer, naturalist, conservationist, zookeeper. Author of memoir *My Family and Other Animals*.

George Eliot (1819–1880). Pen name of Mary Ann Evans, an English novelist, poet and translator. Author of *Middlemarch, Mill on the Floss, Silas Marner*. Partner of writer George Henry Lewes for 25 years, she then married John Cross in 1880.

T S Eliot (1888–1965). Modernist

poet. Despite once writing in a letter that he wanted to 'make ashes' of his letters and professing a wish 'to leave as little biography as possible', Faber & Faber are publishing his complete correspondence of which nine volumes have been published to date (covering 1898-1941).

Ralph Waldo Emerson (1803-1882). American essayist, poet, and philosopher of the Transcendentalist movement which is a belief system encouraging a non-traditional appreciation of nature.

Edward FitzGerald (1809-1883). English poet and writer. He translated *The Rubaiyat of Omar Khayyam*. He corresponded widely and prolifically with key literary figures of the day, including his friend Alfred, Lord Tennyson.

Captain Cecil Frost (1897-1947). A young Canadian soldier who fought at the front during the First World War. Between 1917-1919 he wrote vivid letters about his wartime experiences in France to his parents back home in Ontario.

Robert Frost (1874-1963). American poet who wrote about rural settings and farm life.

Elizabeth Gaskell (1810-1865). English novelist, author of *Cranford, North and South* and *Wives and Daughters*. She also wrote *The Life of Charlotte Brontë* which made extensive use of letters to tell the story of Brontë's life. She was a prolific letter writer.

William Godwin (1756-1836). Political philosopher. He married Mary Wollstonecraft in 1797 but she died a few months later, shortly after their daughter Mary was born (and who was to write *Frankenstein* and marry the poet Shelley).

Kenneth Grahame (1859-1932). English author of children's classic *Wind in the Willows*, the outline of which was contained in letters sent to his young son Alastair.

Woody Guthrie (1912-1967). American singer-songwriter.

Thomas Hardy (1840-1928). English novelist and poet. Hardy spent most of his life in Dorset.

Nathaniel Hawthorne (1804-1864). Author of the classic American novel *The Scarlet Letter*. Hawthorne wrote many love letters to Sophia Peabody whom he married in 1842, 164 of which were later published.

Robert Hayden (1913-1980). Poet and first African American writer to hold the office of Poet Laureate.

Seamus Heaney (1939-2013). Irish poet from County Derry, in Northern Ireland.

Ernest Hemingway (1899-1961). American novelist and short story writer. He served as an ambulance driver on the Italian Front in the First World War, sustaining serious injuries from mortar fire. He also covered the Spanish Civil War as a journalist in the 1930s.

George Herbert (1593-1633). English metaphysical poet and priest.

Gerard Manley Hopkins (1844-1889). English poet and Jesuit priest. The majority of his poetry was published many years after his death. Letters exchanged between him and his friend, poet Robert Bridges, discuss the development of Hopkins' poetry and it was Bridges who published a collection of Hopkins' poetry posthumously.

Langston Hughes (1901-1967). American poet of the Harlem Renaissance.

Samuel Johnson (1709–1784). Towering literary figure and preeminent 'man of letters', Johnson was author of *A Dictionary of the English Language*. His prolific literary output includes letters written to many key contemporary figures such as Hester Thrale, Fanny Burney and James Boswell.

Franz Kafka (1883–1924). Czech novelist whose output includes the novella *The Metamorphosis*. He exchanged passionate love letters with translator Milena Jesenská but they only met twice.

John Keats (1795–1821). The letters of Romantic poet Keats are well-known, from the passionate letters he wrote to fiancée Fanny Brawne, to letters which included first drafts of his poems and contained detailed thoughts on his philosophy of poetry such as the concept of 'negative capability'.

Charles Lamb (1775–1834). Writer and friend of Wordsworth and Coleridge. Brother of Mary.

Mary Lamb (1764–1847). English writer and sister of Charles. She struggled with mental illness.

Philip Larkin (1922–1985). English poet.

D H Lawrence (1885–1930). English novelist and poet. Lawrence was the son of a coal miner and he was brought up in Eastwood, Nottinghamshire. In 1912 he eloped to Germany with the already married Frieda whom he later married after her divorce.

Edward Lear (1812–1888). Best known for his nonsense verse and limericks, he was also a gifted painter. His letters were full of nonsense verse, poems and sketches.

George Henry Lewes (1817–1878). Writer and critic. Partner of George Eliot.

C S Lewis (1898–1963). Author of *The Chronicles of Narnia* and a literary scholar.

Amy Lowell (1874–1925). American poet from New England. Wrote in the Imagist style.

Louis MacNeice (1907–1963). Irish poet.

Katherine Mansfield (1888–1923). A New Zealand short story writer and poet. In 1911 Mansfield met John Middleton Murry, an editor and writer, in London. After a tumultuous relationship, they married in 1918.

Herman Melville (1819–1891). American novelist, short story writer and poet, author of the masterpiece, *Moby Dick*, telling the story of a whale hunting voyage.

Edna St Vincent Millay (1892–1950). Major American lyrical poet and great letter writer.

John Milton (1608–1674). English poet, author of the verse epic *Paradise Lost*, which has been hugely influential. He wrote it by dictation after losing his eyesight. Of the 38 letters that survive, the majority were written in Latin and were sent to diplomats, poets, friends and ambassadors.

Lady Mary Wortley Montagu neé Pierrepont (1689–1762). Poet, travel writer and medical pioneer. When her husband Edward was appointed an ambassador in Turkey, she travelled with him, writing many letters on her experiences which were to form *The Turkish Embassy Letters*, published posthumously.

Michel de Montaigne (1533–1592). Widely read French essayist and philosopher who had a considerable influence on other writers.

Marianne Moore (1887–1972). American modernist poet. She was a prolific letter writer.

E Nesbit (1858–1924). English writer and poet. Author of children's classic *The Railway Children*. Nesbit would always reply to letters she received from her young readers.

Mary Oliver (1935–2019). American poet who drew her inspiration from the natural world.

George Orwell, pen name of Eric Blair (1903–1950). Writer and journalist. Author of *Animal Farm* and *1984* and the memoir *Down and Out in Paris and London* in which Orwell experiences and recounts a life in poverty.

Dorothy Osborne (1627–1695). She became Lady Temple on her marriage to Sir William Temple. She became highly regarded for her writing style when the love letters she wrote to Temple prior to their marriage were published posthumously in 1888.

Wilfred Owen (1893–1918). An English poet and soldier who was killed in the First World War. The majority of his surviving letters were written to his mother.

Sylvia Plath (1932–1963). American poet and writer. She was married to poet Ted Hughes. She was a prolific letter writer and her letters contain in intimate and vivid detail many aspects of her life including her inner turmoil and distress as well as the collapse of her marriage.

Pliny the Younger (c.61 AD–c.13 AD). A Roman writer and public servant. Pliny wrote hundreds of letters, of which 247 survived. He published these in nine books, known as *The Epistulae*, and a tenth book was published after his death. They were composed in a detailed, formal style, and likely were carefully edited before publication. They covered a wide range of topics from politics to every day life.

Plutarch (1st century AD). Greek philosopher, historian and essayist. He wrote 48 biographies of famous Greek and Romen men, now known as *Plutarch's Lives*, in which he used letters as an important source of historical information.

Edgar Allan Poe (1809–1849). American poet and short story writer from Boston, Massachusetts. Themes of mystery and the macabre.

Alexander Pope (1688–1744). English poet and satirist. As well as being a gifted and prolific letter writer, Pope wrote a number of *Epistles*, long poems addressed to a specific person in the style of a letter which explored philosophical or moral subjects.

Beatrix Potter (1866–1943). English children's writer. Some of Potter's stories originated in illustrated letters she wrote to young children, famously the one that was to become her first and best known, *The Tale of Peter Rabbit*.

Sir Walter Raleigh (1552–1618). English writer, explorer, statesman and favourite of Elizabeth I. However, he fell out of favour, and was imprisoned in the Tower of London on three occasions.

Samuel Richardson (1689–1761). English author of the great epistolary novels *Pamela* — considered one of the first English novels — and *Clarissa* (consisting of 537 letters). He was also a prolific letter writer.

Isaac Rosenberg (1890–1918). Anglo-Jewish poet and artist killed in the First World War.

Rainer Maria Rilke (1875–1926). Austrian poet. As well as leaving a large body of correspondence, a collection of ten letters Rilke wrote to Franz Xaver Kappus and known as *Letters to a Young Poet* offering advice on writing and life was published by Kappus after Rilke's death.

Crabb Robinson (1775–1867). Famous for his diaries that described the lives and characters of many Romantic poets, such as William Blake and Wiliam Wordsworth.

Mary Robinson (1757–1800). Poet, playwright, actress and a celebrity of the Georgian era.

Christina Rossetti (1830–1894). English poet and prolific letter writer. One of her brothers was painter and poet Dante Gabriel Rossetti.

Vita Sackville-West (1892–1962). Novelist, poet and gardener. Sackville-West wrote about her experiences in Persia where she travelled with her husband Harold Nicholson. Romantically involved with Virginia Woolf with whom she exchanged many letters.

Ignatius Sancho (c.1729–1780). Sancho was a freed Black slave who settled in London. He was the first known Black Briton to vote in a British election. He wrote letters to newspapers and corresponded with the writer Laurence Sterne urging him to cover the topic of slavery. After his death 160 of his letters were published as *The Letters of the Late Ignatius Sancho, an African*. The book was a bestseller.

Sir Walter Scott (1771–1832). A prolific and hugely popular Scottish poet and novelist from Edinburgh, writing 27 novels and volumes of poetry. He wrote thousands of letters over the course of his life.

Joseph Severn (1793–1879). Painter. He was a close friend of poet John Keats and accompanied him to Rome, remaining with him till his death. It is through Severn's letters to friends back home that we have such a detailed account of Keats's last days.

Madame de Sévigné (1626–1696). French aristocrat and letter writer extraordinaire, in both quality and quantity, covering personal and family concerns and social commentary on Versailles during Louis XIV's reign. Her letters were well-regarded at the time, often circulated and read aloud. They were collected and published posthumously.

William Shakespeare (1564–1616). English playwright, poet and actor. Shakespeare frequently uses letters as a dramatic device in his plays. Letters are often read aloud or alluded to by his characters, and they communicate important news, insights and developments.

Percy Bysshe Shelley (1792–1822). English Romantic poet and revolutionary. Husband of Mary Shelley and friend of Byron, Keats and others.

Mary Wollstonecraft Shelley (1797–1851). English novelist best known for her gothic novel *Frankenstein*. Daughter of early feminist Mary Wollstonecraft and wife of poet Percy Bysshe Shelley.

Thomas Sheridan (1687–1738). Irish actor and poet.

Gertrude Stein (1874–1946). American novelist and poet known for her avant-garde, experimental style.

Leslie Stephen (1832–1904). English writer, biographer and critic. Father of Virginia Woolf.

Laurence Sterne (1713–1768). Novels include *Tristram Shandy*. Supportive of the anti-slavery movement about which he and Ignatius Sancho corresponded.

Robert Louis Stevenson (1850–1894).

Scottish novelist and poet. Novels include *Treasure Island* and *Strange Case of Dr Jekyll and Mr Hyde*.

Bram Stoker (1847–1912). Irish author of *Dracula*.

Alfred, Lord Tennyson (1809–1892). Poet Laureate during Queen Victoria's reign.

Dylan Thomas (1914–1953). Welsh poet. Critic Heathcote Williams described him as 'drunk on language'.

Edward Thomas (1878–1917). English poet who died in action in the First World War.

Henry D Thoreau (1817–1862). American philosopher, poet and environmental thinker. Author of *Walden*, or *Life in the Woods*, an account of living a simple life in a cabin near Walden Pond, Concord, Massachusetts.

Hester Thrale (1741–1821). Writer and friend of Samuel Johnson.

Mark Twain (1835–1910). Pen name of American writer Samuel Clemens. Author of *The Adventures of Tom Sawyer* and *Adventures of Huckleberry Finn*.

Voltaire (1694–1778). French writer and philosopher. Considered one of the greatest letter writers of all time with an estimated 20,000 letters written.

Phillis Wheatley (1753–1784). An enslaved woman who became the first African American author to have a book of poetry published.

Walt Whitman (1819–1892). American poet writing in long free verse. He visited thousands of injured soldiers in hospitals during the American Civil War.

Oscar Wilde (1854–1900). Irish poet and dramatist. Advocate for art for art's sake. Wilde was gay, and was imprisoned in Reading Gaol for two years for gross indecency, when homosexuality was a crime in Britain, from where he wrote the unsent letter *De Profundis* to his former lover Lord Alfred Douglas.

William Carlos Williams (1883–1963). American Imagist poet.

P G Wodehouse (1881–1975). Very prolific author of comic novels, including the *Jeeves and Wooster* series.

Mary Wollstonecraft (1759–1797). English writer, author of *Vindication of the Rights of Women*. She had a daughter with her lover Gilbert Imlay and lived in Paris during the French Revolution. Later she married William Godwin with whom she had Mary (later Mary Shelley, author of *Frankenstein*).

Virginia Woolf (1882–1941). Part of the Bloomsbury set of London. Her novels used the stream of consciousness technique. Diarist and prolific letter writer.

Dorothy Wordsworth (1771–1855). Sister of William Wordsworth. Author of well-regarded journal.

William Wordsworth (1770–1850). English Romantic poet associated with the Lake District. Brother of Dorothy, wife of Mary. A great – if at times – reluctant letter writer.

Mary Wordsworth (1770–1859). Wife of poet William Wordsworth.

W B Yeats (1865–1939). Irish poet.

Index

Sources

Maya Angelou, *Letter to My Daughter* (2008), Little Brown Book Group Limited, Virago. Reproduced with permission of the Licensor through PLSclear. "Mt. Zion" from LETTER TO MY DAUGHTER by Maya Angelou, copyright © 2008 by Caged Bird Legacy, LLC. Used by permission of Random House, an imprint and division of Penguin Random House LLC. All rights reserved.

Elizabeth Barrett Browning, *The Brownings' Correspondence* (1984), ed. Philip Kelley, Scott Lewis, Edward Hagan, Wedgestone Press; Eton College.

Elizabeth Bishop, *The Complete Poems 1927-1979* (1984), Macmillan; Farrar, Straus and Giroux, an imprint of Macmillan Publishers.

Charlotte, Patrick Brontë, *The Brontës: A Life in Letters* (1998), ed. Juliet Barker, Viking, Penguin Random House LLC; The Overlook Press, Abrams Books.

"1 August The red harvest moon, swollen with plenty (Willa Cather to Mariel Gere-Red Cloud, Nebraska 1893)" from THE SELECTED LETTERS OF WILLA CATHER (2013) by Willa Cather, letters copyright © 2013 by The Willa Cather Literary Trust. Introduction, annotation, commentary and compilation copyright © 2013 by Andrew Jewell and Janis Stout. Used by permission of Alfred A. Knopf, an imprint of the Knopf Doubleday Publishing Group, a division of Penguin Random House LLC. All rights reserved.

From *A Life in Letters* by Anton Chekhov published by Penguin Classics. Copyright © Translation Copyright © Rosamund Bartlett and Anthony Phillips, 2004. Editorial Material Copyright © Rosamund Bartlett, 2004. Chronology Copyright © Ronald Wilks, 2004. Reprinted by permission of Penguin Books Limited.

Wilkie Collins, *The Letters of Wilkie Collins, Volume 2: 1866-1889* (1999), ed. William Baker, William M. Clarke; Faith Clarke. Published by Springer Verlag London Limited, an imprint of Palgrave Macmillan Scholarly. Reproduced with permission of the Licensor through PLSclear.

e e cummings, *Selected Letters of E E Cummings* (1969), ed. F. W. Dupee, George Stade, Houghton Mifflin Harcourt; used by permission of W. W. Norton & Company, Inc.

Charles Dickens, *The Pilgrim Edition of the Letters of Charles Dickens: Volume 7, 1853-1855* (1993), ed. Graham Storey, Kathleen Tillotson, Angus Easson, First Edition. Reproduced by kind permission of Commander Mark Charles Dickens.

Emily Dickinson, *Open Me Carefully: Emily Dickinson's Intimate Letters to Susan Huntington Dickinson* (1998), ed. Ellen Louise Hart, Martha Nell Smith, Harvard University Press; reproduced by permission of Wesleyan University Press.

Alice Dunbar-Nelson, *Paul Laurence and His Song* (1947), ed. Virginia Cunningham, Dodd, Mead & Company.

Gerald Durrell, to his fiancée Lee, 31 July 1978. Reproduced with permission of Curtis Brown Group Ltd, London on behalf of The Beneficiaries of the Estate of Gerald Durrell. Copyright © Gerald Durrell.

T. S. Eliot extract from *Letter Writing Among Poets from William Wordsworth to Elizabeth*

Bishop (2015), ed. Jonathan Ellis, published by Edinburgh University Press Limited. Reproduced with permission of The Licensor through PLSclear.

Ralph Waldo Emerson, *The Selected Letters of Ralph Waldo Emerson* (1999), ed. Joel Myerson, Columbia University Press; *The Letters of Ralph Waldo Emerson* (1939), ed. Ralph L. Rusk, reprinted with permission of Columbia University Press, the Ralph Waldo Emerson Memorial Association.

Cecil Frost, *The Wartime Letters of Leslie and Cecil Frost, 1915-1919*, edited by R.B. Fleming (Wilfrid Laurier University Press, 2007).

Robert Frost, *The Letters of Robert Frost Volume I:1886–1920* (2014), ed. Donald Sheehy, Mark Richardson and Robert Faggen, published by Harvard University Press. Copyright Robert Lee Frost Estate and Trust.

Woody Guthrie, *Born to Win* (1965), ed. Robert Shelton, Macmillan Publishers; Simon & Schuster LLC.

Thomas Hardy, *The Collected Letters of Thomas Hardy: Volume I: 1840-1892* (1977), ed. Richard Little Purdy, Michael Millgate, Clarendon Press; reprinted by permission of Curtis Brown Group Limited, and courtesy Dorset Museum & Art Gallery.

Robert Hayden, *Collected Poems* (1997), ed. Frederick Glaysher, Liveright Publishing; used by permission of W. W. Norton & Company, Inc.

The Letters of Seamus Heaney (2023) by Seamus Heaney, ed. Christopher Reid, published and reproduced with permission of Faber and Faber Ltd; Farrar, Straus and Giroux, an imprint of Macmillan Publishing.

The Letters of Ernest Hemingway (2011), by Ernest Hemingway, ed. Sandra Spanier, Robert W. Trogdon, published by Cambridge University Press. Reproduced with permission of the Licensor through PLSclear.

Langston Hughes, *Selected Letters of Langston Hughes* (2015), ed. Arnold Rampersad, David Roessel, published by Alfred A. Knopf, an imprint of the Knopf Doubleday Publishing Group, a division of Penguin Random House LLC; Harold Ober Associates, Inc.

Excerpt(s) from LETTERS TO MILENA by Franz Kafka, translated by Tania Stern and James Stern, edited by Willi Haas, translation copyright 1953 and © renewed 1981 by Penguin Random House LLC. Used by permission of Schocken Books, an imprint of the Knopf Doubleday Publishing Group, a division of Penguin Random House LLC. All rights reserved.

Philip Larkin: Letters to Monica (2011), by Philip Larkin, ed. Anthony Thwaite, published and reproduced with permission of Faber and Faber Ltd.

D H Lawrence, *The Selected Letters of DH Lawrence* (1958), ed. Diana Trilling, Paper Lion Ltd.

Edward Lear, *Selected Letters* (1988), ed. Vivien Noakes, Oxford University Press; Watson, Little Ltd.

George Henry Lewes, *The Letters of George Henry Lewes* (1995), ed. William Baker, ELS Editions, University of Victoria; Jonathan G Ouvery.

Letters of C S Lewis (1966) by C S Lewis, ed. W. H. Lewis, Walter Hooper. Copyright © 1966, 1988 C.S. Lewis Pte. Ltd. Extract reprinted by permission of the C. S. Lewis Company Ltd.

Amy Lowell, The First Wave: Women Poets in America, 1915-1945 (1987), William Drake; Harvard University, Choate, Hall & Stewart.

Selected Letters of Louis MacNeice (2020) by Louis McNeice, ed. Jonathan Allison, published by Faber and Faber Ltd. Reproduction by permission of David Higham Associates Ltd.

Herman Melville, *The Letters of Herman Melville* (1960), ed. Merrell R. Davis, William H. Gilman, Yale University Press.

Edna St. Vincent Millay, excerpts from *Letters of Edna St. Vincent Millay*, edited by Allan Ross Macdougall. Copyright 1952 and renewed © 1980 by Norma Millay Ellis.

Reprinted with the permission of The Permissions Company, LLC on behalf of Holly Peppe, Literary Executor, The Edna St. Vincent Millay Society, millay.org.

Marianne Moore, *The Selected Letters of Marianne Moore* (1998), ed. Bonnie Costello, Celeste Goodridge, Cristanne Miller, Alfred A. Knopf, an imprint of the Knopf Doubleday Publishing Group, a division of Penguin Random House LLC; reproduced by permission of Faber and Faber Ltd.

New and Selected Poems (1992), by Mary Oliver. Reprinted by the permission of The Charlotte Sheedy Literary Agency as agent for the author. Copyright © 1965 by Mary Oliver with permission of Bill Reichblum.

The Letters of Sylvia Plath Volume II (2018) by Sylvia Plath, ed. Peter K. Steinberg, Karen V. Kukil, published and reproduced with permission of Faber and Faber Ltd; Houghton Mifflin Harcourt, an imprint of Harper Collins.

Pliny the Younger extract from *Greek and Latin Letters: An Anthology with Translation* (2003), ed. and translated by Michael Trapp, published by Edinburgh University Press Limited. Reproduced with permission of The Licensor through PLSclear.

Edgar Allen Poe, *The Letters of Edgar Allen Poe* (1948), ed. John Ward Ostrom, Harvard University Press.

Beatrix Potter, *Beatrix Potter's Letters* (1992), ed. Judy Taylor, Frederick Warne, Penguin. MA 2009.8, Potter, Beatrix, 1866-1943. Autograph letter signed: Ambleside, to Noel Moore, 1896 Aug. 7., p. 1, 2, 3 and 4. The Morgan Library & Museum. MA 2009.8. Gift of Colonel David McC. McKell, 1959. Reproduced by permission of The Morgan Library & Museum, New York. MA 2009.8. Gift of Colonel David McC. McKell, 1959.

Isaac Rosenberg, *Poems by Isaac Rosenberg* (1922), William Heinemann; reproduced by permission of the Ben Uri Gallery & Museum, the Isaac Rosenberg Estate.

Rainer Maria Rilke, *Selected Letters of Rainer Maria Rilke 1902-1922* (1946) trans. R. F. C. HULL, Macmillan Publishing. Rilke, *Letters to a Young Poet* (2021), trans. Anita Barrows and Joanna Macy, published by Shambhala Publications.

Christina Rossetti, *The Letters of Christina Rossetti, Volume I, 1843-1873* (1997), The Letters of Christina Rossetti Volume II, 1874-1881 (1999), ed. Antony H. Harrison, University of Virginia Press.

Vita Sackville-West, *The Letters of Vita Sackville-West to Virginia Woolf* (1985), ed. Louise DeSalvo, Mitchell A. Leaska, William Morrow & Co.; Penguin Random House LLC.

Dear Sammy: Letters from Gertrude Stein and Alice B Toklas (1977) by Gertrude Stein, Samuel M. Steward, published by Houghton Mifflin. Reproduced by permission of David Higham Associates Ltd.

Leslie Stephen, *Selected Letters, Volume 2* (1996), Palgrave Macmillan Publishing.

Robert Louis Stevenson, *The Letters of Robert Louis Stevenson* (1994), Yale University Press; Tate Lloyd Schieferle.

Bram Stoker, *With Walt Whitman in Camden: January 21 to April 7, 1889* (1953), University of Pennsylvania Press; The Bram Stoker Estate.

Alfred Lord Tennyson, *The Letters of Alfred Lord Tennyson Volume I, 1821-1850* (1981), ed. Cecil Y. Lang, Edgar F. Shannon Jr, Harvard University Press, the Estate of Alfred Lord Tennyson.

Phillis Wheatley, from the Hugh Upham Clark collection, Massachusetts Historical Society.

Walt Whitman, "To Hugo Fritsch" is reprinted with permission from the University of Iowa Press. Originally published in *Selected Letters of Walt Whitman* edited by Edwin Haviland Miller © 1990 by the University of Iowa Press. *With Walt Whitman in Camden* (1953), ed. Sculley Bradley. Copyright 1953, by Anne M. Traubel. Published by Southern Illinois University Press.

Oscar Wilde, *Complete Letters of Oscar Wilde* (2000), ed. Merlin Holland, Rupert Hart-Davis, Henry Holt & Co. Merlin Holland, by permission of The Estate of Oscar Wilde, HarperCollins UK.

By William Carlos Williams, from THE SELECTED LETTERS OF WILLIAM CARLOS WILLIAMS (1957), ed. John C. Thirlwall, copyright ©1957 by William Carlos Williams. Reprinted by permission of New Directions Publishing Corp.

P. G. Wodehouse, *Yours, Plum: Letters of P. G. Wodehouse* (1992), ed. Frances Donaldson, Penguin Books. Copyright the Wodehouse Estate.

From *Letters* (1910) by Virginia Woolf published by Chatto & Windus. Copyright © Quentin Bell and Angelica Garnett, 1910, 1917, 1919, 1920, 1924, 1975. Reprinted by permission of The Random House Group Limited; HarperCollins Publishers LLC.

Dorothy Wordsworth, *The Letters of Dorothy Wordsworth* (1981), ed. Alan G. Hill, Oxford Paperbacks.

Mary Wordsworth, from *The Love Letters of William & Mary Wordsworth 1770-1850* ed. Beth Darlington. Copyright © (1981) Cornell University Press. Used by permission of the publisher, Cornell University Press.

William Wordsworth, *Letters of William Wordsworth* (1984), ed. Alan G. Hill, Oxford University Press.

Acknowledgements

A very big thank you to the great team at Batsford, particularly to my editors Magda Simões-Brown and Nicola Newman. Thank you to my family and friends who continue to support and encourage my literary adventures.

About the Editor

Liz Ison studied English Literature at the University of Cambridge. Since 2015, Liz has been leading shared reading groups in person and online as well as workshops and walks encouraging people to enjoy and rediscover poetry and literature. She is a museum educator at the Charles Dickens Museum. Her anthologies include *A Poem to Read Aloud Every Day of the Year*, *Poems for Tortured Souls* and *100 Poems to Help You Heal*. Liz lives in London.